Finding God in All Things

Finding God in All Things

Celebrating Bernard Lonergan, John Courtney Murray, and Karl Rahner

EDITED BY
MARK BOSCO, S.J.,
AND DAVID STAGAMAN, S.J.

FORDHAM UNIVERSITY PRESS
NEW YORK 2007

Library of Congress Cataloging-in-Publication Data

Finding God in all things : celebrating Bernard Lonergan, John Courtney Murray, and Karl Rahner / edited by Mark Bosco and David Stagaman,—1st ed.
p. cm.
Includes bibliographical references and index.
ISBN 978-0-8232-2808-9 (clothbound : alk. paper)
1. Lonergan, Bernard J. F. 2. Murray, John Courtney. 3. Rahner, Karl, 1904–1984. 4. Catholic Church—Doctrines—History—20th century. 5. Theology, Doctrinal—History—20th century. I. Bosco, Mark. II. Stagaman, David J., 1935–

BX4705.L7133F56 2007
230′.20922—dc22

2007043733

Printed in the United States of America
09 08 07 5 4 3 2 1
First edition

Contents

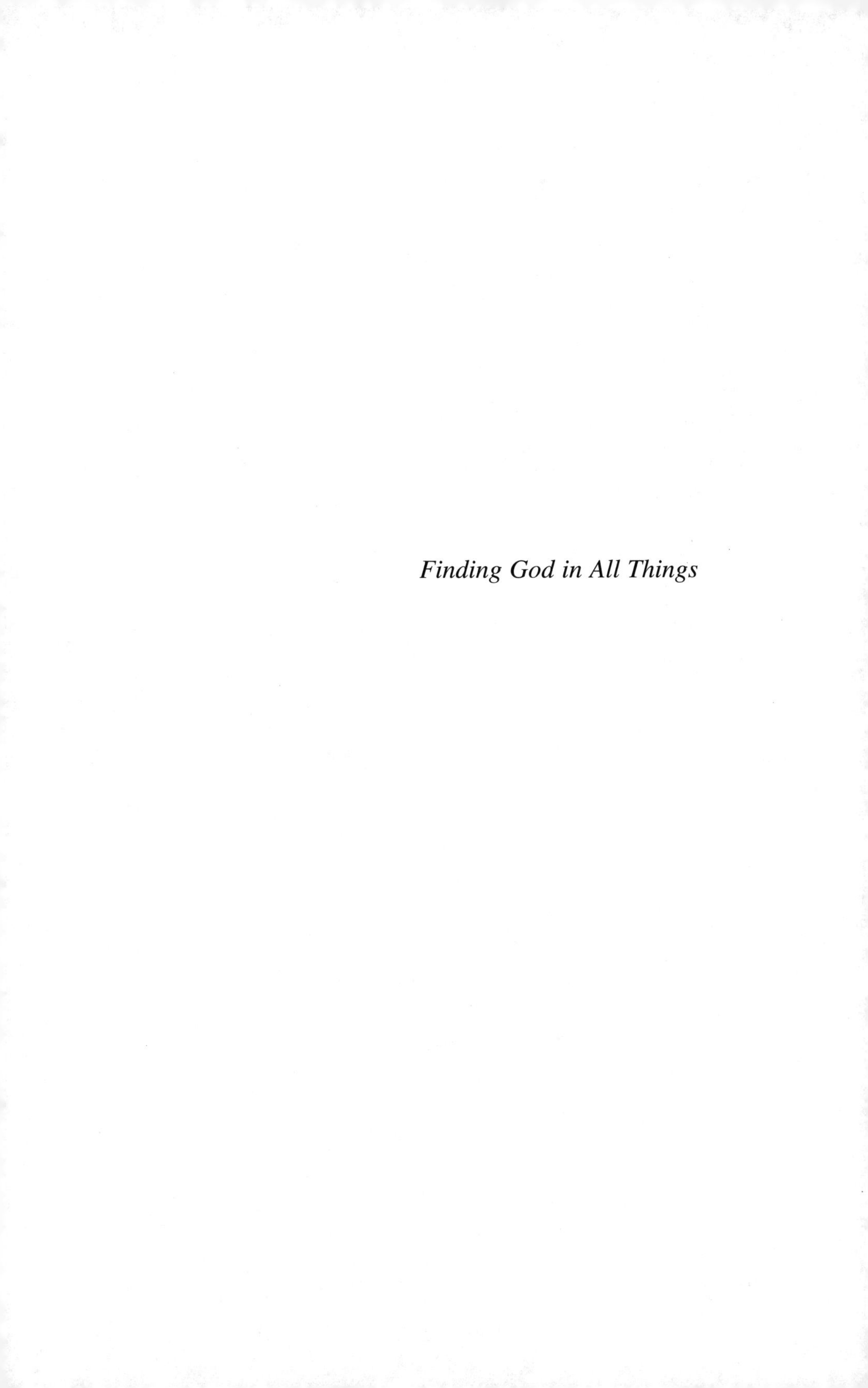

Finding God in All Things

1. Introduction

Mark Bosco, S.J.

> *In every age, the church carries the responsibilities of reading the signs of the times and of interpreting them in the light of the Gospel, if it is to carry out its task. In language intelligible to every generation, it should be able to answer the ever recurring questions which people ask about the meaning of this present life and of the life to come, and how one is related to the other. We must be aware of and understand the aspirations, the yearnings, and the often dramatic features of the world in which we live.*
>
> —*Gaudium et Spes*

The above sentiments of the Second Vatican Council's *Pastoral Constitution on the Church in the Modern World* capture a transitional moment in the Catholic Church's attitude in its relationship with modernity. This shift is seen most remarkably in the language of the Council, what Jesuit historian John W. O'Malley notes is a change from "the rhetoric of reproach" so prevalent in documents from previous church councils to an embrace of the "rhetoric of affirmation and invitation." The rhetorical change in attitude that permeates the Council documents was matched by a new formulation of the Church's consciousness of itself since the Council of Trent and the First Vatican Council. Such pivotal themes about the nature of the Church found new expression and emphasis: the acceptance of historical consciousness in the articulation of the Church's history and doctrine; the importance of an active role for the laity; the spirit of détente between the Church and the modern world; the modification of the Church's identity beyond clerical terms to the more inclusive "people of God"; the renewal in liturgical practice; the affirmation of religious freedom to worship according to one's conscience; and the stress on human rights as fundamental to religious faith. Thus, the previously "agonistic" tone of Roman Catholic theology at war with the Reformation and the Enlightenment is, for the first time, given what O'Malley calls a humbler, "irenic" timbre. A more pastoral and temperate sensibility suffuses the Council documents in order to express in a new way the "substance" of the Roman Catholic tradition. Indeed, O'Malley argues that if we want to understand the Catholic Church of the past forty years we need to think about this distinctive theological "style," this change in attitude towards methodology and expression of Catholic belief and faith.[1]

O'Malley's formula is an apt way to introduce this collection of centenary essays on the theological vision of three of the greatest Jesuit thinkers of the twentieth century. Bernard Lonergan, John Courtney Murray, and Karl Rahner were influential in bringing to fruition—or deliberatively extending—the rhetorical and methodological style of the Second Vatican Council. It might be said that to understand the past forty years of Catholic theology one must understand the contribution of these men. Interestingly, they were each born in 1904 during the height of the Church's most militant, agonistic rhetoric against all things modern. Just three years after their birth, the Vatican's Congregation of the Holy Office issued the decree *Lamentabili* (1907), a sweeping condemnation of sixty-five propositions against the "errors of the age." Two months later in the same year, the encyclical *Pascendi Dominici Gregis* (on the doctrines of the modernists) was promulgated, followed by an antimodernist oath for all Catholic bishops, priests, and theologians. Under this umbrella of suspicion and oaths, Lonergan, Murray, and Rahner were nurtured in their Catholic faith and underwent theological training in the Society of Jesus. Each of them in their own way felt the burden of the antimodernist policies in their theological formation. And yet by the time of their mature work during the 1950s and 60s, these three individuals were instrumental in helping the Church usher in a critical dialogue between modernity's historico-philosophical expression and contemporary Catholic theological scholarship. In an era of détente with science and Enlightenment thought (due in no small part to Pope John XXIII's Council), each of these Jesuits brought their understanding of the Catholic theological tradition into closer relation with modern outlooks in philosophy, history, and political science.

Lonergan, Murray, and Rahner were also loyal sons of St. Ignatius of Loyola. They shared a spiritual as well as intellectual "way of proceeding" in their life and work, a certain Jesuit style encapsulated in the motto "finding God in all things." Though their theological engagement differed in emphasis and focus, the spiritual grounding of their work was remarkably similar, steeped as it was in the *Spiritual Exercises* of St. Ignatius. One can see the elements of this Ignatian style in their incarnational embrace of the world as a potential dwelling place of the divine, their probing realism concerning the human condition in all its sublime and sinful manifestations, and their respect for historical consciousness in light of their developing faith in God and God's Church. Whether in the form of Lonergan's theological method, in Murray's reasoned defense of religious liberty, or in Rahner's countless theological investigations into Catholic doctrine and practice, each contributed to the Catholic renaissance encapsulated in the Second Vatican Council's *aggiornamento*, the "bringing up to date" of the ancient truths of Christian faith.

In honor of the centenary of their birth in 2004, theological journals such as *The Way* and *Theology Today* created special centenary issues, while many public lectures and academic conferences were held at Jesuit universities and theological centers throughout the world. Many of these anniversary celebrations focused on how the theological investigations of Lonergan, Murray, and Rahner still impact the style and content of Catholic discourse today. My academic home at Loyola University Chicago, for example, sponsored a university-wide conference in the spring semester of 2004. Speakers shared personal memories of having known Lonergan, Murray, or Rahner, and offered scholarly analysis on how these twentieth-century figures are still important for the doing of theology in the Church of the twenty-first century.

This present collection represents a sampling of the many essays and lectures from those anniversary celebrations, written for, produced by, or presented at a variety of venues throughout 2004. Four essays on each of these men, varying in style and content, have been chosen in order to give a broad range of perspectives on their life and work. Some of the essays are personal, anecdotal accounts of having lived with or studied under Lonergan, Murray, or Rahner, showing the humanity often hidden under their erudite intellects. Other essays, coming from scholars of their work, are more academic in their focus, assessing how these three figures still have much to offer contemporary theological discussion; and some essays fall in between these two poles, offering the lay person an introduction to the import of their work and how it still helps to shape the way Catholics think and talk about God, church, and state. It is our hope that the collection gives the reader a multifaceted composite that honors each man's contribution and shows the ongoing relevance of that contribution in theological discourse today.

The essays begin with Bernard Lonergan, born in Canada on December 17, 1904. Lonergan entered the Society of Jesus at Guelph, Ontario, in 1922 and had a truly international Jesuit education, studying philosophy at Heythrop College in England and theology at the Gregorian University in Rome. Sometimes referred to as a Transcendental Thomist, he was highly influenced by the works of both Thomas Aquinas and John Henry Newman during the course of his studies. Lonergan's two great works, *Insight: A Study of Human Understanding* (1957) and *Method in Theology* (1972), still attract significant attention at many universities and institutes and at conferences held annually by academic societies throughout the world.[2] Lonergan's dense, philosophical work, *Insight*, takes as its task the critical manner in which the human person acquires possession of his or her own consciousness. He attempts to illustrate the structure of personal insight, of what he called "insight into insight." *Method in Theology*, on the other hand, aims, among other things, to give the variety of ways that theological investigation is grounded in its own complex methodology. Both works have helped to reconceive Catholic theology as an interdisciplinary enterprise that influences—and is influenced by—all of human culture.

The theologian Donald L. Gelpi, S.J., begins the four essays that celebrate Lonergan's achievement. Gelpi gives a concise treatment of Lonergan's major philosophical breakthroughs in theological method and offers clear synopses of what he thinks are the primary issues at play in the ongoing application of his work. Gelpi then describes how he has tried to appropriate Lonergan's intellectual project for his own theological reflection, while at the same time coming to terms with what he sees as the limitations of Lonergan's theory of method in theology. Critical of Lonergan's endorsement of Kantian transcendental logic, Gelpi argues that the American philosophical tradition represented by Charles Sanders Peirce provides a sounder philosophical grounding for Lonergan's theories. Elaborating on how this insight into Peirce's logic transformed his own fundamental reorientation as a theologian, Gelpi extends how Lonergan's thought can be reimagined and reworked for the ongoing journey of intellectual, moral, and religious conversion that is necessary to do meaningful theology in the twenty-first century.

Patrick H. Byrne's essay picks up where Gelpi's leaves off, discussing the importance of Lonergan's thought by explicating his use of the phrase, "the passionateness of being." He traces the import of this phrase to Lonergan's notion of the implicit and explicit paradigms that shape human ways of thinking, feeling, and judgment. Each individual has an unconscious, implicit "metaphysics" operating in one's life: one's assumptions and ideologies—inherited from parents, friends, culture, and religion—become the unconscious paradigm of one's reality. Byrne notes that Lonergan's contribution is to propose that there is another "First Philosophy" inherent in human beings as well, one which does not come from the world around us but from the sense of reality built into our cognitional structure. We human beings get passionate about our insights into ourselves in a profoundly different way than the implicit paradigms operating in our lives. Indeed, this innate, explicit metaphysics or First Philosophy has to do with reflective self-awareness, what Lonergan calls "self-appropriation." Byrne shows how the notion of self-appropriation is connected to theology, how it becomes, in effect, the major task of theology: to self-appropriate God's self-gift of passionate, unconditional love as rendered in the Christian traditions, so as to move us to preach this passionate love and transform the world.

Elizabeth A. Murray delves even deeper into Lonergan's understanding of human consciousness in order to find what she calls the "key" to his philosophy. Arguing that Lonergan starts in the polymorphic nature of human interiority, she charts the stages of consciousness that emerge in the dynamic, intentional process of self-appropriation. This moment of insight is Lonergan's methodological key. Murray suggests that Lonergan's philosophical methodology can be employed in order to safeguard the complex nature of consciousness, a methodology that keeps in tension the understanding of consciousness as an "act of knowing" and consciousness as an "act of identity." She defends Lonergan's idea of the appropriated self against modern and postmodern reductions. Indeed, she shows that Lonergan's focus on the pivotal act of insight into one's self-appropriation helps us to steer clear of the denial or neglect of the self that is so prevalent in modern varieties of philosophical empiricism, rationalism, and phenomenology.

John C. Haughey, S.J., concludes the section on Lonergan with his somewhat humorous title, "Lonergan's Jaw." The title refers to a recent newspaper article about the discovery of the mutation of a gene about 2.4 million years ago that lead to much weaker jaws in certain primates. But the upside of these weaker jaws was the growth of larger brains in the development of the human species. Haughey uses this recent scientific discovery as a springboard to discuss Lonergan's worldview of "emergent probability," a view that describes how the ongoing accumulation of scientific and humanistic data helps account for the complex interdependency of cosmic evolution. Haughey illuminates how Lonergan's notion of emergent probability changes the very nature of how we speak about "God talk" and about human transcendence. For Lonergan, emergent probability has its greatest referent in the intersubjective experience of love, a self-transcending, transformative act that changes the world. Haughey notes that for Lonergan, the human person is a co-creator, actively intervening in the drama of the cosmos, assisting its progress or halting its decline. We are, in Lonergan's word, "emergents" whose primary act is to announce the good news of Jesus, he who "spans the divide between us and the apes and us and the Trinity."

The second set of essays concern the very public theologian-intellectual, John Courtney Murray. Born on September 12, 1904, in New York City of Irish and Scottish ancestry, Murray entered the Society of Jesus in 1920 and, like Lonergan, earned his doctorate in theology from the Gregorian University. He would spend the major part of his career teaching the theology of grace and Trinity to Jesuit seminarians at Woodstock College in Maryland; he also served as an editor of *Theological Studies* and *America*, the Jesuit national weekly magazine. Though Murray is perhaps best known today for his contribution to the public theology of church-state relations, his ecclesiastical superiors forbade him from publishing on this topic for a time in the 1950s because it veered too close to modernist, Americanist controversies in the Church. In 1960 Murray was finally given permission to publish what would become his most famous work, *We Hold These Truths: Catholic Reflections on the American Proposition*, advocating the compatibility of American constitutionalism with Roman Catholicism.[3] Later that same year, he gained national notoriety as a celebrity intellectual when he was chosen as the cover piece for *Time* magazine's December 12 issue. At the invitation of Francis Joseph Cardinal Spellman, archbishop of New York, Murray was named a theological adviser at Vatican II, in which he helped write the Council document on religious liberty, *Dignitatis Humanae*. In 1967, shortly after returning from the Council, John Courtney Murray died. His published work reflected his deep concern to promote genuine dialogue about the common good in a pluralistic society—a dialogue often sadly lacking in contemporary public life. As Peter McDonough notes, "Murray's renown rested on his capacity to persuade Catholics and non-Catholic alike that religious tolerance and political pluralism were acceptable and even praiseworthy."[4] His understanding of pluralism envisioned statesmanlike leaders involved in reasoned debate about the civil and moral law that could help defend the common good.

Michael J. Schuck's "John Courtney Murray's American Stories" begins this set of four essays by highlighting the important relationship between Murray's consciousness of the American proposition and the Murray family's own immigrant roots in New York City. Schuck gives us a unique perspective on how the lived experience of the Catholic immigrant story of America—with its accounts of freedom, courage, and hard work—nurtured the ground from which Murray builds his understanding of a public theology. Schuck notes that the pillars of Murray's theology focused on an immigrant's vision: human freedom, the courage to open up to genuine dialogue, and the hard work it would take to maintain it.

The next essay in this section is the most personal of the four, written by Mark Williams, the nephew of John Courtney Murray. A graduate of Georgetown University, New York University Law School, and a successful businessman, he was asked to give his thoughts at Georgetown's centennial celebration on his "Uncle Jack." Williams reveals an intimate portrayal of Murray's relationship to his family through the often humorous and always insightful anecdotes that he remembers about his famous uncle. If Schuck illustrates the importance of the lived experience of the immigrant on Murray's theological imagination, Williams allows us to see the humanity of Murray and how his family played a large part in confirming his American immigrant sensibilities.

"Murray on Loving One's Enemies," the ingenious title of the essay by Leon Hooper, S.J., uses the biblical exhortation to illustrate Murray's spiritual and intellectual journey. He shows how Murray grew deeper in his Catholic tradition before having to transcend and transform the limitations of that tradition in order to enter genuine dialogue with the world. Hooper notes that "while Murray never wrote much on loving one's enemies, he did have a clearly identifiable enemies list." He takes us through Murray's list—the idea of Americanism, the professors and administrators at Catholic University of America (who helped to silence him), American Protestants in general, and atheists in particular. Hooper deftly describes Murray's "hatred" toward each, how his own Catholic tradition consciously and unconsciously fostered that hatred, and how he found hidden in that tradition a way to "bear the cross" of others and come to love one's enemies.

Thomas Hughson, S.J., ends the section with his essay "Murray: Faithful to Tradition in Context," further excavating Murray's relationship between the American experience and the legacy of Roman Catholic political thought. Hughson first shows how Murray's Catholic, natural-law style of moral theology overlapped with the Enlightenment deism of the Founding Fathers. Murray saw that the Christian tradition was what Hughson calls "a biblical leaven working from within upon Western political self-understanding and practice." What Murray foregrounded through both his scholarship and in his participation at the Council was the richness of the Anglo-American legacy of constitutionalism, a legacy seemingly unknown to the Catholic world of Latin Europe and certainly missing from Leo XIII's 1901 encyclical *Graves de Communi Re* on Christian democracy. Hughson argues that it is time to retrieve Murray's vision for the Church today, especially in terms of the relationship between the church and the state, and the distinction of the moral and legal orders that must be weighed in a pluralistic state. Murray believed that conscience should always be protected in this tension, not because freedom is its own reward, but because conscience is the point where the gospel and political life meet and interact.

Perhaps the best known and most published of the three theologians of the centenary year is Karl Rahner, born on March 5, 1904 in Freiburg, Germany. He entered the Society of Jesus in 1922, following in the footsteps of his brother, Hugo. Ordained in 1932, Rahner began his academic career as a philosopher, spending four semesters attending the lectures of Martin Heidegger at the University of Freiburg. Rahner would later say that though he had many good professors in his studies, "there is only one whom I can revere as my teacher, and he is Martin Heidegger."[5] In 1936 Rahner withdrew from philosophy and took his doctorate in theology, now fully convinced of the need to reshape Thomistic theology in light of Heidegger's critique of philosophy. Rahner would go on to publish over 3,500 essays (collected in fourteen volumes), six dictionaries and encyclopedias of theology and, late in his life, his book *Foundations of Christian Faith: An Introduction to the Idea of Christianity*, which is still in print today.[6]

Rahner, like Lonergan, is sometimes referred to as a Transcendental Thomist, taking seriously the Kantian turn toward the subject in light of Aquinas's epistemological and ontological claims about reality. Rahner posits that human beings are by their very nature self-transcendent and that God is the endpoint of that human drive toward self-transcendence. One of his greatest legacies was his reformulation of the way theologians speak about experience of God: an encounter with infinite mystery, an uncategorical experience deep within the structure of the human being that draws forth one's desire for truth, goodness, and beauty. Rahner's perspective is seen everywhere in Catholic theology during the time of the Council, most especially in the manner of style that O'Malley articulates as one of the hallmarks of the Second Vatican Council. His contribution at the Council rests in his ability to reframe the dogmatic formulas of Catholicism so that their tenor was radically reinterpreted in a more inclusive, ecumenical, and pastoral language, even as the scholastic language of formal orthodoxy was maintained.

"On Reading Rahner in a New Century," by Leo J. O'Donovan, S.J., is the first essay of this section. He attempts to answer why Rahner is a necessary companion for theological reflection in the coming decades. Contrary to the usual classification of Rahner as a theologian engaged with modernity, O'Donovan holds that Rahner more rightly qualifies as a postmodern theologian, arguing that there is an explicit critique of modernity traced throughout his oeuvre. O'Donovan traces this line of reasoning by analyzing what he calls "pivotal interpretive issues" in Rahner's thought that are decisive in reading him today and into the twenty-first century.

Harvey D. Egan, S.J., follows with "Karl Rahner's Theological Life," a very personal reflection and assessment of the man whom he studied under in his own theological training. Egan reminds us that though there were many thinkers who influenced the formation of

Rahner's theology, Rahner always contended that it was the Christian mystics and his own Jesuit spirituality that had the greatest significance on his work. Egan argues that Rahner deserves the title "Doctor Mysticus" of the Church, for God's self-communication to human persons is always at the heart of his theological vision, however difficult or hidden that experience of God might be. Egan recalls his own memories and those of friends who remember Rahner as a disciple of the *Spiritual Exercises of St. Ignatius*, serving others generously as spiritual director and pastor. It is not by accident that Rahner's long list of publications begin and end with a book on prayer, bookends, as it were, for a man whose theological task came out of his desire to know and to love the end of all theological endeavors, the God of Jesus Christ.

The essay of George E. Griener, S.J., picks up where both O'Donovan and Egan leave off, further developing an understanding of Rahner as a pastoral theologian. The "heart," Greiner notes, is the major theme of Rahner's theological project. Greiner begins by giving the historical context of the German world in which Rahner lived: the Protestant Reformation, the Enlightenment thought of German philosophy, the work of Kant and Hegel, the Kulturkampf on the Catholic Church in 1872, the criminalization of the Society of Jesus in Germany until 1917, the oath against modernism, and the two world wars. All of these events helped to hone the pastoral vision of Rahner's theology. Greiner then tries to touch upon some of the overriding themes that come out of Rahner's grappling with such a world. Like Egan, he notes that Rahner's theology of grace as God's self-communication is the lens by which all of his theology is based.

James Voiss, S.J., offers a final, constructive essay on Rahner by pairing him up with another twentieth-century theologian who is undergoing a renaissance of study, the German-Swiss theologian, Hans Urs von Balthasar. Born a year after Rahner and himself a Jesuit for many years, von Balthasar's theological project has often been juxtaposed to Rahner's theological methodology and optimistic tenor. If Rahner was hopeful about the Church's engagement with modernity and the progress of Vatican II, von Balthasar was highly critical of what he called the "epic" pretensions of the modern theological project. Von Balthasar's starting point in theological aesthetics is a markedly different starting point than Rahner's Transcendental Thomism. The two theologians, often at odds in their theological judgment of the other's work, continue to represent two competing visions of theological investigation today. Voiss's contribution is to attempt to find a conciliatory reading of these thinkers by arguing that it is false to conclude that Rahner lacks a theological aesthetic, albeit one that is only implicit in his work. Voiss first engages von Balthasar's critical appraisal of Rahner's theological method and then attempts to respond to these charges by offering a much nuanced interpretation of Rahner's theology in light of these charges. Voiss finds that throughout Rahner's more than 4,000 titles, one can find evidence to suggest that Rahner was theologically sensitive to a theological aesthetics, even if it is never fully articulated in his work. In effect, Voiss helps both to expose the somewhat artificial gap that exists between Rahner and von Balthasar's theology and to extend paths in which future Rahner scholarship might lead.

Finally, David Stagaman, S.J., offers a postscript to the essays on Lonergan, Murray, and Rahner. He looks back on the history of twentieth-century Catholic theology, charting his own absorption of their work as he matured as a Jesuit theologian and scholar. Stagaman first situates his discussion of their work in the philosophical questions that arise from the father of Transcendental Thomism, Joseph Maréchal. Lonergan, Murray, and Rahner were deeply affected by Maréchal's attempt to place Immanuel Kant and Thomas Aquinas into a fruitful dialogue. Stagaman then turns to each of our centenarians, offering his own sense of the reception of their work by the theological community in the United States in the past century. He ends by noting that the Dominican priest Yves Congar was another important theologian of the year 1904, connecting the theological dots of the twentieth century to make it a very good year indeed.

What all of the essays share is a deep regard for these pioneering theologians. They celebrate their life and work and point to new avenues of reflection and research for the contemporary Church. The many threads of their theological focus were bound together into one large pattern in the defining moment of the Second Vatican Council. Each found in the Council an opening to explore the meaning of Christian faith in the midst of the "joy and hope, the grief and anguish of the people of our time." Each in his own way was able to integrate the wisdom of the Church's past with the novel possibilities of the present and suggest a future search for meaning.

Bernard Lonergan

2. Learning to Live with Lonergan

Donald L. Gelpi, S.J.

Before joining the faculty of the Jesuit School of Theology at Berkeley, California, I taught philosophy and supervised the academic program of the Jesuit scholastics studying at Loyola University in New Orleans. I taught in the philosophy department because I had done my doctorate in philosophy with a special focus on American philosophy. I wanted to spend my professional academic career doing theology; but I had studied enough theology as a Jesuit scholastic to realize that unless one brings to systematic theology a new set of categories, one winds up rehashing history. I wanted to create an inculturated theology for the United States church, and I wanted to use American philosophy both as a point of entry into American culture and as a source of speculative theological categories.

In the spring of 1973, the semester before I came to Berkeley, three Jesuit scholastics asked me to teach them a seminar in the thought of Bernard Lonergan. I had no special interest in Lonergan, but I had no objection to getting deeper into his thought. Moreover, Lonergan's last and greatest work, *Method in Theology*, had just appeared, and, since I would be teaching theology here in Berkeley the following year, it made sense to me to get on top of that important work.[1]

That semester seems to me in retrospect providential. *Method in Theology* remains in my judgment the best analysis to date on how theology works, even though I have strong reservations about a number of the presuppositions that Lonergan uses to ground his theory of how theologians ought to think. By the end of the seminar on Lonergan, I had decided that in Berkeley I would test Lonergan's method by using it. I have been doing that in a systematic way for over thirty years, and in this essay I would like to share with you some of the things I have learned from thirty-some-odd years of living with Lonergan.

I shall attempt to do three things. First, I would like to give you some sense of who Bernard Lonergan was. Second, I will try to sketch for you the scope of his intellectual project. Third, I would like to share with you what I perceive as the strengths and limitations of Lonergan's theory of method in theology.

Bernard Lonergan was born on December 17, 1904, in Buckingham, the province of Quebec, Canada. He would acquire two younger brothers. It quickly became apparent to both his father, Gerald J. Lonergan, who worked as a land surveyor, and to his mother Josephine, that they had begotten a very precocious child. He attended elementary school with the Christian Brothers in his hometown. Later he got a thorough grounding in Latin and Greek, in the humanities, and in mathematics at Loyola High School in Montreal.

He joined the Jesuits at the age of seventeen and received his philosophical training at Heythrop College in London from 1926 to 1929. He subsequently earned a bachelor of arts in the classics at London University between 1929 and 1930. By his own account he felt significantly struck at the modesty of the English Jesuits who taught him philosophy. His tutor Charles O'Hara, S.J., deepened his grasp of mathematics. Lewis Watt, S.J., introduced him to issues in economics and to Catholic social teaching; Lonergan claimed that reading John Henry Newman's *An Essay in Aid of a Grammar of Assent* made him into something of an existentialist. That work was destined to influence significantly his thinking in *Insight*, his most important philosophical work. During these years, Lonergan sought to find in sociology, in economics, and in history a speculative basis for the realization of the great social encyclicals.

In the late 1940s, Lonergan taught at the Thomas More Institute for Adult Education in Montreal. His life-long friend and collaborator, R. Eric O'Connor, S.J., had founded the Institute. These years of lecturing and research produced *Insight: A Study of Human Understanding.*[2]

In 1953, Lonergan became a professor of dogmatic theology at the Gregorian University in Rome. His lectures in Latin on Christology and the Trinity appeared as published Latin texts. Lonergan characterized these examples of textbook theology as the product of a "hopelessly antiquated" teaching situation at the Gregorian. The primitive state of theological thinking combined with his studies of European scholarship, hermeneutics, and critical history, launched him on his most significant theological project: namely, rethinking method in theology.

Toward the end of his twelve years in Rome, Lonergan developed lung cancer. One of his lungs was removed, but his superiors made it possible for him to complete the writing of *Method in Theology*. After his retirement, he held the Stillman Chair in Catholic Studies at Harvard Divinity School and spent several years teaching at Boston College. Bernard Lonergan died at Pickering, Ontario, on November 26, 1984.

I will begin my attempt to describe the scope of Lonergan's speculative project by looking at his deep roots in the Thomistic tradition. This first appears in his early studies in the 1940s of operative grace in Aquinas. A subsequent probing of the mind of the Angelic Doctor produced a second series of scholarly articles on the role of the *verbum*, or inner word, in Aquinas's account of human cognition. In his study of operative grace, Lonergan dramatized, through the study of a specific theological problem, that medieval theology exhibited a spontaneous drive toward systematization; and, as his thought developed, Lonergan would exhibit a growing preoccupation with understanding the nature of systematic thinking. His *verbum* articles began to define how Lonergan would undertake to grasp the nature of systematic thinking: namely, through a study of human interiority.

Lonergan's early probing of the thought of Aquinas located him solidly in the Thomistic revival occasioned by Pope Leo XIII's encyclical *Aeterni Patris*, (*On the Restoration of Christian Philosophy*), issued August 4, 1879 (DS 3135–3140). The encyclical stimulated a more systematic scholarly retrieval of Aquinas's thought; but the Thomistic revival at the beginning of the twentieth century also sought to demonstrate the contemporary relevance of the Thomistic synthesis by putting it into dialogue with modern and contemporary thinkers. During his years at the Thomas More Institute in Montreal, Lonergan set himself to advance this second aspect of the Thomistic revival in a very systematic manner. His efforts produced his first major work: *Insight: A Study of Human Understanding*.

Here I should warn you that one cannot understand what Lonergan is talking about without probing his philosophy. Lonergan began his career as a philosopher and developed into a systematic theologian; but his systematic theology, including his theory of method in theology, incorporates into it many of the philosophical positions he developed in writing *Insight*. I will try to explain some of the more important philosophical issues without oversimplifying them.

Lonergan derived his most immediate inspiration for advancing the Thomistic tradition speculatively from the work of Joseph Maréchal, a Belgian Jesuit. Maréchal tried to demonstrate Aquinas's contemporary relevance by putting his philosophy into dialogue with that of Immanuel Kant, who had tried to deduce a priori the conditions for the possibility of scientific knowing, of moral judgment, and of aesthetic judgment.

Kant began his philosophical career as a rationalist, but his reading of David Hume wakened him from what he called his dogmatic slumbers. Through Hume, Kant absorbed the conceptual nominalism of the British empirical tradition. Nominalism denies the reality of universality or of real generality. It reduces the objects of knowledge to concrete sensible things: this chair, this rock, this tree, this horse, this automobile. Classical nominalism reduces universals to a *flatus vocis*, which John Deely, in his history of semiotics, translates as a kind of fart of the lips. Put less colorfully and less crudely, for classical nominalists what philosophers call universals are simply the same concrete sound, like "horse" repeated again and again over a concrete, long-necked, long-faced, maned, tailed, hooved, herbivorous mammal. Conceptual nominalists allow that real generality or universality exists but maintain that it exists only in human subjectivity, not in the objects which human thinking grasps.

One cannot summarize as subtle a thinker as Kant in a few sentences; but I think that it is fair to say that Kant derived the universal generalizations of scientific thinking from human subjectivity. Kant argued that scientific thinking imposes these subjectively derived universals on the concrete sense data it studies. Concrete sense data do not itself possess any universality. As a result, scientific thinking can never grasp reality as such, what Kant called the *Ding an sich* (thing in itself). The scientific mind can only know reality reconstructed through the imposition on concrete sense data of a subjectively derived universality, which the sense data themselves do not possess.

Worse still, from the standpoint of Thomistic philosophy, Kant denied the possibility of metaphysical knowing. Metaphysics, of course, offers a systematic account of the nature or reality, of Being. Kantian epistemology requires that every theoretical judgment have a concrete, sensed object. Metaphysical categories like God, the world, the soul exemplify no concrete sensed object and therefore fail to qualify as knowledge in the strict sense. On these nominalistic presuppositions, Kant buried metaphysics.

Maréchal undertook to refute Kant on Kant's own terms. He endorsed Kantian transcendental method. Like Kant in his *Critique of Pure Reason*, Maréchal undertook to deduce a priori the conditions for the possibility of theoretical knowledge; but while he endorsed Kant's philosophical logic, Maréchal took issue with his conceptual nominalism. Maréchal argued that by restricting human knowing to the subjective interrelation of concrete sense data and subjectively derived universal concepts, Kant had failed to take into adequate account an important aspect of human cognition, which forms the centerpiece of Aquinas's theory of knowledge, namely, the judgment of being, the cognitive grasp of existence as such.

The human intellect's ability to grasp being as such endows it in a Thomistic theory of knowledge with its formal object. A formal object defines the scope of a human power's activity. The formal object of a power of knowing consists of the reality the power grasps and the aspect under which it grasps that object. For example, the five senses all know physical, sensible things. Physical, sensible realities provide, then, the objects, which the five senses grasp. Sight, however, grasps them as colored, scent as odoriferous, touch as extended, hot or cold, etc. In a Thomistic theory of knowledge, the human intellect, too, grasps physical, sensible realities as its proper object, because Aquinas agreed with Aristotle that all human knowledge derives from the senses. The human intellect, however, grasps physical, sensible things as existing, as being. Being therefore, supplies the formal object of the intellect, the aspect under which it knows the things it encounters in the physical world.

In Thomistic metaphysics, God and Being coincide. Aquinas therefore concluded that the human spiritual intellect has a natural, inbuilt orientation to God. Maréchal seized upon this aspect of Aquinas' thought and developed it. He portrayed the active human intellect as an insatiable appetite for more and more being, more and more knowledge, and ultimately as an intellectual longing for union with God. As a result, Maréchal resurrected and gave special prominence to a forgotten

Thomistic doctrine: namely, that the human intellect's essential orientation to God, to Being as such, transforms it into a natural desire for the beatific vision, for the perfect, graced, face-to-face knowledge of God, which the saints enjoy in the life to come.

In *Insight*, Lonergan endorsed many of these fundamental Maréchalian positions, although he did not pursue the theme of the human intellect as a natural desire for the beatific vision. He left that to Henri de Lubac. Lonergan, however, went beyond Maréchal by incorporating into his version of Transcendental Thomism a much more detailed analysis of the structure of human intentionality. In *Insight*, he undertook a detailed analysis of the structure of mathematical, scientific, and common sense judgments. On the basis of that analysis, he claimed to have deduced a priori an unrevisable starting place for all human knowing. That starting place consisted in an invariant pattern of cognitive operations, which one could not deny without reproducing those very same operations in the same terms and relations as Lonergan had deduced a priori from the data of consciousness.

According to Lonergan human knowing begins with experience, which provides the raw material for thought much as the sense manifold does in Kant. Human knowing next advances to understanding, to the moment of insight when the mind grasps how hypothetically to explain a particular problem or set of experienced data. It then advances to the moment of judgment, which either verifies or falsifies one's insight into the data under investigation. In the act of judgment, one grasps the being, the reality of whatever one is trying to understand. Judgment provides the realistic ground for a final operation, namely, decision.

Like Maréchal, Lonergan portrayed the human intellect as an insatiable thirst for Being and truth. He characterized the human mind as an unrestricted desire to know, as an insatiable thirst for more and more knowledge and truth. Having answered any given question, the human mind longs to ask and answer more and more questions until its thirst for Being as such and for truth as such finds ultimate satisfaction through union with the Being and truth of God. (I have been teaching all my life and have never encountered such a mind, including my own; but we need to postpone any criticism of Lonergan's position until later.)

Lonergan's distinction between knowledge and consciousness provides a fundamental presupposition of his epistemology. Knowledge advances human understanding of the created world and invokes the hypothetico-deductive method of the positive sciences. Consciousness focuses not on the world around us but on the operations of the human mind, what Lonergan calls the data of consciousness. The exploration of consciousness does not use the method of sciencc but invokes Kant's Transcendental logic in order to deduce a priori the invariant, intentional structure of human self-awareness: namely, that it advances from experience, to understanding, to judgment, and finally to decision.

All these philosophical presuppositions lie at the basis of Lonergan's theory of method in theology, his last and greatest work. In my own theological thinking, I endorse three aspects of Lonergan's account of method in theology: his description of the fundamental task of theological thinking, his definition of method, and his theory of functional theological specialties.

The first sentence of *Method in Theology* asserts: "A theology mediates between a cultural matrix and the significance and role of a religion in that matrix." At the Jesuit School of Theology in Berkeley we take pride in promoting a culturally contextual theology. In my judgment, more than any other theoretician of theological method, Lonergan places inculturation at the heart of the theological enterprise.

The term *culture* entered Western speculation in the nineteenth century. Even to this day it ranks as one of the great weasel words of the English language, and of any other language for that matter. Weasel words mean so many different things that one frequently finds oneself at a loss to say exactly what they do mean. The same vagueness dogs the term *inculturation.* I know of only one way to use a weasel word responsibly: namely, to say from the beginning precisely what one does mean by it. By "culture" I mean anything in space and time conditioned by communication among embodied persons.

Theological inculturation for me connotes three things: it connotes, first of all, the actualization of a religion in symbols and categories derived from the culture which any given religion addresses and therefore in symbols and categories likely to prove intelligible to the people living in that culture. Second, in the case of Christian theology, inculturated theological thinking also invokes gospel values to challenge the sinfulness of a culture and to bring the persons and institutions in that culture repentance. Christians repent initially by replacing commitment to sin with the commitment of justifying faith. Church institutions repent by reforming themselves in ways compatible with Jesus' vision of the reign of God. Finally, given the unprecedented internationalization of culture, inculturated theological thinking needs to overcome the myopia inherent in any given culture by keeping it in creative dialogue with other cultures and with the great tradition of the Church.

Lonergan himself distinguished two different ways of understanding culture. A classicist understanding of culture recognizes only one culture, normally one's own culture, as both universal and permanent and dismisses all other cultures as barbaric. An empiricist notion of culture views culture as developmental, as the set of meanings and values which inform a way of life and which may enjoy relative stability, gradual development, or rapid dissolution. Cultural classicists view theology as a permanent achievement. Cultural empiricists view theology as an ongoing process. Since Lonergan's theory of method in theology presents theological thinking as an ongoing process, he clearly rejects the classicist notion of culture as inadequate and opts for what he calls an empiricist notion of culture.

In my own theological thinking, I also endorse Lonergan's definition of the term "method." In the introduction to *Method in Theology*, Lonergan observes that: "Method is not a set of rules to be followed meticulously by a dolt. It is a framework for collaborative creativity." In his first chapter he defines method as "a normative pattern of recurrent and related operations yielding cumulative and progressive results."

I find much to recommend in such a definition of method. I like its focus on operations. One understands a method if one can name the operations one needs to perform in order to get something done. In the practical sciences like animal husbandry or mining, method seeks a practical outcome—healthy cows, mine shafts that do not collapse. In a theoretical scholarly enterprise like theology, operations seek to effect a speculative result: namely, a true account of the reality one is trying to understand.

A sound method has related operations because it exemplifies an organized technique for getting something done either practically or theoretically. It has recurrent operations because one can apply a successful method to one related question after another and achieve satisfactory answers or results.

Lonergan correctly asserts that one ought to judge a method by its ability to produce results, whether theoretical or practical. Those results have a cumulative character when they build on one another. In the theoretical sciences, a successful method produces conclusions, which throw light on one another and yield a greater and greater insight into the reality under investigation. Such an insight also has of necessity a progressive character.

Finally, in the theology I have been creating, I also endorse and continue to invoke Lonergan's theory of functional specialization in theology. Lonergan called his book *Method in Theology* rather than *Theological Method* because his argument in that work implicitly denied the very existence of theological method as such. Lonergan argues, correctly in my estimate, that different kinds of questions require different methods to answer them. Each question and its corresponding method gives rise to eight different kinds of theological thinking, which Lonergan calls functional specialties within the total theological enterprise.

Four functional specialties—research, interpretation, history, and dialectic—comprise what Lonergan calls mediating theology. Mediating theology retrieves a religious tradition and clarifies problematic issues in need of rethinking and reformulation.

Lonergan understood theological thinking as an ongoing dialogue among all eight theological specialties. Research theology provides those who ply the other functional specialties with the materials they need in order to think theologically. *Research* theologians excavate the Holy Land and other historical religious sites. They edit and update dictionaries and grammars of sacred languages. They produce critical editions of religious texts.

Theological *interpretation* envisages more than just Biblical exegesis although it includes the interpretation of the Bible. Theologians must interpret all the artifacts and texts made available by theological research. They must give an account of what those texts and artifacts meant to the people who created them and what they might mean to contemporary Christians living at the beginning of a new millennium.

Theological *history* tells the story of the development of a religious community. It provides the context for interpreting the texts and artifacts produced by theological research. Historians face two interrelated scholarly tasks. They first need to establish an accurate chronology of the events they narrate. Then they need to formulate a hypothesis, which explains why history took this turn rather than that, when at some point in the past it might have gone in either direction.

The dialogue character of Lonergan's theory of method appears when one realizes that any of the functional specialties in theology might raise questions for other specialties to solve. For example, the archaeological discovery of the Dead Sea Scrolls and their subsequent publication in critical editions raised important questions for the interpreters of both the Old and the New Testaments to resolve, questions like "What impact, if any, did the beliefs and practices of the Essene monks at Qumran have on the rise of Christianity?" The feminist retrieval of women's histories and the liberationist attempt to retell the history of the Church and of human society through the eyes of the oppressed have both created new contexts for interpreting religious documents.

Dialectic completes the retrieval of a religious tradition. Any study of a living religious tradition reveals that the people who create that tradition are always arguing with one another about what the tradition really means. Theological dialecticians attempt to clarify the terms of that debate. In studying different doctrinal debates within the Church, dialecticians compare and contrast the different frames of reference in which different thinkers approach the formulation of Church doctrines. Dialecticians do so in an attempt to identify when the thinkers in question agree, when they disagree, and, if they do really disagree, the specific issues which divide them.

If mediating theology retrieves a religious tradition, mediated theology undertakes its critical reformulation. One cannot reformulate a religious tradition critically until the first four functional specialties have retrieved it in an ongoing way. In this sense, in Lonergan's theory mediating theology mediates mediated theology.

Four functional specialties constitute mediated theology: foundations, doctrines, systematics, and communications. *Foundational theology* articulates a normative account of the conversion experience that lies at the basis of a religious tradition. Moreover, Lonergan revolutionized a traditional theology of conversion by arguing that it comes in more than one form.

A traditional theology of conversion, which you will find very clearly explained in the first volume of Bernard Häring's *The Law of Christ*, portrayed conversion as an essentially religious event with moral and religious consequences.[3] Conversion always involves a turning from and a turning to. Christian conversion requires one to turn away from a life of sin and unbelief to the obedience of faith. That turning endows Christian conversion with moral consequences.

Lonergan did not question the truth of a traditional theology of conversion, but he did question its adequacy. Lonergan clearly derived his notion of intellectual conversion from the critical appropriation of the structures of human consciousness he had articulated in *Insight*. He believed that the uncritical, unreflective mind tended to remain trapped in the fallacy of the already-out-there-now real. The fallacy of the already-out-there-now real underlies all forms of intellectual fundamentalism. It uncritically objectifies truth as a set of fixed and unchanging propositions for memorization. These allegedly eternal truths need defending by memorizing the ready answer.

By the time Lonergan wrote *Method in Theology*, however, his own philosophical thinking about the structure of intentionality had evolved. In *Insight*, following Maréchal, he had argued from the essential orientation of the human spiritual intellect to Being as such to a fairly traditional Thomistic metaphysics of Being. In *Method in Theology*, the turn to experience and, specifically, normative thinking about the different kinds of conversion experience, replace the metaphysical concerns of *Insight*. Moreover, in *Insight* Lonergan's account of ethical thinking had largely extended the consequences of his metaphysics into the realm of practical reasoning. By the time he wrote *Method in Theology*, Lonergan had, correctly in my estimate, come to regard moral deliberation as a different kind of thinking from theoretical metaphysics. This insight led him to distinguish between intellectual and moral conversion. In *Method*, therefore, Lonergan spoke of three kinds of conversion: intellectual, moral and religious.

In *Method*, moreover, Lonergan invoked Joseph de Finance's distinction between the exercise of vertical and horizontal freedom in order to explain what happens when one converts. Horizontal freedom happens within an accepted horizon, or frame of reference. Vertical freedom creates a new horizon, or frame of reference. Moreover, the new horizon offers a deeper, broader, richer frame of reference for interpreting reality. Every conversion for Lonergan exemplifies an exercise in vertical freedom. It offers one a new perspective on reality that forces the reevaluation of one's attitudes, beliefs, habits, way of life.

I find this explanation true enough as far as it goes; but it reflects Lonergan's embrace of the Kantian turn to the subject and his preoccupation with anatomizing the structures of subjective human intentionality. In my judgment, to describe a conversion as a decision that creates a new horizon of consciousness fails to take into adequate account a fundamental dimension of conversion: namely, that it involves a turning from and a turning to. With hints from H. Richard Niebuhr's *The Responsible Self*, I prefer to define initial conversion as the decision to turn from irresponsibility to responsibility in some identifiable realm of human experience.[4] I would, however, concede to Lonergan that such a decision does indeed create a new evaluative frame of reference, which Lonergan calls a "horizon." I would also concede that the creation of a new converted frame of reference requires the reevaluation of everything in one's earlier perceptions of reality.

Robert Doran subsequently caused Lonergan to admit that in writing *Method in Theology*, he should have taken into account what Doran called psychic conversion. Lonergan's thought reflects the strong intellectual bias of Thomistic philosophy and of his own personality. Most of what he says about human affectivity, human imagination, and intuitive forms of thinking he derives from other thinkers. This obtuseness on his part in dealing with a very important realm of human experience no doubt explains in part why we failed initially to speak of conversion at an affective, psychological level.

Doran and I reached the same insight into the need to complete Lonergan's account of the different kinds of conversion quite independently of one another. I prefer to talk of affective rather than of psychic conversion; and, if I understand Doran's position correctly, I mean something different by affective conversion from what Doran means by psychic conversion. Doran seems to me to portray psychic conversion largely in terms of shining the rational light of intellectual conversion on affective, intuitive forms of thinking, whereas I would insist that affective, intuitive thinking grasps reality in its own right, and that most of the thinking which characterizes affective conversion engages affective, intuitive thinking rather than rational, inferential thinking. I agree with Doran, however, concerning the need to expand Lonergan's three forms of conversion—intellectual, moral and religious—with a fourth: namely, what I call affective, rather than psychic, conversion.

In addition, I have over the years come to realize that personal morality and public morality define two distinct but interrelated ethical frames of reference, with the result that one can convert ethically in two ways. When one takes responsibility for one's personal dealings with others and commits oneself to respecting their rights and to fulfilling one's duties toward them, one experiences an initial personal moral conversion. When one commits oneself to collaborating with others in order to achieve the common good and to insure the justice of human institutional arrangements, one converts politically. In other words, I have come to expand the number of conversions to five: affective conversion, intellectual conversion, personal moral conversion, political conversion, and religious conversion, with Christian conversion exemplifying one form of religious conversion.

It would appear that Lonergan became fascinated with the question of theological method as a result of reading a lot of bad, garbled theology. In *Method in Theology* he observes that the fact that meaning can incarnate itself entails that "the meaningless, the vacant, the empty, the vapid, the dull" can do so as well.

Concern with theological truth caused Lonergan to distinguish the functional specialty of *doctrines* from that of *systematics*. Lonergan looks to the norms elaborated by foundational theology to provide the criteria for distinguishing sound from unsound doctrines. Sound doctrines will advance the conversion process. Unsound doctrines will tend to distort the conversion process, even to subvert it altogether.

In my own development of Lonergan's theory of method in theology, one must invoke a normative insight into the five forms and seven dynamics and counterdynamics of different kinds of conversion which foundational theology examines in order to distinguish between sound and unsound doctrines. Moreover, I thoroughly agree with Lonergan that only after one has used the normative insights of foundational thinking in order to identify sound doctrines should one go about the task of organizing those doctrines into a system. This the functional specialty of systematics does. In my judgment, a number of methodological problems beset Paul Tillich's *Systematic Theology*.[5] Moreover, this work exemplifies well, I believe, the dire consequences of overhasty systematization before doctrinal theology has had a chance to do its work.

Communications provides the fourth and final functional specialty of mediated theology. Here again, Lonergan's theory of method exhibits a refreshing originality. By communications Lonergan means much more than the popularization of the fruits of the other functional specialties. Ideally, communications ought to address the breakdown of communications in the Church, like that currently dividing left- and right-wing Catholics. In cases like this, communications theologians should design a catechesis, which seeks to summon all those involved in that breakdown, to the level of conversion that will put them back into communication with one another.

Among the functional specialties, three of them play a key role in the critical reformulation of a theological tradition: dialectic, foundations, and doctrines. Dialectic names the debated issues with which the critical reformulation of a theological tradition must deal. The normative insights of foundations provide the criteria to the results of dialectic. In my own theological work, I have attempted to develop these three functional specialties in a systematic way.

After looking at the scope of Lonergan's theological process, I will now describe how the use of Lonergan's method in my own theological thinking forced me to call into question a number of the presuppositions which ground that method.

As I have already indicated, Lonergan's method requires one to reflect critically on the relationship between a religion and the culture in which that religion seeks to actualize itself. Even as a Jesuit scholastic, I had already decided that thinking in a theologically inculturated manner would require me, if I ever would succeed in creating a theology, to take into account the best insights of the philosophical tradition in the United States. As I reflected on *Method in Theology*, I realized that in order to do that in a systematic way, I had to apply the four specialties of mediating theology—research, interpretation, history, and dialectic—not only to the systematic retrieval of the religious tradition on which theology reflects, but also to the development of culture in the United States. I therefore undertook a dialectical examination of the principal issues, which shaped the development of religious philosophy in this country. I have published some of the results of that dialectical analysis in *Endless Seeker: The Religious Quest of Ralph Waldo Emerson* and in *Varieties of Transcendental Experience: A Study in Constructive Postmodernism*.[6]

The more I immersed myself in the philosophical tradition in the United States, however, the more I found that it forced me to call into question many of the presuppositions that lay at the basis of Lonergan's theory of method in theology. As we have seen, Lonergan, following Maréchal, invoked Kantian transcendental method in order to deduce a priori the conditions for the possibility of theoretical knowing. Both thinkers claimed to have deduced a priori the truth of a Thomistic theory of knowledge and metaphysics. Charles Sanders Peirce, the founder of American pragmatic philosophy, began his philosophical career as a Kantian. He read Kant's *Critique of Pure Reason* so often as a college student that he could recite large sections of it by heart. He said he stopped doing that when he saw through Kant's argument in that work.

Peirce seems to have felt something like a divine vocation to rethink the foundations of logic and of metaphysics, and astonishingly he succeeded. The greatest logician this country has ever produced, Peirce very early immersed himself in scholastic logic and particularly admired the thought of John Duns Scotus. Peirce's revision of the logic of the syllogism convinced him that one could reduce any act of inferential reasoning to three irreducible kinds of argument.

Peirce argued, correctly in my judgment, that every act of inferential thinking interrelates a rule, a case, and a result. By a "result" he meant our descriptive account of the data you are trying to explain. By a "case" he meant the way you choose to categorize the data you are trying to explain. By a "rule" he meant your conception of some law ingredient in that data which justifies categorizing the data in question as one has chosen.

Abductive, or hypothetical, reasoning concludes to a case because it categorizes the data in a new way on the basis of some rule, which it vaguely perceives operating in nature. Deductive, or predictive, reasoning concludes to a result because it argues that if one's rule holds in nature, then other data not yet in evidence will become evident under specifiable conditions. Induction, or verifying reasoning, concludes to a rule because it argues that, if the data appears under the conditions one specified deductively, then the rule which one assumed to operate in nature actually does so.

Let's try to clarify these logical abstractions with a concrete example. Christopher Columbus sitting on a dock in a harbor observes that, as ships approach him, he first sees the top of their masts, then the whole mast, then the whole ship getting larger and larger as it approaches. He reasons abductively, or hypothetically, that if the surface of the ocean were flat he would see the whole ship from the beginning getting larger and larger as it approached in the way a car or person does in topping a hill. If, on the other hand, the surface of the ocean were curved, then he would see first the top of the mast, then the whole mast, then the whole ship getting larger and larger. If the surface of the ocean curves, then the bottom of the ocean must curve as well. Columbus concludes abductively that the world is round, not flat, as many of his contemporaries supposed. In re-categorizing the world as round, he assumes that the laws of nature tend to make planets like the earth round rather than flat.

Next, Columbus predicts deductively that, if the laws of nature have made the earth round, not flat, then he can reach what Europeans called the Orient, the East, by sailing west. This inference qualifies as a deduction because it predicts that facts not yet in evidence (sailing to the Orient) will become evident under specified conditions (by sailing west, not east).

When the crew of Ferdinand Magellan finally circumnavigated the globe by sailing west, it proved that Columbus had gotten it right when he assumed that the laws of nature had made the earth round, not flat. This inference counts as an induction because on the basis of a verified deduction, it asserts the reality of a rule, or of a certain conception of a law of nature.

Peirce saw through Kant's *Critique of Pure Reason* once he realized that his own revised account of inferential reasoning invalidated Kantian transcendental logic. In attempting to deduce a priori the way scientific thinking works, Kant had in fact only formulated a fallible abduction about the way scientists think and presented it as a conclusion or induction, while simultaneously calling it a deduction. From the standpoint of Peirce's revised logic of inference, one could hardly come up with a more confused formula for reasoning inferentially than that. Moreover, Peirce as a practicing scientist saw that Kant's account of scientific thinking had gotten things exactly backwards. The last thing a scientist wants to do is to impose on reality an intelligibility it does not have. Instead, scientists look to things to tell them the kinds of laws they obey by the way they behave.

The fact that Lonergan, who imitated Maréchal in endorsing Kantian transcendental logic, had invoked an invalid logic in allegedly arguing to an unrevisable starting point for all thinking forced me to call that particular speculative claim into question. Not only had Lonergan not come up with an unrevisable account of human knowing, but his theory of knowledge seemed to me to need revision at several key points. For example, Lonergan, in my judgment, made a mistake when he treated what he called "experience" as the raw material of inferential reasoning. With Peirce, I recognized that people do not live their lives at the level of abstract, rational inference but at the level of intuitive thinking: of feeling, memory, and imagination. One does not grasp Being, reality, only in verified inductions, whether abstract or concrete, as

Lonergan seems to suggest. Intuitive thinking grasps reality in its own right and does so with judgments of feeling.

In addition, Peirce's logic of abduction and deduction gave a more precise logical account of what Lonergan called "understanding." It did so by naming with logical precision the operations and relations which make up abductive and deductive thinking, just as Peirce's account of inductive inference gave a more precise logical account of what Lonergan called judgment. After a close study of John Dewey's *Logic: The Theory of Inquiry*, I also concluded that Dewey had formulated a more precise account of practical, deliberative thinking than Lonergan had.[7] In other words, not only had Lonergan failed to discover an unrevisable starting point for all thinking, but also his alleged unrevisable starting point needed serious revision at several points.

Moreover, the more I studied the logic and metaphysics of Charles Sanders Peirce, the more convinced I became that it provided a much sounder philosophical grounding for Lonergan's theory of functional specialization in theology than Lonergan himself had. Lonergan, as we have seen, had a social, dialogic, collaborative understanding of the way the functional specialties operate. Any specialty can raise questions and issues for another specialty. Peirce's logic had not only invalidated Kant's transcendental deduction a priori of the nature of human knowing, but it also forced him to replace the Kantian turn to the subject with the Peircean turn to community.

Peirce's turn to community followed logically from his theory of inference. Let's try to understand why. Peirce's theory of inference grounded his doctrine of fallibilism. Since deductive prediction deals only with possibilities, Peirce realized that the reasoning mind couches reality only in formulating what might prove wrong. In investigating any matter of complexity, Peirce argued, the scientist has first to decide how much of one's life one intends to devote to the project. Since one can give only limited time to searching for the truth, one must formulate one's hypothesis before one knows that one has taken all the relevant data into account. As a result, an overlooked fact can, in principle, always turn up, calling one's hypothesis into question. Similarly, one can verify an induction only in a representative sample of the reality one is investigating. As a result, inductive inference normally enjoys only a measure of probability. Once again, facts could turn up in the future to call one's provisionally verified induction into question.

Peirce's doctrine of fallibilism required one to admit the fallibility and limitations of the human mind. Peirce did not look on fallibilism as a gloomy doctrine. On the contrary, he insisted that one has a much better chance of reaching the truth if one admits that one might be wrong, than if one claims an infallibility for one's conclusions which they do not in fact possess, as Lonergan had done in claiming to have found an unrevisable starting point for all knowledge. It also seemed to me that in insisting on the finitude and fallibility of the human mind, Peirce had understood better than Lonergan exactly how the human mind does work. Lonergan claimed for the human intellect a virtual infinity and an insatiable thirst for the totality of truth, which as far as I can see, the human mind does not in fact possess. Close studies of human cognition among developmental psychologists tend, in my judgment, to falsify Lonergan's theory of an unrestricted human desire to know by providing some empirical evidence that the human mind begins finite and remains finite. In my humble judgment, ego inertia tends to characterize the human mind more than insatiable curiosity.

Peirce drew another conclusion from the finitude and fallibility of the human mind: namely, that shared systematic inquiry in a community of colleagues committed to getting at the truth offers the best way to fix human beliefs about reality. In the process, Peirce replaced Kant's turn to the subject with a turn to community. It seemed to me that a social, communitarian logic provided a much better grounding for Lonergan's social, dialogic theory of functional theological specialization than the logically invalid a priori exploration of individual human subjectivity.

Peirce's logic also allowed me to clarify some of the vagueness under which Lonergan's theory of functional theological specialization labored. Lonergan argued that the normative insights of a foundational theology of conversion provide the criteria for discriminating between sound and unsound doctrine. In his logical division of the sciences, Peirce argued, again correctly in my estimate, that the normative philosophical sciences of aesthetics, ethics, and logic mediate between the phenomenological description of what appears in experience and the formulation of a fallible metaphysical hypothesis about the nature of reality. Moreover, I saw very quickly that one could use the insights of aesthetics in order to explore the normative shape of personal moral conversion and of political conversion. Theology, of course, explores Christian conversion.

I came to Berkeley intent on drawing on the American philosophical tradition in order to develop a normative account of the different forms and dynamics of conversion. Lonergan requires that one approach foundational theological thinking in a cross-disciplinary context. One's normative account of conversion needs to use metaphysical categories, theological categories, and the categories of the secular sciences that study human experience and human religious experience. In *Method in Theology*, however, Lonergan fails to tell one how to derive a unified account of the forms and dynamics of conversion by drawing on different speculative disciplines, with different sets of presuppositions, and with different methods for thinking.

Peirce's logical division of the sciences, however, enabled me to clear up this bit of methodological vagueness in Lonergan by naming the specific contribution that each of these disciplines makes to a unified, normative, foundational account of conversion. Metaphysics does not yield an a priori, necessary, universal insight into reality, as Karl Rahner naively believed. Metaphysics offers only a thoroughly fallible hypothesis about the nature of reality in general. It predicts that its philosophical categories have the ability to interpret any reality whatever. One needs only discover one fact, which one's metaphysical hypothesis cannot interpret, and one has to take one's hypothesis back to the drawing board.

Not only will a successful metaphysics interpret shared, lived human experience as lived, but it will also successfully interpret the results of those sciences which study only limited aspects of reality. When a metaphysical theory succeeds in this enterprise it contextualizes the results of the other sciences by situating them within one's conceptual schematization of reality in general. When the sciences do verify one's metaphysics, they simultaneously amplify it by providing more information about the shape of reality than philosophical reflection on lived experience as lived can ever come up with. The same thing happens when one can verify one's metaphysical hypothesis in a theological interpretation of the events that reveals to us the triune God. In other words, the revelatory events, which theology studies, provide the means for verifying or falsifying metaphysical God-talk.

I could dwell more on how I have drawn systematically on the philosophical tradition in the United States in order to revise the philosophical presuppositions that lie at the basis of Lonergan's theory of method in theology; but that would take us far afield. I will conclude, then, by noting that, while the systematic application of the first four functional specialties to the American philosophical tradition forced me to revise the presuppositions which grounded Lonergan's method, it did not lead me to discard his theory of functional theological specialties. Why not? Because John Dewey had taught me to believe that only a method capable of revising its own presuppositions qualifies as a sound method. Moreover, having regrounded Lonergan's theory of functional theological specialization in the sounder logic and metaphysics of Charles Sanders Peirce, I concluded that, so revised and regrounded, that theory offers the best applied logic for doing theology that I have found to date.

3. The Passionateness of Being: The Legacy of Bernard Lonergan, S.J.

Patrick H. Byrne

It is daunting to be asked to communicate why Bernard Lonergan is such an important thinker. The magnitude of his achievement is great, and I owe a great personal debt for all that I have learned from him. Over the course of his life, Lonergan wrote extensively and profoundly about an amazing range of topics—painting and music; economics and politics; epistemology, metaphysics, and ethics; quantum mechanics and relativity theory; statistics and evolution; sexuality and marriage; logic, ordinary language, and symbolic meaning; religion and feelings; common sense; the theory of history; sin, grace, and the theology of the Christian doctrines of Incarnation and the Divine Trinity.

Certainly Lonergan's gifts of genius enabled him to wade into so vast a range of topics and to make original and substantial contributions in each. But just as importantly, he was able to make such contributions because of what he learned about being a human being through grappling with the greatness of Thomas Aquinas, the subject of his doctoral work at the Gregorian University in Rome. He wrote of this time: "After spending years reaching up to the mind of Aquinas, I came to a two-fold conclusion. On the one hand, that reaching had changed me profoundly. On the other hand, that change was the essential benefit."[1] The changes that Lonergan underwent during his studies of Aquinas became the core of his greatest achievements and his great contributions to philosophy and theology. The discovery about the meaning of being human provided him with a basic framework that he brought to all of his further investigations. For this reason, he invited his readers to also undertake the challenge of self-discovery and promised that they too would find it would yield rich rewards in all sorts of endeavors.

His contributions cover so many fields and are often so sophisticated that it is difficult to find of a way of communicating his achievement concisely. But one day a phrase from one of his later essays struck me—"the passionateness of being." Let me quote the entire passage where that phrase occurs:

> We experience, understand, and judge to become moral: to become moral practically for our decisions affect things; to become moral interpersonally, for our decisions affect other persons; to become moral existentially, for by our decisions we constitute what we are to be.
>
> Such vertical finality is another name for self-transcendence. By experience we attend to the other; by understanding we gradually construct our world; by judgment we discern its independence of ourselves; by deliberate and responsible freedom we move beyond merely self-regarding norms and make ourselves moral beings.
>
> The disinterestedness of morality is fully compatible with *the passionateness of being*. For that passionateness has a dimension of its own: it underpins and accompanies and reaches beyond the subject as experientially, intelligently, rationally, morally conscious. . . It ushers into consciousness not only the demands of unconscious vitality but also the exigencies of vertical finality."[2]

I take it as my task to try to understand what Lonergan meant in this passage by "the passionateness of being."

For many centuries students at Jesuit universities regarded the study of metaphysics as the most abstract, static, and incomprehensible of all their studies. There are many reasons for this reaction, but one of them originates with what was called the theory of "the three degrees of abstraction." According to that theory, there are three increasingly abstract levels of universal concepts. A universal concept is a concept that can have many instances. Roughly speaking, the first level of universal concepts would be our ordinary concepts, such as tree, car, cat, MP3 player, justice, person. For each of these abstract concepts, there are many concrete instances, and each of these instances can undergo change.

The second degree of abstraction was associated with mathematics: concepts like number, point, line, plane. This second degree is more abstract than the first. In particular, it has to do with concepts of things that don't change. A concept like the number seven contains fewer familiar qualities than a concept like cat; and unlike cats, numbers don't change. But mathematical concepts can pertain to far more individuals; just about any group of individuals can make up a group of seven, but far fewer individuals can be classified as cat.

The third degree of abstraction was called metaphysical abstraction and was concerned with being as being. Metaphysical abstraction had to do with what every being had in common with every other being. Here even the wispy qualities associated with a concept like number are stripped away to leave only the characteristic that each existing entity shares with every other existing entity.[3] Well, what characteristic is that? If you don't know, then you must not have the metaphysician gene. You can begin to see why metaphysics conceived in this way got less than favorable reviews from students in Jesuit schools. And if being is what is left when you abstract everything palpable away, where is the passionateness in that?[4]

Much of modern and twentieth-century philosophy involved a ferocious reaction against this way of thinking about metaphysics. Rene Descartes complained strongly about his classes at the Jesuit school *La Fleche.* At the beginning of the twentieth century another major philosopher who had a Jesuit education, Martin Heidegger, called for a "destruction of metaphysics." Lonergan himself once quipped that one of the three most important elements of his education was the fact that the professor for his metaphysics course was appointed to an administrative post, so that the class only met once during the whole year.

This abstract, traditional conception of metaphysics was, and still is, attributed to Aristotle and Thomas Aquinas. But Lonergan's study of these two authors led him to conclude that this was not at all their understanding of metaphysics, and that this way of thinking about a third degree of metaphysical abstraction was a bad distortion of their actual thoughts.

When Aristotle wrote his great work on the philosophy of being, he himself called it *First Philosophy*.[5] Now it bears the title, *Metaphysics*, but that is a title supplied by some later editor. It has actually been suggested that the title was invented when Aristotle's writings were put in a collected edition well after his death. In that collection, this book came after (*meta* in Greek) the books on physics. Hence, meta-physics. That word has a spooky ring to it nowadays. But Aristotle himself called it *First Philosophy*. What he was really after was what is and should be first for us.

It turns out that each and every one of us has an implicit First Philosophy, whether we study Aristotle or not. Each of us has an implicit metaphysics. For each of us, something comes first. Our implicit First Philosophy, our sense of being, settles what seems real to us; it also settles what seems unreal to us, what is believable and what is unbelievable. Think of what people mean when they say: " that's not realistic." They are implicitly relying on some sense of what is or is not real, what is or is not being.

For some people, what comes first, what counts as real, can be what you see or touch, and everything else is just idealistic or fantastic. Samuel Johnson, the great British man of letters, had an implicit metaphysics that what is real is what you can touch. He once became quite annoyed with a brilliant Irish philosopher, Bishop George Berkeley. Berkeley had written that matter is ideal, meaning that matter is an idea that someone came up with. Dr. Johnson did not care at all for Berkeley's philosophy, and Johnson allegedly one day kicked a rock hard and said: " I refute his philosophy thus!" Johnson's primary sense of reality was that which was hard to the sense of touch. Berkeley's sense of reality was what was real to the mind but not to the aching toe.

For some people what comes first is money; this is what people mean by applying the divine attribute "the almighty buck." When money is first, when profit is the bottom line in life even more so than the ledger sheet, the reality of everything else is measured in those terms. Things become less and less real the more removed they are from money. Endangered Northern Spotted Owls or endangered urban neighborhoods are indeed quaint, but let's be realistic; they are standing in the way of opportunities for investment. Students majoring in literature or music or theology or, God forbid, philosophy, are unrealistic and impractical. When such students are asked, "What are you going to *do* with that?" They are really being asked the realistic question, "How are you going to earn money with that?"

Or, if for someone else, human suffering comes first, then the reality of everything else is measured in terms of its relevance to causing or alleviating suffering. People who have been to war zones or disaster areas witness the overwhelming reality of suffering. When they return to their homes and see what people do with their time—see people absorbed, frivolously watching television, or shopping for cosmetics—they have the overwhelming sense that these people are out of touch with reality. The sense that nothing matters as much as suffering can even affect people's judgments about art. Picasso's *Guernica* is regarded as real, but Renoir's *Girl with a Watering Can* is viewed as merely self-indulgent.

People can hold that the most real thing in the world is celebrity or tolerance or violence or love or sex or equality or fun or their children. So we all have an implicit First Philosophy, an implicit metaphysics. As you can tell, what is first in *these* senses is something that people are indeed very passionate about, in sharp contrast to the aridity of the metaphysics of abstraction.

Lonergan was very emphatic that everyone has a First Philosophy in the sense I have just been describing. Certainly, he wasn't the only twentieth-century philosopher to hold that each of us has a passionate, implicit metaphysics of this sort. But Lonergan was unique among philosophers in saying that we actually have *two* First Philosophies.[6] We have a First Philosophy in the sense that I was describing—where something that we are familiar with and are passionate about has become our paradigm of reality. This is an implicit metaphysics that we usually inherit from someone, even when we think that we made it up all by ourselves. We usually inherit this primary sense of reality from our parents or by rebelling against our parents or from our friends or our political allies, or from the entertainment media, from our ethnic or other cultures, or from our religion. About this, Lonergan agreed with other twentieth-century philosophers.

But Lonergan was unique in saying that we have an additional First Philosophy that we are all born with, a primary sense of reality that we do not get from any other human being. According to Lonergan, there is also a sense of reality built into our questioning and inquiring spirit. We all ask questions, and our questions and inquiries are founded in a kind of "knowing" what reality is. Before we fully know what is included in reality, we *desire* to know it by asking questions. Our questioning desire orients us toward reality, toward being. Our first and most basic sense of reality is in our desiring to know it without restriction. We are able to have a kind of anticipation about all that is by *desiring* to know about it, by asking questions about it.

As Lonergan put it, every question "supposes some notion of being."[7] That is to say, each question supposes the deep, anticipatory, unlimited desiring that is oriented toward being—oriented toward the totality of all that is. Our questioning, inquiring, desiring spirit forms the basis of our second, alternative First Philosophy. Unlike the other primary sense of reality that I previously described, this is not a sense of reality that is at all familiar. It is rather a mysterious sense of reality because we don't yet know what the totality of being is. We don't yet know everything about every thing that is. But we do have a sense about that totality because our questioning spirit keeps pointing us toward it by raising more and more questions about everything. The reality that we wonder about and that we desire to know provides us with an alternative, a strange but even more basic, paradigm of reality.

Reality in this sense is also clearly something that we are passionate about, because we *desire* to know it. Our passion for this broader sense of reality resides in our desire for it. This desire runs in and through our inquiring, questioning spirit. To be human is to be a dynamic, inquiring being. As soon as children can talk, they bombard their parents with a barrage of questions. Even as adults, each day we continue to ask hundreds of questions: What did she mean by that? How am I going to get the kids to practice on time? How can I get over this feeling? How can I make ends meet? Why is there so much violence in the world? How should I handle this new problem at work? Am I being told the truth? Questions also form the heart of the university professions of scientists, historians, and scholars. In academia, we ask: What was the cause of the breakup of the Soviet Union? Is globalization really eliminating more jobs than creating? What does economic theory say is the optimum level for the prime rate of interest? What keeps galaxies from flying apart? Questions are omnipresent and at the very heart of our quests for knowledge and understanding, in both ordinary life and in the academic pursuits of the university, whether those quests are mundane or highly sophisticated.

In all the work that he did in philosophy and theology and other areas, Lonergan built his contributions on his conviction about the great importance of our desiring, passionate quest to understand and know being. Yet we hardly notice that desire. We seldom pay attention to how many questions we have or how influential they are in directing the things we do each day. We focus our attentions elsewhere. For Lonergan, this woeful neglect of our questioning is a symptom of the spiritual loss of our time. In a deep sense, the human spirit is the spirit of inquiry, the spirit of wonder.

But Lonergan was not content merely to draw our attention to the depth and pervasiveness of inquiry in our lives. Imagine going to a university where *all* that your professors did was to ask questions and all he or she expected back from you was more questions. If students or teachers become satisfied only with questions without any answers, something important is missing. We ask questions *in order* to find answers. Questions without answers are unfulfilled desires, and in the long run unfulfilled desire turns first to frustration and then to bitter emptiness. Some people try to pass this off as the true objective of higher education—to indoctrinate young people to question everything. But this is only a partial and therefore a distorted picture. There is a subtle dishonesty in absolving higher education of its responsibility for answers. Real education absolutely rests on our restless inquiring spirit, but it is also dedicated to arriving at the best possible answers to our questions.

So, while for Lonergan First Philosophy does indeed rest on our questioning and inquiring spirit, he also took the next step to explore how we respond to our inquiring and how we answer our questions. We don't respond to our relentless desire to know with one big answer—one big metaphysical intuition. We respond to our questioning desire incrementally, through answers to our questions one at a time. That is because our questions and our desire for being set a very high standard that our answers have to live up to. Our desiring is a grand desire to know being, but the way we actually come to know being is by answering our limited questions one after another.

There are of course many different kinds of questions and answers. But from his studies of Thomas Aquinas, Lonergan came to one of his most important discoveries: namely, that all of our questions and answers about reality are of two fundamentally different kinds. The first kind of question is what Lonergan called questions for intelligence. There are questions that typically begin with what, why, how, who, which, where, when. These are questions that are provoked by our encounters with our sense experiences: What was that noise? How did that watermark get there? Why did that structure collapse? What are those unusual features in my data? Who am I? And so on. These questions seek innovative and creative discoveries and inventions. Lonergan called the answers to this first kind of question "insights," and he regarded insights as the most basic and common manifestations of human intelligence.

Yet oddly we are never completely satisfied with our insights, no matter how intelligent, clever, or brilliant. Once we have an insight of our own, or when we hear about one from someone else, we raise a second kind of question—we raise critical questions. This second kind of question manifests our desire to know at an even deeper level. However intelligent or creative our insights are, we desire to know more deeply whether they are true insights, whether our insights correctly understand being, correctly understand reality, correctly understand the way things really are. We follow our insights with critical questions that seek what Lonergan called unconditioned judgments. It is through our experiences, our insights, and our judgments that we move from *desiring* to know being to *actually* knowing being, step by step.

These two different kinds of questions and answers follow upon each other in alternating sequences. We ask our questions for intelligence about our experiences. Once we have answered these questions with intelligent and often inventive insights, we ask critical questions about whether they are correct insights. When we answer our critical questions with unconditioned judgments, new questions occur to us that never would have occurred before. We experience things in a new light, and we ask all sorts of further questions, followed by still further original insights and critical judgments. By means of this cyclical pattern of questions and answers, our knowledge of reality, of being, gradually grows. Lonergan called this cyclical pattern our "self-correcting process of learning and knowing."[8] We respond authentically to our unrestricted, desiring spirit of inquiry not by one big metaphysical intuition, but by participating in the self-correcting cycle of knowing.

Insights and judgments are not rare things that only rare philosophers like Lonergan have. Each of us has a thousand insights into our experiences every day, and certainly we reach hundreds of unconditioned judgments every day. The difficulty is that we do not notice this. We do not pay attention to the fact that we are doing this all the time, day in and day out, in all walks of life. This lack of attention in itself would not be such a bad thing; after all, parents and health professionals and plumbers and lovers and scientists have to devote their attention to actually answering the questions that crop up in their lives and to acting on the basis of their answers. If they directed all of their attention to the questioning and answering processes as such, they would never get their very important work done.

But there is also a great downside to this neglect. The more that we become inattentive to our questioning and answering, the more we fail to notice when we have not actually answered our own questions. We even begin to overlook many of the questions that do arise. Our unanswered questions get pushed further and further to the edge of our concerns. Instead of acting intelligently and critically, we become satisfied with just getting by. We begin to rationalize and to substitute flashy rhetoric for genuine answers. We become satisfied with pat answers rather than engaging in the often difficult and challenging work of finding creative insights and critically grounded judgments that truly do satisfy our questions.

We get passionate—Lonergan said ecstatic—about our insights. We also get passionate in our criticisms of insights when we are pursuing reality. But people are not always passionate in their criticisms and debates out of a desire to know what is really so. Instead people advance arguments with a passion about things like tolerance or suffering or money. This kind of passionateness advances some questions while ignoring and even hiding other questions. This kind of passionateness is different from our passionate desire to know what is really so.

Lonergan observed that our passionateness for being is profoundly different from the passions that underpin our other First Philosophy. Those passions often have greater intensity, but they are also very limited. Those passions can shove aside the gentler and subtler passion for wanting to really know being. But they cannot do so forever. Tolerance and suffering and money all have their place and their realities, but we can ask questions about their limits. Our questions have a mild but unflagging persistence. They can be ignored and deferred, but they cannot be eliminated. They keep coming back to nag us and unsettle us and leave us with uneasy consciences until we really and adequately answer them with creative, intelligent insights and with critical and thoughtful judgments.

There is, then, a struggle within us between our two First Philosophies. A First Philosophy, whether grounded in a passion about money or suffering or tolerance or reliance on the solidity of matter, can take over. The paradigm of reality it offers becomes first for us. And the notion of reality that resides in our unlimited, unrestricted inquiring spirit becomes smothered and comes to seem unrealistic. Our world contracts from the rich and wondrous realm of everything about everything that we can ask about, into the narrow confines of what we find is real in a much more limited sense. And we ourselves, we also shrink. We stop becoming what we are called to be by the passionateness of being, and we become the instruments of some less grand and less noble purpose.

Lonergan saw the need for a great remedy for this shrunken horizon, and he called his remedy "self-appropriation." By self-appropriation Lonergan meant a reawakening of our experience of ourselves as inquirers, a recognition of ourselves as people who desire and who can attain intelligent insights, who desire and who can attain limited but nonetheless unconditioned judgments. Self-appropriation means, first of all, to become much more attentive to the things that we do all the time. It also means really understanding the selves that this heightened attentiveness reveals. But at bottom, it means accepting the challenges that this new self-knowledge presents to us. Once we discover that our knowing of reality means responding intelligently, critically, faithfully to our inquiring spirit, we are posed the question: "Will I accept the challenge of this call, or will I turn away to follow some lesser First Philosophy?"

Now something interesting happens to us as we begin to take up this challenge of self-appropriation. As our self-appropriation grows, our sense of reality grows. Increasingly we become assured that reality *really is* what we pursue when we are faithful to our passionate desire to understand and judge what truly is. When we allow ourselves to be guided by our unrestricted questioning spirit, we become knowers of being, not in its totality, but nonetheless one bit at a time. There is therefore a fundamental sense in which each of us is already and always has been a latent, implicit, metaphysician. The concept of form was central to traditional metaphysics. Regarding this traditional metaphysical category, Lonergan himself once remarked, "If one wants to know just what forms are, the proper procedure is to give up metaphysics and turn to the sciences."[9] According to Lonergan at least, knowledge of the metaphysics of form does not require a special metaphysical intuition or even special metaphysical training. When we are authentically answering our questions, we are already implicit metaphysicians.

Still, Lonergan did recognize that there is a significant difference between having an implicit metaphysics and having an explicit metaphysics. What is the difference? This goes back to the theory of the "third degree of abstraction." Traditional metaphysicians conceived of it as taking away from something all of its palpable qualities, every quality that could distinguish it from any other existing being. But Lonergan turned back to the writings of Thomas Aquinas himself and found that the real meaning of metaphysics and the third degree of abstraction has to do with reflective self-awareness, or in other words, with self-appropriation. Aquinas said that the third degree of abstraction is a matter of reflecting, of relating things known back to their ultimate principle, to the passionateness of being.[10] Lonergan recognized that what Aquinas was getting at was that the third degree of abstraction is not an impoverishing move but an enriching one. The true metaphysician is the person who has added a second, reflective self-awareness of the passionateness of being, to their awareness of the objects in their world. The so-called third degree of abstraction is what happens in a person who engages both in the hard work of knowing something about the world and simultaneously knowing what she or he is doing while they are knowing.[11] The true metaphysician is the person who has therefore also developed a heightened responsibility for his or her efforts to know reality as it really is.

When it is put this way, it is clear that what Lonergan meant by self-appropriation does not fall victim to an excessive and obsessive inward gazing that would distract us from the legitimate demands on us as workers, citizens, friends, parents, and lovers. In fact, quite the opposite is the case. Self-appropriation demands of us periods of serious self-attentiveness, self-understanding, and self-criticism. But these are occasions of withdrawal for the sake of a return, as Lonergan liked to put it.[12] In that return we come back to our responsibilities to the world and to our fellow human beings with a heightened sense of our inquisitive desiring, and what it means to intelligently and critically respond to that desiring.

Self-appropriation is an expansion of our capacity for attentiveness and of the authenticity of our responsiveness. This is because our desiring, inquiring spirit is really a call. In our desire to know being we are called forth by being. We desire to know being because reality is inherently passionate. The passionateness inherent in being stirs our desire for its passionateness. We can be passionate about being because there is something about being that attracts our passion.

This is a very different picture of the nature of reality and the nature of knowledge than the view that pictures objective knowledge as a cold, detached, bloodless affair. So perhaps it would be best to pause for a moment and dwell on an illustration of the passionateness of knowing. Since the natural sciences are widely regarded as the paradigms of genuine knowledge of reality, of objectively and dispassionately facing the cold, hard facts of reality, a good test case can be drawn from one of the greatest scientists, Albert Einstein.

Far from pursuing his scientific objectives dispassionately, Einstein pursued them with great passion. In his autobiography, he speaks of the great excitement he experienced as a boy when his uncle gave him a directional compass. He was fascinated by the way the needle "knew" how to point north without anything from the outside touching it to push it in the right direction. (By way of contrast, recall how Dr. Johnson held tangibility to be the fundamental paradigm of reality.) To Einstein this experience of the magnetic compass awakened in him a sense of its strange wondrousness. It awakened in him a desire to understand magnetism anew, and then light, and then motion, and then space and time, and then gravitation. This desire drove him to thousands of insights and judgments that issued forth in hundreds of scientific articles, lectures, and speeches. His passionate desire to understand the universe knew no bounds. Toward the end of his career, he said that he wanted to comprehend the mind of God.

Einstein detected this same desire in the best of his fellows, that extraordinary generation of physicists at the beginning of the twentieth century. He said that "the scientist . . . makes the cosmos and its construction the pivot of his emotional life."[13] Elsewhere he wrote that:

> Feeling and longing are the motive force behind all human endeavor and human creation. . . . [We] want to experience the universe as a single significant whole. . . . [This] feeling is the deepest and strongest motive for scientific research. [14]

Einstein also attributes this same passionate desire to correctly understand and judge reality to earlier scientists such as Johannes Kepler, Sir Isaac Newton, and James Clerk Maxwell. I agree with Einstein that this desire to comprehend the intelligibility of the universe can be found to permeate the work of every genuine scientist.

No less than Lonergan, Einstein attributed the source of this passion for knowing to the passionateness of being itself: "The most incomprehensible thing about the world is that it is at all comprehensible." This is quite a remarkable observation. Why should our ideas inside our heads have anything to do with reality? This question has vexed some of the greatest minds in Western and non-Western philosophy. Why should our insights and judgments have any connection at all with reality? Lonergan's answer, and implicitly Einstein's as well, is that the comprehensibility, the intelligibility, the passionateness of being calls forth in us a desire for it. Our knowing is a dynamic, passionate response to our being called forth by the passionateness of being.

Whence comes the passionateness of the universe and of being that calls our spirit to transcend its narrow concerns? For Lonergan the answer is that it comes from God who breathed God's own passionateness into all of creation. Concerning God, Lonergan wrote: "Our subject has been the act of insight or understanding, and God is the unrestricted act of understanding, the eternal rapture glimpsed in every Archimedean cry of 'Eureka!'"[15]

That is to say, the blaze of unlimited, infinite intelligence, which is the passionate being of God, touches us in each of our insights every time we attain some limited understanding about something finite. Even if we were to correctly understand everything about the natural universe and the entire wretched and glorious history of human affairs, our desire to understand would not yet be stilled. We would still desire to know: But why is the universe that way? Why did everything have to be that way and not some other way? What purpose has been served by the fifteen billion years of the universe and the millions of years of human history? Why is there being rather than nothing? Our desire for being draws us even beyond the being of the universe to the Being that makes sense out of the universe's existence. As St. Augustine put it, "Our hearts are restless until they rest in Thee, O Lord."[16]

Later in his career Lonergan began to realize that our questioning desire for this unlimited passionateness of being comes to us in two forms. The first form is the passionate intelligibility breathed into the universe, which calls us forth through our inquiring and our intelligent and critical responses.[17] But there is also a second, more intimate passionateness that arises directly and immediately within our consciousness. Lonergan called this second form of passionateness the religious experience of "being in love in an unconditional fashion." He characterized this experience as the "basic fulfillment" of our unrestricted desiring.[18] In referring to this more intimate sense of the passionateness of being, Lonergan frequently quoted St. Paul's *Letter to the Romans*, Romans 5:5: "God's love flooding our hearts through the gift of the Holy Spirit given to us."[19] He agreed with St. Paul that this experience is not primarily a matter of our love for God. It is rather, God's own love poured into us. It is God's infinite and unconditional love of everything about everything and everyone. Just as God breathes the rapture of intelligibility into all of the created universe, so also the Holy Spirit breathes the passionate, unconditional, and unrestricted love that God is into the consciousness of each and every human being. We participate in the passionate love that God is, because God breathes God's own loving self into us. This is the unconditional self-gift of God's own passionateness into our hearts.

This of course is Christian terminology; after all, Lonergan was a Catholic priest. But he was nevertheless quite emphatic that the self-gift of God's love is not at all limited to Christianity. Lonergan argued that this experience is transcultural.[20] He used to underscore this point by citing with approval the researches of the Jewish psychiatrist Abraham Maslow.[21] Maslow interviewed people to learn more about a phenomenon that he called "peak experiences." Initially people would say that they never had such experiences. But as Maslow would begin to tell them about his research, they would suddenly say, "Oh, I did have an experience like that one time," and they would go on to describe the peak experience in detail.[22] Based on his reading of Maslow's research, Lonergan became convinced that most if not all people's peak experiences were indeed instances of being in love in an unrestricted fashion, the experience that St. Paul described two millennia ago.

It isn't that some special, select people are given this gift while others are not. Maslow was led to the conclusion that just about everyone has such experiences, but some people notice and appropriate the experience, while others do not. He further concluded that the right sort of descriptions could facilitate the process of noticing, appropriating, and living in the light of peak or religious experience. In this connection Lonergan would also refer repeatedly to the Catholic doctrine of God's universal salvific will.[23] Lonergan read this doctrine as saying that God unconditionally bestows upon every human being an experiential participation in God's passionate loving.

Christians rely upon the language of St. Paul and call this experience the self-gift of the Holy Spirit; but other religious traditions speak about this same transcultural experience in various other terms. The self-gift of God's passionate loving self is unconditional; it does not wait upon a prior act of faith in Christ Jesus to be bestowed. Quite the opposite, Lonergan claimed, the faith that is capable of affirming Jesus as divine is conditioned by the prior gift of the Holy Spirit. Hence Lonergan argued that all religions, non-Christians as well as Christian, grow out of this ineffable religious experience of being in love unconditionally. Just as human insights and judgments grow out of the transcultural unrestricted desire to know, so also the variety of religious expressions arise out of this unconditional gift of loving. It is the transcultural reality of this experience of being in love unconditionally that provides a basis and the hope for the inter-religious dialogue that the world needs now more than ever.

If we were to ask Lonergan himself what he regarded as his greatest contribution, I think that he would probably say that it was his book, *Method in Theology*. In a way he spent most of his life building up to that achievement. As a young man in the 1930s he was inspired by the great Catholic historian Christopher Dawson, who remarked that Thomism "has devoted comparatively little attention to the problem of history."[24] In his youth Lonergan set himself the task of working out a genuinely Christian philosophy of history that would surpass the works of Hegel and Marx.[25] Soon he came to realize that Catholic theology itself was imperiled unless it faced up to the challenges posed by modern historical studies of Scripture and the development of the Church. As Lonergan would later write: "Christianity is a religion that has been *developing* for over two millennia."[26] So his project in the philosophy of history expanded into providing a project of providing a new foundation for Catholic theological method that took seriously the historical, developing reality of the Christian faith and Catholicism. He originally intended his great philosophical book, *Insight,* to be part of a larger work on theological method. But he had to "round off" that book at 748 pages, as he humorously put it,[27] when he was called to teach at the Gregorian University in Rome. Over the next fifteen years his thought on history and theological method continued to develop until he finally published *Method in Theology*.

Does this book have anything to do with the passionateness of being? Put in extremely simple terms, Lonergan conceived of method in theology as a heightened form of self-appropriation. Just as he revolutionized metaphysics through the self-appropriation of questioning and knowing, so also he revolutionized theology through reflective self-appropriation of the expanded sense of passionateness. This means that in order to do theology in the most effective way, the theologian must become aware of and faithful to both of the sources in us of passionateness for being: the passionate desiring to know being and the passionate love for all being.

In theological method, the reflective self-awareness of metaphysics becomes reflexive self-appropriation of what Lonergan eventually called "development from below upward."[28] In the context of his book *Insight*, this meant engaging in the work of intelligent discovery and critical judgment with regard to some realm of being, while at the same time being reflectively self-aware and taking responsibility for that work. "Below upward" refers to the movement from experience through inquiry to insight and further inquiry to judgment and beyond. In the context of theology, it comes to mean self-reflective responsibility directed toward understanding and judging the sources of the Christian religious traditions—especially Scripture and the historical records of Christian practices and teachings.

But theological method is broader than metaphysics, even in Lonergan's enriched form. In theology the reflective self-awareness of "development from below upward" is complemented by reflective self-awareness of what Lonergan called "development from above downward."[29] If indeed, as Lonergan claimed, every human being is gifted with God's love in the intimacy of her or his consciousness, this loving is still unconditional, unrestricted, and therefore ineffable. Each person is left with the immense, almost impossible task of trying to give finite expression to that ineffable gift in deeds and in words.

Still, Lonergan argued, the effects of the gift of love show up as a shift in people's values, people's experiences, and people's insights and judgments. When we fall in love with another human being, our experiences of the world dazzle and sparkle. This is even more true when we fall in love in an unconditional way. The natural world, other human beings, one's own life, pleasure, money, status, sex, poverty, power—they all take on dramatically new meanings when one is in love.

Likewise, the corrosive effects of bias, bitterness, hatred, despair, and sin begin to melt slowly when love begins to grow in a person's heart.[30] When the love that one falls into is a participation in God's love of everything about everything, all of being becomes precious in a dramatically new way. This shift in a person's values is what Lonergan called conversion, and it begins to change what a person is willing to accept as real and true. It affects people's judgments about reality, and they seek to better understand the new realities revealed by the new eyes of love. It brings about keener attention to experiences previously ignored. This is what Lonergan meant by "the way from above downward" that flows from being in love unconditionally.

There is a general resemblance between "the way from above downward" and the form of First Philosophy mentioned toward the beginning of this essay. According to Lonergan, we all have *two* First Philosophies—one that resides in our unrestricted, inquiring desire to know being, and the other that comes from some paradigm of reality. Initially our two First Philosophies are in conflict with and contradict one another. But when the divine self-gift of unconditional love becomes paramount in a person's life, it displaces the self-limiting paradigm of reality that is that other First Philosophy. Then, the sense of being that is the unrestricted objective of the inquiring spirit, and the sense of being that is unconditionally loved come into harmony.

In *Method in Theology* Lonergan made reflective self-appropriation of the way downward also a task of theology. The theologian is now charged with two challenging tasks: the task of authentically understanding and judging Christian sources and the Christian traditions, but also the task of going forth to preach the good news of God's passionate love to all nations and to transform the world: to "Set the world aflame" as St. Ignatius of Loyola charged his followers. Of course Ignatius meant the flame of God's passionateness. Bernard Lonergan was a Jesuit faithful to the commission set down by the founder of his order. As such he devoted his entire life to discerning and appropriating the passionateness of being, and in developing methods of self-appropriation to help us all to go forth and set the world aflame. This, I believe, is the great legacy of Bernard Lonergan whose life we celebrate this centennial year of his birth.

4. Lonergan and the Key to Philosophy

Elizabeth A. Murray

Insofar as a philosopher is obscure, insofar as he is saying things that you do not get the hang of or that you do not see any importance in, insofar as you do not see where his ideas are leading, the philosopher is providing you with evidence of the existence of your horizon.

—Lectures on Existentialism[1]

Lonergan as an Original Thinker

Bernard Lonergan is counted among the major Catholic thinkers of the twentieth century. His contribution to philosophy with his major work, *Insight*, and to theology with his crowning achievement, *Method in Theology*, has been widely recognized at international conferences and is evidenced by a growing body of scholarly publications. Some consider Lonergan to be primarily a philosopher; more consider him to be a theologian. There is also growing interest in his economic manuscripts, the fruit of his life-long avocation. Yet, he himself once remarked: "Fortunately, I don't think I come under any single label."[2]

He was, nevertheless, willing to refer to himself late in life as a "methodologist."[3] But what he means by this designation is not obvious. There is no single discipline of methodology. In fact, most disciplines have their own methodologies, and specialists in various fields often focus on methodological questions. Lonergan is not unique in his focus on method, but it is his single-minded focus on method in every investigation that breaks the disciplinary mold.

The radical and comprehensive nature of Lonergan's thought points to its epochal originality. The pioneering nature of his contribution can be indicated in its relation to the sciences, to philosophy, and to theology. Frederick Crowe in *The Lonergan Enterprise* writes of Lonergan as supplying a new *organon*, a new tool or instrument for inquiry. As Aristotle provided the *organon* of deductive logic, which was surpassed at the dawn of modernity by Bacon's *Novum organum* of inductive scientific method, so Lonergan's method of intentionality analysis provides a new *organon* for our age.[4] This methodological tool enables Lonergan to formulate a new scientific worldview. With his transcendental method, Lonergan formulates the worldview of emergent probability. This is a post-Einsteinian, post-Darwinian scientific worldview, which takes into account quantum physics and statistical method. Further, Lonergan transcends the epistemological roadblocks of post-Kantian immanentism with his account of judgment and objectivity. Lonergan is postmodern in his recognition of the futility of the conflict of theoretical positions, but he neither bemoans nor rejoices in the death of metaphysics. Rather, he invites us to become fully engaged in the next historical stage of metaphysic—the stage of explicit metaphysics. Finally, Lonergan's originality comes to fruition with his articulation of a fundamental and dialectical method for theology.

The originality of Lonergan's thought can be indicated in numerous ways, but let us here note the general nature of his originality. He understood his work to be a contribution to the program *vetera novis augere et perficere*, (ancient teachings enhanced and made new) initiated by Leo XIII in his encyclical *Aeterni Patris*.[5] Lonergan spent years, in his words, "reaching up to the mind of Aquinas."[6] Aquinas is not the only influence on Lonergan's thought, however, and he explicitly rejected the label neo-Thomist. Early influences on his thought, before his doctoral work on Aquinas, include Mill, Suárez, Augustine, Plato, and Newman, and later he studied Marx and Hegel.[7] Lonergan's creation is not, then, *ex nihilo*, but it is original. In sum, Lonergan accomplished for the twentieth century a synthesis of Christian thought and Aristotelian science and hermeneutics that is comparable to the synthesis of Christian thought and Aristotelian science accomplished by Aquinas in the thirteenth century.

The Key to Philosophy

In the present work, I shall consider Lonergan the methodologist, primarily in his role as a philosopher, and I shall focus on what he considers to be "the key to philosophy."[8] Wittgenstein once wrote that: "Philosophy is like trying to open a safe with a combination lock: each little adjustment of the dials seems to achieve nothing, only when everything is in place does the door open."[9] To complicate the metaphor, for Lonergan there is a key to the employment of this combination lock. How do we find this key to philosophy, what is its nature, and what does it unlock?

Lonergan identifies the key to philosophy in his discussion of the language of philosophy in the chapter, "The Method of Metaphysics," in *Insight.* In outlining the possibility and limitations of a technical meta-language, he explains:

> There also would be the difficulty of explaining to people as they are before they begin philosophy just what is meant by the terms and syntax of this meta-language, and at the same time of convincing them, as well as those with philosophic opinions of a different color and shade, that the polymorphism of human consciousness is the one and only key to philosophy.[10]

How do we find this one and only key to philosophy? What is our access to the polymorphism of consciousness?

Interiority and Self-Appropriation

The starting point of philosophy for Lonergan is the concrete, existential subject.[11] But this subject, who I am, seems elusive. The term "subject" is logical and grammatical in original usage. It is the correlative of the object intended. As such, it is like the operator behind the camera who rarely appears in the scene he shoots. Must we rely on accidental shadows and traces or on tricky introspective reflections to catch glimpse of the subject? In his monograph, *The Subject*, Lonergan explains:

> The study of the subject is quite different [from any metaphysical account of the soul], for it is the study of oneself as one is conscious. It prescinds from the soul, its essence, its potencies, its

> habits, for none of these are given in consciousness. It attends to operations and to their center and source which is the self.[12]

The subject is the concrete self whose unity is already simply given in consciousness. The given unity is neither the soul of classical metaphysics nor is it the pure ego of Husserlian phenomenology.[13] The self given is a unity, not in the sense of a transcendent object, but in the sense of the very field of consciousness out of which one may come to know distinct unities including the self as an object known. There follows then the distinction between mere self-consciousness and self-knowledge.

As conscious, we are already and always self-conscious. This double complexity or reflexivity is an essential characteristic of consciousness. Just as consciousness is ever intentional, as Brentano established, so consciousness is also self-conscious. Consciousness of a sound heard is simultaneously self-consciousness of the hearing. This reflexivity is not, however, a self-reflective knowledge of the self. A self-cleaning oven does not clean the self; it is simply self-cleaning. Consciousness is similarly simply self-conscious in its acts and states. To come to know the self or the subject is a different matter, and so Lonergan distinguishes between self-consciousness and self-knowledge.[14] The painstaking task of arriving at self-knowledge is what Lonergan calls, in *Insight*, the project of self-appropriation.

Self-appropriation requires deliberate exploitation of spontaneous self-consciousness, the presence to oneself that is presupposed by the presence of anything to the subject.[15] It requires an advertence to one's conscious and intentional acts and states, which Lonergan calls a heightened consciousness. What does it mean and how is it possible to heighten one's consciousness? Is it possible to simultaneously attend to an act without doubling one's conscious and intentional acts? "The trick in self appropriation," Lonergan remarks, "is to move one step backwards."[16] This suggests that heightening of consciousness is a broadening of perspective. To include more of the scene in a photograph, one takes a step backwards; one does not take two photos—one of the initial more limited scene and another photo of the additional perimeter. Yet the suggestion of taking a step backwards employs a spatial metaphor, which is misleading. Lonergan is not prescribing an infinitely regressive chain of reflecting upon one's reflecting, in which the subject ever recedes behind the last reflective act. The advertence presupposed by self-appropriation is not introspective. Lonergan explains: "So it is not a matter of introspection in any spatial sense, in any sense of 'looking back into,' because what counts is not the presence of what is looked at, but the presence of the subject that looks, even when he is looking as himself."[17] Avoidance of the pitfalls of the spatial metaphor does not deflect a serious contemporary challenge to Lonergan's notion of a heightened consciousness, which rises out of the postmodern critique of the metaphysics of presence.

Even if self-advertence is not introspective, does not the very nature of our temporal existence preclude any self-advertence that is not the matter of recollection? While a spatial difference is not required, is not temporal distancing ineluctable? The idea that temporal distance is required for self-advertence results from the mistaken view that the presence of the subject to the subject requires two distinct intentional acts. One imagines that to advert to one's conscious act is a second act. So, either these two acts occur in a present spacious enough to accommodate two simultaneous acts or the two acts must be successive. Even if the former were possible, how am I to attend to both operations simultaneously? And, if we must conclude that self-advertence is a matter of recollection, then the data of consciousness, which serve as the evidentiary ground of self-appropriation or of any phenomenological investigation, are derivative and thereby suspect.

The apparent difficulty can be resolved without positing a pure ego whose present contains simultaneous conscious acts. The self-advertence required does not require temporal distance any more than spacial distance. The presence of the subject to the subject becomes a feature of the original self-conscious and intentional act itself. As one senses, understands, questions, or formulates, one can be aware of oneself, the act and the content of the act. "To heighten one's presence to oneself, one does not introspect, one raises the level of one's activity."[18] For an analogy to the experience of heightened consciousness, let us consider an account of contemplative practice. Thomas Keating asks what the relationship of contemplative prayer is to the rest of life. He writes: "The presence of God should become a kind of fourth dimension to all of life. . . . It is like adding a soundtrack to a silent movie. The picture is the same, but the soundtrack makes it more alive."[19] It is especially helpful to use this auditory metaphor for the heightening of consciousness meant by Lonergan. It is not misleading like the visual, spatial metaphors that have been used, and it captures the intensification of consciousness experienced in advertence to the self-presence.

If one has not adverted to one's conscious intentionality in this way, then this account will not resonate. On the other hand, if one is familiar with this experience, or even better is engaged in it now, then its rehearsal may still be welcome, because the perspective of heightened consciousness is not an easy one to sustain. The reason for the difficulty of sustaining this perspective lies in the polymorphism of consciousness to be described in the next section.

What we have been referring to as a perspective of heightened consciousness or self-advertence is what Lonergan means by the term "interiority." Interiority in this sense is the subjective correlate to an objective pole consisting of a historically emergent stage of meaning. In *Method in Theology,* Lonergan traces the historical development of three stages of meaning: an initial stage of undifferentiated, commonsense meaning; a second stage in which theoretical meaning differentiates itself from commonsense meaning; and a third stage of interiority in which the critical ground is sought for distinguishing realms of meaning.

Lonergan also used the term "interiority" to designate one of the realms of meaning. In addition to defining three *stages* of meaning, Lonergan names four *realms* of meaning: the two outer realms of common sense and theory, the inner realm of interiority, and the ultimate realm of transcendence. A realm of meaning in general is a field or a world of objects with its own implicit procedures or explicit canons, its own expectations, and its own language. It is related to a mode of consciousness in the following way: "Different exigencies give rise to different modes of conscious and intentional operations, and different modes of such operation give rise to different realms of meaning."[20] Interiority as a mode of consciousness, then, gives rise to interiority as a realm of meaning, which emerges in the third stage of meaning, the stage of interiority. This interiorly differentiated mode of consciousness arises in response to an exigence.

An exigence is a specification of the underlying, operative, and normative finality of conscious intentionality. In other words, it is the felt-pressure of the pure desire to know in its normative force. Lonergan names a number of exigencies—the systematic, the methodical, the critical, and the transcendent. The interior mode of consciousness is a response to the critical exigence. Lonergan sums up the correlation in the following:

> With these [critical] questions one turns from the outer realms of common sense and theory to the appropriation of one's own interiority, one's subjectivity, one's operations, their structure, their norms, their potentialities. Such appropriation, in its technical expression, resembles theory. But in itself it is a heightening of intentional consciousness, an attending not merely to objects but also to the intending subject and his acts. [21]

The stages of meaning, realms of meaning, and the correlative modes of consciousness emerge historically and individually. Thus, while philosophies of interiority have already emerged, large segments of the population have undifferentiated consciousness, and even notable philosophers remain in the second stage of theoretical meaning. To the ears of a second-stage theorist, Lonergan's account of conscious intentionality and the heightening of consciousness will sound just like one more theory. But the pronouncements of interiority are subtly different. Their authority does not lie in the theory nor does it lie in the status of the author, but it lies in the self-appropriated subject. Lonergan, incidentally, would not consider himself to be the only representative of interiorly differentiated philosophy. Kierkegaard, for one, challenges us to the task of becoming a self through inwardness; Husserl also grounds phenomenological method in the pure seeing of the intentional act. While not unique, Lonergan's philosophy is distinctive in its articulation of interiority as a mode of conscious intentionality and as a realm and stage of meaning.

To answer the question with which we began this section, the key to philosophy, that is, polymorphism of consciousness is found within the realm of interiority through the mode of interiorly differentiated consciousness. In other words, in order to investigate one's consciousness to uncover the key to philosophy, one must advert to one's own intentional and self-conscious acts. It should be noted, however, that this advertence alone is not self-appropriation, although it is the sine qua non of self-appropriation. The project of self-appropriation involves the identification of distinct acts, states, and drives within the conscious data, the correlation of terms, the testing of hypotheses regarding correlates, and judgments regarding the nature of conscious intentionality.

Even still, this is only half of the story, for there is a dialectical side to the picture. Lonergan explains:

> The business of self-appropriation is not a simple matter of moving in and finding the functionally operative tendencies that ground ideals [of knowledge]. It is also a matter of pulling out the inadequate ideals that may be already existent and operative in us. There is a conflict, there is an existential element, there is a question of the subject, and it is a personal question that will not be the same for everyone. [22]

So, in addition to the cognitive task of coming to one's own conscious intentionality, there is the existential task of orienting oneself in light of this self-knowledge.[23]

The Polymorphism of Consciousness

With this account of our access to the key to philosophy, we can proceed to the second question stated at the outset: What is the nature of that key? What does Lonergan mean by the "polymorphism of consciousness?" There are many forms of consciousness, and we have already seen how Lonergan distinguishes some forms. First, we distinguished a consciousness that is experienced but not adverted to and a consciousness that is adverted to, which we can call "ordinary consciousness" and "heightened consciousness." We have also mentioned modes of consciousness, which emerge historically and in the individual as differentiations of consciousness. We can distinguish, then: an undifferentiated consciousness, a theoretically differentiated consciousness, an interiorly differentiated consciousness, and a transcendently differentiated consciousness. By the last, I mean that consciousness enjoyed by the contemplative or mystic. For the most part, ordinary consciousness corresponds to the first two modes, and heightened consciousness corresponds to the second two modes. Yet, when one is interiorly or transcendently differentiated, one is not necessarily engaged in adverting to one's conscious intentionality. Phenomenologists and contemplatives experience ordinary consciousness most of the time, but when they are engaged in deliberate reflection or prayer, ordinary consciousness occurs as an interruption. Similarly, those of undifferentiated consciousness and theorists are in the mode of ordinary consciousness as a general rule, and moments of advertence to their own conscious activity are rare and occasioned by extraordinary circumstances.

The third way of distinguishing forms of consciousness, which was only implicit in the above account, is in terms of levels of conscious intentionality. There are four levels of conscious and intentional activity distinguished by Lonergan: first, empirical consciousness, which qualifies the intentional acts of sensing, imaging, and perceiving; second, intelligent consciousness, which qualifies the acts of questioning, understanding, conceiving, and formulating suppositions; third, rational consciousness, which qualifies acts of critical questioning, reasoning, verification, and judging; and fourth, rational self-consciousness, which qualifies the acts of questions of conscience, evaluating, moral judging, and deciding. I shall not articulate these levels in any more detail; however, there are a few points about levels of consciousness that should be noted.

Lonergan speaks of "levels" of conscious intentionality, because the operations listed above are functionally related and self-assembling. They need not all occur, but one kind of act will call forth another in sequence. For example, imagining may give rise to questioning, which in turn, when one is lucky, gives rise to an act of understanding. The acts then are not random occurrences. They are distinguished as on different levels, because the quality of the acts changes as the fundamental intentionality, which evokes them, is transformed. The simple conation or interest of empirically conscious acts becomes the wonder of intelligently conscious acts. The direct questions of wonder give way to the critical, reflective questions of doubt, and one moves from intelligent consciousness to rational consciousness. When moral questions arise regarding what one ought not to do, doubt becomes conscience or, in other terms, rational consciousness becomes rational self-consciousness. Conation gives way to wonder, wonder gives way to doubt, and doubt gives way to conscience, not in the sense of a four-tiered structure, but in the sense of an ever-widening, sublative intentionality.

I have been speaking of conscious intentionality and of conscious and intentional acts. It should be noted that for Lonergan consciousness and intentionality, as well as self-consciousness, are characteristics of the act. Consciousness itself is not strictly speaking an act of intentionality. We are speaking loosely when we speak of being conscious of something, as in, "I am conscious of the knock at the door." We may agree with Brentano's dictum that "consciousness is consciousness of," but we should understand that consciousness is simply a quality of the intentional act. As the nature of the intentional acts change, as the underlying dynamic intentionality is transformed, the quality of those acts change. They are qualified by different types of consciousness.[24]

Further, in listing the types of acts, which occur on the different levels of consciousness, I have prescinded from discussing the affective states and acts of the four levels of conscious intentionality. Lonergan does not restrict his account of acts to cognitive acts, but in *Insight* the question is the nature of human understanding, so the emphasis is primarily cognitive and rational. He does make mention of the feelings and desires of empirical consciousness and of the exigence for rational consistency felt in rational and rational self-consciousness. His account of affectivity is enriched in *Method in Theology* and later writings. The language of intentionality analysis replaces the classical language of faculty psychology. So, in *Method,* rather than analyze the act of will and willingness, he writes of the motive force and normative role of emotional responses to values and disvalues.

A final point regarding the four levels of consciousness pertains to the meaning of the term "experience." Lonergan speaks of the level of experience and of empirical consciousness as the first of four levels. "Experience" in this sense denotes sensory, imaginative, and perceptual acts. But all four levels of conscious intentionality are experienced. As discussed above, this experience of intentional acts, even on the empirical level, are commonly not adverted to, but they are all nevertheless experienced. So, the term "experience" may refer either to the first level of consciousness or to the entire structure of conscious intentionality as given. It is experience in the broader sense to which we advert with heightened consciousness.

So far, we have discussed ordinary and heightened consciousness, four modes of differentiated consciousness, and four levels of consciousness. All four levels of consciousness occur as either ordinary or heightened consciousness, and all four levels may occur in any of the modes of consciousness. Our account of the variety of forms of consciousness can be complicated still further by the introduction of Lonergan's notion of patterns of experience.

When Lonergan refers to a pattern of experience, he is using the term "experience" in the sense explained above, in the broader sense of conscious intentionality on any level of consciousness. Experience in this sense is the flow of consciousness. We speak of consciousness as flowing or as a stream because of the succession of different acts and contents, but there is another dimension to the succession. It has a direction, an orientation and a dominant interest, which patterns the experience. The patterning of the flow of consciousness is variable. In his discussion of patterns of experience in chapter 14 of *Insight,* Lonergan identifies seven patterns of experience: biological, aesthetic, artistic, dramatic, practical, intellectual, and mystical.[25]

It might be helpful to describe briefly the orientations, which define the various patterns. Lonergan describes the stream of consciousness in the biological pattern of experience simply as a "higher technique for attaining biological ends."[26] The animal's consciousness is directed outwards towards possible opportunities to satisfy appetites and to avoid dangers. He writes: "If we endeavor to understand the sudden twists and turns of both fleeing quarry and pursuing beast of prey, we ascribe to them a flow of experience not unlike our own. Outer senses are the heralds of biological opportunities and dangers. Memory is the file of supplementary information. Imagination is the projection of courses of action."[27] In man, too, experience may be patterned by such elemental purpose, but it is rare for us to be dominated exclusively by biological aims. To illustrate, when one is forced to bivouac unexpectedly at 13,000 feet at the edge of a glacier in a driving wind, one's consciousness is dominated by the aim of retaining body heat and staying hydrated. All of one's bodily actions and conscious acts are directed to that end.

Commonly, our flow of consciousness is the dramatic pattern of experience, in which mere biological aims are transformed by our concern with how we stand in relation to others. Our conscious acts are patterned by the fundamental aim of human dignity. We act with an orientation to the presence of others, whether others are actually present or not, as we learn from Heidegger with his conception of *Mitsein.* The climbers huddled together are not mere wind blocks like any rocky outcropping, and so in watching out for each other's welfare they will share extra layers of clothing and any remaining water and food.

When the immediate demands of biological needs are met, playfulness may emerge in the animal as well as in man. The aesthetic pattern of experience liberates us from elemental purposes. It is experiencing for the sake of experiencing; it is "spontaneous, self-justifying joy."[28] Bear cubs roll and tumble in mock fighting, and hawks glide on wind currents. Lonergan's account of the aesthetic pattern of experience introduces two additional patterns of experience—the artistic and the intellectual. The aesthetic pattern of experience is oriented to free symbolic creation. As the immediate threat to survival passes, the freezing climbers may begin to notice the beauty of the starry sky and the dramatic views, and humor may help to fill the hours before dawn. This free creation of the artistic pattern is a twofold liberation: "As it liberates experience from the drag of biological purposiveness, so it liberates intelligence from the wearying constraints of mathematical proofs, scientific verification, and commonsense factualness."[29]

One is in the intellectual pattern of experience when one is engaged with such proofs and verification. The dominant drive of the intellectual pattern of experience is the desire to know, the intention of being and truth. When one is in the intellectual pattern of experience, one's seeing, remembering, and imaging all conspire to aid in the pursuit, and other conflicting aims and interests fall away. One may forget to eat and feel no need for sleep.

The last two patterns of experience identified by Lonergan are the practical and the mystical. The practical is a pattern of experience aimed at getting things done. It is related to both the biological and the dramatic patterns. It is aimed at survival but not simply the survival of an animal in a natural environment. It is an orientation to human survival in a world mediated by meaning. Before one can become immersed in the intellectual pattern of experience, one may find that one has to make another trip to the library or have one's computer repaired, and these are practical concerns. The aim of the practical pattern of experience is getting by the interpersonal world of everyday commerce.

Finally, there is the mystical pattern of experience. The mystical pattern of experience is a consciousness dominated by the love of God. It is similar to the dramatic pattern of experience in that it is primarily concerned with the presence of another, but it is not restricted to concerns about one's own dramatic interaction. It has in common with the intellectual pattern a detachment from the everyday world of practical concerns, although it is not restricted to the pursuit of intellectual ends. It is "without conditions, qualifications, reservations." "This lack of limitation, though it corresponds to the unrestricted character of human questioning, does not pertain to this world."[30]

The seven distinct patterns alternate. One does not remain in one pattern exclusively, although one pattern may dominate one's waking life more than the others. In fact, one may find it difficult to break out of a pattern and allow one's consciousness to flow in a different direction. How difficult is it for a stock investor pressed by practical deadlines to pause and enjoy the strains of a sonata? How difficult is it for a musician engrossed in a new composition to turn to balancing the checkbook? In addition to alternating, patterns of experience can also mix and blend, so we may speak of the practical-dramatic pattern of everyday living, or the dramatic-intellectual pattern of classroom pedagogy. The patterns also may conflict and interfere with one another. While in the intellectual pattern and engrossed in writing, someone may enter the room and suddenly one's stream of consciousness is no longer dominated by one's intellectual pursuit, but now is patterned dramatically.

Experience or the flow of consciousness, then falls into various patterns—the seven pure patterns and various blends of patterns. These patterns of experience can now be added to our account of the sets of forms of consciousness. The four levels of conscious intentionality can be operative in any of the seven patterns of experience. One may advert to the flow of one's consciousness while in any patterns of experience with heightened consciousness; although typically patterns of experience are orientations of ordinary consciousness. The harrowing stories of survival in death camps by authors like Frankl and Solzenitzyn reveal that one's consciousness can be self-reflectively heightened even when one's consciousness is most narrowly focused on biological aims. And, it seems that the seven patterns of experience are also to be found in all four of the historically differentiated modes of consciousness. Lonergan, for example, in introducing the notion of patterns of experience retells the legend about Thales and the milkmaid:

> We speak of consciousness as a stream . . . the direction of the stream is variable. Thales was so intent upon the stars that he did not see the well into which he tumbled. The milkmaid was so indifferent to the stars that she could not overlook the well. [31]

But Thales, who represents here the intellectual pattern of experience, lived in the stage of undifferentiated consciousness prior to the theoretical differentiation initiated by Socrates and Plato.

The many forms of consciousness, which we have articulated so far—ordinary and heightened consciousness, the four levels of consciousness, the four modes of differentiated consciousness, and the seven patterns of experience—occur within one's horizon. The nature of one's horizon, in turn, influences and transforms the nature of one's conscious activity. So, to complete our account of varieties of forms of consciousness, let us review what Lonergan means by horizon, and how he differentiates the various horizons.

By "horizon" Lonergan means not the limit of one's visual range, but rather what lies within the range of one's knowledge and interest. As such, one's horizon could be seen as the objective pole corresponding to the subjective pole of conscious intentionality. Lonergan identifies three ways of differentiating horizons: genetically, complementarily, and dialectically. Horizons may differ genetically in terms of stages of development.[32] One may call to mind the work of the developmental psychologists, Jean Piaget and Lawrence Kohlberg. Horizons may differ in a complementary fashion. On a university campus, for example, we find the complementary horizons of: librarians, campus ministers, campus police, groundskeepers, classics scholars, basketball coaches, and public relations staff. In any one of these complementary horizons, there will also be genetically different horizons. Horizons may also differ dialectically. This third way of differentiating horizons bears the greatest significance for philosophy.

Horizons differ dialectically on the basis of the presence or absence of conversion. By conversion is meant a 180-degree shift brought about through a decision—an act of freedom—that radically transforms one's orientation and world. Lonergan writes of three conversions: intellectual, moral and religious.[33] Briefly, intellectual conversion is the shift from the common myth that knowing is like looking to the view that knowing is a process of acts of intelligence and rationality, and that the real is what is known in judgment, not what is given in experience. Parmenides writes of a kind of intellectual conversion when he writes of choosing which way to take: the way of truth or the way of opinion. Augustine recounts the difficult intellectual journey he went through to finally come to the realization that God is not any object of sense or imagination.[34]

Moral conversion is the shift from basing one's decisions and actions on self-interest and satisfactions to basing one's decisions and actions on values. One thinks of a figure like Cesar Chavez, who decided one afternoon in California's Central Valley to put aside considerations of his family's welfare to fight for justice for his fellow migrant farm workers. And thirdly, there is religious conversion, which is the transformation of one's horizon that takes place when one surrenders unconditionally to a total being in love. Lonergan acknowledges that it is interpreted differently in different religious contexts, but "for Christians it is God's love flooding our hearts through the Holy Spirit given to us."[35]

With the three pairs of dialectically related horizons, there are eight possible concrete permutations. One may be religiously converted but lack moral and intellectual conversion; one may be morally converted but lack religious and intellectual conversion. One may have all three conversions or lack all three conversions, and so on. But one is in one of these eight dialectically defined horizons. Further, these eight possible dialectical horizons combine with the complementary horizons. We may encounter a philosophy professor with intellectual and moral but not religious conversion, or a campus minister with religious and moral but not intellectual conversion. One's dialectical horizon permeates all four levels of one's conscious intentionality, and so the varieties of horizons and their combinations pertain to our question of the nature of the polymorphism of consciousness.[36]

The forms of consciousness are then: ordinary and heightened consciousness, four levels of consciousness, four modes of differentiated consciousness, seven patterns of experience, and the transformations of consciousness corresponding to the differences in horizons. The sets of terms we have been developing to define the variety of forms of consciousness are what Lonergan calls, in *Method in Theology*, "general theological categories."[37] These general categories along with special theological categories constitute the foundations of theological method. Lonergan, however, does not consider these categories per se to be the ultimate foundation of theology or philosophy. Lonergan is not a foundationalist; he does not attempt to base his thought in a set of fixed categories or principles. The general categories we have defined are themselves discovered within the dynamic basis, which is the concrete, existential subject.

Polymorphism and the Duality of the Subject

We have been investigating the nature of the key to philosophy—the polymorphism of consciousness—by articulating the sets of terms and relations that define the variety of forms of conscious intentionality.

How could anyone make use of such a key? In what way is the polymorphism of consciousness a key to philosophy? In fact, at this point polymorphism of consciousness is more like one of those large, heavy key rings loaded with keys that jailors in penitentiaries once carried. The set of terms and their many combinations, which promise to proliferate into innumerable possible forms of consciousness, seems to be an unwieldy tool indeed.

We can simplify our account of the protean nature of consciousness by returning again to the starting point of philosophy for Lonergan. If we begin again with the concrete, existential subject, we find that the self is a unity in tension. There is a duality in the subject's basic operation, in knowing, and in the philosophies that issue from the tension of that duality. Lonergan is not a metaphysical dualist in a Cartesian sense, though he finds the duality of knowing juxtaposed in Cartesian dualism.[38] Material extension corresponds to the knowing of the subject as naturally extroverted, as an animal in a habitat. The cogito corresponds to the knowing of the subject as awakened by a detached desire to know, as intelligent and rational. Lonergan calls these two forms of knowing, animal knowing and human knowing. But they are both human inasmuch as we engage in empirical acts of consciousness as well as in intelligent and rational acts of consciousness.

The polymorphism of consciousness, which we have been describing in its great variety, is at its root the fact of a basic antithesis, a radical either/or. The nature of the subject for Lonergan is dialectical in his post-Hegelian sense of dialectic.[39] This fundamental either/or is not one that can be resolved or transcended. How does the polymorphism of consciousness in the simplified sense of an ineluctable duality serve as a key to philosophy? Lonergan conceives of philosophy as concerned primarily with "the subject in his free and intelligent self-constitution."[40] Lonergan sees the subject's consciousness as fundamentally polymorphic, so in writing *Insight* he extends an invitation to the reader: "to know oneself in the tension of the duality of one's own knowing."[41] He also views philosophy as fundamentally historical, in that the philosopher must respond to the problems of his age, of his environment.[42] Lonergan's own characterization of the fundamental problem of our age might come as a surprise. He writes: "At the present time, it seems to me that the real issue does not lie in the possibility of a world order without grace; the real issue, the one momentous in its consequences, lies between the essentialist and conceptualist tendency, and, on the other hand, the existentialist and intellectualist tendency."[43]

Difficulties arise when, as philosophers, we identify human knowing with simple animal knowing or when we assume that all cognitive acts, even understanding and conceiving, must be like looking, that is, a kind of confrontation. "For the consciousness of man is polymorphic, and it ever risks formulating its discoveries not as positions but as counterpositions."[44] Lonergan formulates a radical either/or in the form of a "position"/"counterposition"position as the ground for his method of philosophy:

> It will be a basic position (1) if the real is the concrete universe of being and not a subdivision of the 'already out there now'; (2) if the subject becomes known when it affirms itself intelligently and reasonably, and so is not known yet in any prior 'existential' state; and (3) if objectivity is conceived as a consequence of intelligent inquiry and critical reflection, and not as a property of vital anticipation, extroversion, and satisfaction. On the other hand, it will be a basic counterposition if it contradicts one or more of the basic positions. [45]

Typical of counterpersonal opposition to the basic position is denial of the significance of the act of understanding. Overlooking insight is what otherwise disparate philosophic positions like empiricism and conceptualism have in common. And so, along with the promotion of the self-appropriation of one's own rational self-consciousness, the coequal aim of the book *Insight* is a campaign against the flight from understanding. The flight from understanding in the history of philosophy can be traced in systematic oversight of the significance of the act of understanding.

The polymorphism of consciousness, the fundamental duality in knowing, is fertile ground for the flight from understanding. This is not because the dual orientation is in itself corrupt, but because the refusal to acknowledge this basic tension is obfuscating and corrosive. In writing a philosophy that reduces, ignores, or denies acts of understanding, one is embracing just one side of the dialectic, as if that would somehow resolve the tension. Such philosophies are numerous, varied, and inventive.[46] Lonergan does not consider the existence of many disparate philosophies to be surprising. The mind is polymorphic, and its own complexity is at the root of antithetical solutions. When the discoveries one makes in the intellectual pattern of experience are articulated under the sway of a different pattern of experience, the discoveries will likely be formulated as counterpositions rather than as positions.

Appropriation of the polymorphism of consciousness, of the basic duality in our orientation and knowing, yields a set of normative criteria. These criteria can be employed as a tool in the dialectical interpretation of various philosophies in order to promote what is positional in them and reverse what is counterpositional. For example, let us consider how this tool can be employed to correct a persistent misunderstanding of the nature of consciousness itself. Lonergan distinguishes between two competing conceptions of consciousness: consciousness as perception and consciousness as experience. The ground of these two conceptions lies in the opposition of two theories of knowledge: one, which is confrontational, modeled on intelligence and more Aristotelian.[47] Schools of thought as disparate as naïve realist, empiricist, and phenomenological, assume for the most part the confrontational view of knowledge, and consequently, a confrontational view of consciousness. Lonergan's nonconfrontational account allows for both an ordinary consciousness, which is not restricted to sense and perception, and a heightened consciousness, which makes possible self-appropriation.[48]

Lonergan's bold claim to have uncovered "the one and only key to philosophy" is grounded in the concrete, existential subject. It is neither an unfounded presupposition nor a conclusion deduced from foundational principles. This key is articulated as the set of differentiated terms and relations and as the more basic duality in conscious intentionality. The interiorly differentiated philosophy which takes full account of the polymorphism of consciousness has implications not only for a dialectic of conflicting philosophies, but also for the subject who is invited by Lonergan to the task of self-appropriation. "You get all sorts of pique and indignation and emotion and resentment in philosophic debates because philosophic issues are concerned with the horizon of the subject."[49] But, for Lonergan, to be a philosopher is to be willing to push through one's anxiety to a horizon more coincident with the unrestricted intention of being.

5. Lonergan's Jaw

John C. Haughey, S.J.

Bernard Lonergan, who lived from 1904 to 1984, would have been delighted to become aware of the scientific discoveries that have occurred in our times. He remains a favorite mentor of mine, and when I indulge my amateur's interest in science I turn to him, not because he was a scientist, but because he gives me a way of looking at these new realities with a worldview that makes room for them, however unexpected or disconcerting they might be.

One scientific discovery that alters our worldview comes from the field of biology. Scientists have discovered that a mutation of the myosin gene occurred in a portion of the ape population about 2.4 million years ago. This mutation caused muscle tissue in these chimpanzees to contract, which lead to weaker jaws and much larger brains. Smaller jaws developed from this because the thick muscles that worked like bungee cords and anchored the ape's jaw to the crown of the head weakened and receded. Over time, the brain tripled in size with the onset of this mutation.[1]

It is this change that seems to have enabled the emerging species of Neanderthals to develop tools and possibly the primitive beginnings of language. This now extinct species were our immediate forerunners. Human beings like us emerged about 2.5 million years ago in Africa and migrated into Europe about 40,000 years ago. This discovery of the myosin mutation has been a breakthrough moment in understanding the emergence of the human species from its ape ancestors in East Africa.

Another scientific discovery that alters our worldview comes from the field of physics. In 1992 the Nobel Prize-winning scientists George Smoot and John Mather found through the instrument of their Cosmic Background Explorer (COBE) satellite what they daringly called "the footprints of God." They saw background radiation so much more deeply in the universe than had ever been seen before. This discovery enabled cosmologists not only to verify the fact of the big bang but also to narrow the time of its happening from the highly speculative guess of from ten to twenty billion years ago to a much more precise 13.7 billion years.

Although my knowledge of these discoveries is only as deep as what I read in daily newspapers, they confirm for me the value of the worldview that Lonergan was intent on developing. He called that worldview "emergent probability." I continue to find that his idea of emergent probability can make room for the ever-unfolding discoveries from all these sciences, as well as make room for the less volatile developments in the humanities.

In contrast to the largely preevolutionary worldview that Lonergan grew up with, his emergent probability worldview is a heuristic, cognitional device that orients the knower to a known that is also admittedly still largely an unknown. What does this mean? It is like a map that heads you in the right direction, but the final destination isn't on any map which you have in your possession. Or it is a guide that incites questions and anticipates insights into answers that, while satisfying one up to a point, only leads to further questions. For Lonergan it was largely from his learning of statistics, science, mathematics, and history that changed his mind.

That change was from someone with a classical consciousness to someone with an historical consciousness. The former was impressed by the harmony and predictability of the objective order and was able to speak in terms of well-defined essences or natures that applied universally. Among the known, of course, was human nature. Hence the authority of church and school was intact and honored. So the duties or obligations that followed from this kind of objective knowledge were relatively clear. With his historical consciousness, which he kept developing, he came to see the world much more dynamically. His mind was always open to revision and conditioned by new findings. He learned to begin with experience and to give it as much attention as it needed before he let in the understandings available to him. It was from this latter consciousness that emergent probability emerged.

A classical consciousness claimed more knowledge about God, nature, and the natural law; or the way things could be expected to go, than this worldview of emergent probability would claim. So the Creator who says in Genesis: "Let there be light and waters and creeping things," would more likely in Lonergan's new understanding have said: "Let there be the emergence of things, cosmic process, evolution, schemes of recurrence, the interdependence of things on things, movements to higher integrations, and vertical jumps beyond their prior state."

I will analyze the two words, *emergent* and *probability*, as Lonergan uses them. The implication of the word "emergent" is to give preference to an inductive approach in looking at reality. He was always open to data in the micro and the macro worlds that forces us to look anew at the previous worldviews we inherited from Aristotle, Thomas Aquinas, Galileo, and Darwin. Each of them have developed models of the world in the light of what they knew at the time. As new data and interpretations come to light, we build on or modify these models. For example, Darwin, by looking at individual species one by one and extrapolating from them, neglected to look at the larger schemes of recurrence that were affecting each species as they emerged or declined or became extinct.

The implication of "probability" becomes richer and more complex as statistical knowledge grows, and the observables with the naked eye don't always give trustworthy information. Goodbye to so many of our certitudes! The import of this? This gives us the modesty, humility, and awareness about our proclivities that we need to keep from projecting onto unfolding data either our categories or conclusions that have proven to be premature. This proclivity might be especially operative with those whose categories are theological; and I take myself as a case in point. We have to ask ourselves anew: "Who do you say that you are, human being?" Because we now have to account for so much more than we ever knew existed.

Let us look again at the event that occurred over two million years ago which makes us so different from our ape antecedents. The mutation in the myosin gene seems to account for the tripled brain size of humans in comparison to our pre-Neanderthal ape ancestors. Granted, as the scientists who discovered this gene admit, this doesn't fully explain the coming into being of new species, hominids or Homo sapiens, but now there is an empirically new known that was unknown before. This new information about the mutated gene, among the myriad other findings already acquired and still to come, leaves us more informed but paradoxically less ready to give a complete explanation about what a human being is and will become. This is why emergent probability as a heuristic worldview is so useful: it expects and can take in ever unfolding, often intriguing and sometimes disturbing data about our humanity and our world/universe. Yet emergent probability can bring this data into a much larger field of the known while at the same time giving us less clarity about the relationship of the human species to the myriad of other emergents, their source and their telos. Emergent probability gives great value to our questions because they keep our understanding alert for answers beyond what we know or thought we already knew. And the great value of answers is that they take on a tentativeness that keeps the desire to know ever ready to transcend what was thought to be already fully known. When insights "combine, cluster, coalesce, into the mastery of a subject; they ground sets of definitions, postulates, deductions." In brief, higher viewpoints develop.[2] It is, of course, also possible that one finds oneself having gone down the primrose path only to find that the insights we gain don't lead anywhere. Lonergan calls an insight that doesn't work a cul de sac, an "inverse insight."

There are two other descriptors used by Lonergan that give further understanding of his worldview of emergent probability. One of these is his "theorem of the supernatural." This is his way of saying that there is a dynamism and logic at work in this universe that opens us to find things out at both the micro and macro levels hitherto not even suspected. So, what is seen as natural for a given, living thing can at times exhibit a jump beyond its natural processes to that which is supernatural to it. For example, the ape world some 2.5 million years ago had a branch break off from its modus operandi, a break off from what eventually became us. We, Homo sapiens, are an instance of the supernatural vis-à-vis the species of apes. In this case the designation "supernatural" is not a theological term but a descriptive term that describes the jumps that take place within the worlds of emergents. And since these jumps cannot be predetermined, probability is an appropriate descriptor. Of course, there are instances of theologically supernatural emergents: the light of glory, the beatific vision, the hypostatic union, and, in a word, grace.

Building on this, Lonergan distinguishes what he calls horizontal finality from vertical finality in fleshing out his worldview. Horizontal finality refers to the activities of a creature that are proportionate to what that being is. An ape's acts, for example, come from its "ape-icity"—food gathering, eating, fighting, mating, and the rearing of little apes. But "an exercise in vertical finality" is when a given activity of a being is an instance of a more complex or higher integration than that which has been deemed natural to it. So when one branch of apes evolves into Homo sapiens there is a case where over time the vertical finality obtains. It was this evolutionary worldview that Lonergan marveled at—the evolving movements of species in our world, including their interdependent interaction. He could see and marvel at how subatomic particles somehow enter into the elements of the periodic table; and chemical elements enter into chemical compounds, compounds into cells, cells into myriad combinations and configurations into the constitution of plant and animal life. Relative to what went before, all this upward mobility represents something "super-natural" or vertical. (Vertical finality is not inevitable, only possible.)

Vertical finality in the case of human beings is most germane but still only probable. The trajectory is obscure because, though one can believe in God as our absolute end and know that within each of us a vertical finality pulls us to self-transcendence, nonetheless there is also the pull to inertia and to remaining within the world of horizontal finality.

All this having been said, once there is an aggregate of self-transcending individuals, a new possibility develops within the human order. Lonergan refers to this in various ways, but his references are several: e.g., the new creation, the body of Christ, the Church. But these terms are less clarifying than the interiority of this aggregate. These self-transcending individuals haven't totally jettisoned the old, nor are they entrenched conservatives who are "determined to live in a world that no longer exists." What he hoped for and foresaw was the development of "a numerous center, big enough to be at home in both the old and the new, painstaking enough to work out one by one the transitions to be made, strong enough to refuse half measures and insist on complete solutions even though it has to wait."[3] These are all of a piece with his emergent probability worldview.

One of the effects of Lonergan's proposed worldview is that it makes one much less clear about the character of the so-called end times, the future of matter, the beginning and end of creation, and even how God goes about being God—obviously God has proven unbelievably patient, now that we have some grasp of the length of time it took for humans to emerge from their evolutionary beginnings. There is so much more that we know just about the physical universe alone than when our Judeo-Christian worldview was formed and articulated for us. With this new-found, ever-developing information, beginning with the unmistakable evidence of there having been a big bang, our cherished ideas, whether these be theological or biological or anthropological or cosmological or whatever, what the human enterprise is all about and where it is all going, can stay stuck in past clarities or they can be seen in a new light. There can be wisdom only by accepting our nescience and letting our presumed certainties be affected by ever developing evidence. These developments did not weaken Lonergan's faith: they only strengthened his resolve to map out a method that would help him and the rest of us make our judgments with full advertence to the structures of our consciousness. He was aware of our responsibility as humans to take hold of the resources we already have going for us, chief of which is our intelligence, about this still emerging and dangerous yet promising future so as to marvel at it and affect it.

I celebrate Lonergan's seeing that "the challenge of history is for humanity to progressively restrict the realm of chance or fate or destiny and progressively to enlarge the realm of conscious grasp and deliberate choice." Lonergan himself is the best example of this enlargement. At certain times in his life it was not at all clear whether he himself would be an emergent or the opposite, a failure psychically, physically, relationally—hence, he was a long shot, like the rest of us, a probability rather than a certainty. His advice about this has to do with two aspects of ourselves. One is our desire to know and our ability to achieve some degree of intelligibility in the face of the otherwise unintelligible. From there we can act intelligently and responsibly. His earliest experience of the unintelligible was the devastating effect of unemployment on the little town where he was born and grew up in Buckingham, Quebec, a town of 300 people put out of work by its only industry. This began a lifelong hunger to understand economics. He spent the last years of his life creating a theory of economics that, aside from its other values, sought to make that early trauma intelligible. Therefore, he went from experience to understanding economic theory to judgment to human intervention that in this case could have staunched the devastating social decline the town experienced and never got over.

This effort at understanding with a view to taking responsible action is an intrinsic component of the emergences that we have the responsibility for taking. We have the ongoing need to eke out what is intelligible in our own situations and in that of those around us so that with our intelligence we might see how to reduce or undo the absurdity of decline, and have our lives and situations regain the progress that emergent probability augurs. If we settle for absurdity or unintelligibility or decline we are not being faithful to our calling as intelligent creatures or as instances of Homo sapiens. Since our braincases are so much larger than those of our still brachiating ancestors—those who are still swinging from tree to tree—we can affect emergences and the conditions of our immediate situations and beyond. So beginning with the sensory perception apparatus that we have in common with the apes we seek to use our intelligence to increasingly affect the conditions that surround our lives and do this through understanding and judgment. This is basic to the calling given to each instance of the species of Homo sapiens, you and me.

It is important to keep emergence only probable in the universe, not inevitable. It is too easy to cover over this worldview with too glossy a coating and overlook the suffering, not just of humans, but also of all the species. There have been at least five mass extinctions, probably from asteroids that have struck the earth since the beginning of multicelled life. The greatest of these hits happened 251 million years ago, when 95 percent of ocean and land species were destroyed. This data is published in the Fall 2006 issue of the journal *Science*. The result was not all bad, at least in the oceans, since there was a shift from sedentary sea creatures to mobile sea creatures, a much more complex marine life for which we are all the beneficiaries. The point to be remembered, however, is that unlike the rest of nature, which is both adaptive and reactive, humans are equipped to take much of the probability out of nature by their cognitional and voluntary capacities.

But there is another, a further and even more important piece to emergence that Lonergan's own life represented. This development makes it clear that he was not all cognition or intellect or abstraction, as he has seemed to many who have read him superficially. When Lonergan was fifteen years old he was gravely ill; so ill that his mother moved into the hospital room with him where he lay between life and death. She loved him back to health and life, and three years later he joined the Jesuits. Forty years later, after having written his monumental tome *Insight* on understanding "understanding" (first and foremost, his own), and before starting on *Method*, the second book for which he is also famous, he was again gravely ill, this time with lung cancer—he was a smoker. He hovered between life and death for 82 days in the hospital after his lung was removed. A nun, a Sister Florian, and a nurse whose name is unknown to us, did what his mother had done for him forty years before. More than just nursing him, they loved him back to life. The tangibility of their love changed not just his physical condition. He began to appreciate at a much deeper level something he had not sufficiently adverted to before. He found his heart simply flooded with love of God and for Florian and the nurse and his Jesuit brothers and his academic colleagues. It is not that he went from a life without love to a life with love. Rather he went from a relative inadvertence to it to giving it the primacy it warranted all through his life but which his extraordinary intellect crowded out, it seems, for a time.

From now on the ingredient in emergence that intrigued him most was love. He knew from experience that it started intersubjectively, but he was more attentive to seeing that this love we have for one another could not be explained except by the Love that comes down from above, so to speak. To abide in and act from that love was to attain self-transcendence, or be further evidence of the "theorem of the supernatural." He so clearly moves from horizontal finality to vertical finality—with *gusto*. After his serious illness his favorite text, at least judging from his writings, was Romans 5:5, about God's love flooding our hearts through the Holy Spirit who has been given to us. He was certain of one thing now: that being in love with God and abiding in that love "is the basic fulfillment of our conscious intentionality."[4] And the fruit of this experience? Love of neighbor and great zeal to bring about the kingdom of God on this earth. Without this gift of God he foresaw in himself and in others the great likelihood of "the trivialization of human life in the pursuit of fun, a harshness arising from the need for power, a despair about human welfare springing from the conviction that the universe is absurd."[5] He would now write what he could not have written in *Insight*: This gift of love "is not the product of our knowledge and choice. On the contrary, it dismantles and abolishes the horizon in which our knowing and choosing take place, and it sets up a new horizon in which the love of God will transvalue our values and the eyes of that love will transform our knowing."[6]

He extrapolated from his own experience and that of others to conclude that the main operator behind the emergence of all species and events in the history of the universe is love, in particular, God's love for the world. He could see that the Spirit of Love has been the operator within all the operations of all the creatures that have been evolving all these millennia. Love is now the factor that has center stage in Lonergan's consciousness. He is also aware that "though this dynamic state is conscious this is not to say that it is known."[7] This gift of God's love is an experience of the holy, of mystery, and though he experienced it, he did not require of himself that he would comprehend it. Love, self-sacrificing love, was the lubricant that was given so as to make the use of intelligence efficacious, human progress more frequent, and intimate knowledge of the source of all these things more evident.

So, what is incumbent upon us as members of the species *Homo sapiens*? That we understand ourselves as emergents and seek to reduce some of the probability from life on earth by actively taking our part in the unfolding drama of creation, intervening where necessary, to assist in its progress or halt its decline. Humans whose brains have developed enough to see what has been evolving all these millions of years can now become active participants in the direction of the emergence of the *creata* in history. Though we might not appreciate it, we are the only species who can know and choose progress and at the same time marvel that our now distant relatives were the apes. But our most important task as the chosen species, the species that has been chosen to do what all the other species can't do, is to use our intelligence. It is this that makes us chips off the old block, if we may refer to the Creator in this way. God is praised by our intelligence being fully alive and with it our species (Isaiah 43:21). For Lonergan there is a whole new emergent. Although Paul called it the new creation, in Lonergan's understanding it wasn't limited to members of one faith.

For Catholic Christians the most formal acknowledgment of this new creation is in the Eucharist. It is when and where everything that is part of the immanent in our lives is lifted beyond its rightful autonomy to the Source. Our primary act of the praise of God as Christians is Eucharistic. At Mass, we offer to God the best thing about our humanity: Jesus who is consubstantial with us; we lift up to God whom he called his Father. "And I, if I be lifted up from the earth, will draw everyone to myself" (John 12:32). Jesus' humanity was a priceless moment in the evolution of our humanity from the apes. We the successors of the apes offer him as the zenith instance of humanity to God. And God will not be outdone by our praise and thanksgiving and the offering of ourselves that accompanies this act of offering of Jesus to the Father. God, in turn, offers Jesus to us so that our evolution might proceed apace toward the consummation God envisioned in having Jesus become one of us in all things save sin (Hebrews 4:15). We might even praise God now for Jesus' jaw and ours, for Jesus' humanity and for ours. Talk about emergence! Since at the Eucharist we also receive from God an assurance of our consubstantiality with Jesus' divinity. That is what is so marvelous about him—he spans the divide between us and the apes, us and the Trinity.

John Courtney Murray

6. John Courtney Murray's American Stories

Michael J. Schuck

When I began graduate studies twenty-five years ago, "narrative theory" and "story-discourse" did not surface as topics in my political philosophy, social theory, or theology courses. Systems theory, Kantian rationalism, Marxian analyses, existential phenomenology, personalism—all these were discussed, but not narrative and story. That soon changed. By the end of my course work in 1982, narrative approaches to politics, society, and theology were ubiquitous.

John Courtney Murray died well before this academic interest in narrative and story effervesced. His scholarly imagination was animated by the *philosophia perennis* and by Roman Catholic philosophical, theological, and historical debates adjoining the Second Vatican Council. Ironically, Murray's legacy to Catholic scholarship since his death in 1967 has been not only the learned monographs he produced, but also the compelling story he lived while producing them.

Catholic scholars have amply recounted Murray's personal drama as contributor to Roman Catholic teaching at Vatican II. Less recognized is the impact of the American stories Murray lived *within* as he conducted his research and writing. Murray's scholarly life spanned the years from Herbert Hoover's depression-era presidency to the 1967 student protests against the Vietnam War. The shifting, overlapping, and fractious national stories Americans lived through during this thirty-year period are staggering; that Murray maintained his analytic aplomb and ripened his thought over these tumultuous years is highly impressive. Yet behind the remarkable poise of Murray's writings, one detects the restlessness of a rapidly changing nation. The following essay briefly discusses three of these dynamic stories and suggests their bearing on Murray's scholarship, particularly his notions of freedom and truth. To open the first of these stories, I return to elements of my own narrative that share in a theme central to Murray's thought.

I am, like many North American, Roman Catholic baby boomers, a second-generation descendant of immigrant grandparents from Europe. Though narrated more often and in greater detail a generation earlier, my paternal grandparents' story still engaged my imagination as I grew up: old-country poverty and oppression, risky departures to America, difficult adaptations to a new land, arduous work, rewards of freedom and security. When I read Oscar Handlin's Pulitzer Prize–winning *The Uprooted* in college, I found its powerful immigrant story completely familiar.

Also central to my grandparents' experience was their immersion in the rituals and religious truth-claims of the Roman Catholic Church—the only institution that accompanied them on both sides of the Atlantic Ocean. Shortly after the fall of the Soviet Union, I stood inside my grandmother's childhood church in what was once Kandel, Russia. St. Michael's church was then (as it had been for the previous sixty years) an enormous grain storage building for the area's collective farm. I told the collective's *apparatchik* that my German-Russian ancestors had long ago built this imposing structure. He asked me what people once did inside it. I was five thousand miles from home and a visitor in the village for less than an hour. I felt strange telling this man the religious details of a building I had never seen before this moment, but one he had driven grain trucks in and out of all his life. As with my grandparents' immigration saga, the lineaments of their religious world were thoroughly familiar to me.

Though today I neither retain all the details of my grandparents' story, nor live their religious "first naiveté," a clear message perdures from both: be strong, work hard, preserve freedom, and practice your faith. I recently sat for the homily at the noon Mass at another St. Michael's church—this one my deceased grandparents' adopted parish and the longtime religious oasis for German-Russians in Grand Forks,

North Dakota. Summer was at its peak. As I squirmed in one-hundred-degree heat and wiped sweat beads off my forehead, the pastor clarified why St. Mike's was (unlike the nearby Lutheran church) without air-conditioning: "If our grandparents didn't need it, we didn't need it." When he said this I knew exactly where I was—and the story behind it.

John Courtney Murray had a profound understanding of where he was—and the story behind it. Born of Irish and Scottish immigrants in 1904, Murray had a vivid, first- generation knowledge of the American immigrant saga and the religious world of Roman Catholicism. The values of inner strength, hard work, American freedom, and Catholic truth were surely the ambient refrains of his youth. When Murray later applied his conviction and industry to theological studies, it was precisely the topics of freedom and truth that drew his attention.

Murray celebrated America's historical experiment with freedom. He joined a Catholic esteem for American freedom begun by John Carroll, the first American Catholic bishop, and carried through the nineteenth century by bishops such as John England of Charleston, James Gibbons of Baltimore, John Spalding of Peoria, and John Keane, first rector of the Catholic University of America. Murray's scholarship brought this long-standing Catholic endorsement of American freedom into the twentieth century.

Murray also had profound respect for the truths of the Roman Catholic *depositum fidei.* He insisted that "anyone who really believes in God must set God and the truth of God above all other considerations."[1] A faith grounded in this truth was, for Murray, "a force for the renovation of the world." Murray encouraged lay Catholics to profess their religious truths through actions promoting the common good. Such faith-inspired work, said Murray, "wears very humble outward garbs—an apron or a business suit; for it is in the worlds of the apron and the business suit that the renovating must be done."[2]

Rome had long allowed American Catholics to *live* the practical coexistence of their social freedom and religious truth; what was not allowed was the *thought* that such coexistence might be theologically acceptable. The chilling effect of Pope Leo XIII's odd, fifty-year-old criticism of "Americanism" was still felt in the early years of Murray's career—tacitly sustained in Pope Pius X's 1907 condemnation of modernism and echoed in Pope Pius XII's 1950 encyclical *Humani Generis.*

Though enjoying their personal religious freedom and the mutual separations of their church's affairs from the affairs of their state, American Catholics were to understand this situation as a tolerable *hypothesis,* not as an acceptable *thesis* of Church teaching.

The American hypothesis became the Roman Catholic thesis at the Second Vatican Council. Murray's contribution to this seismic shift in Church teaching is well known. His contributory treatises on religious freedom and church-state relations published in *Theological Studies* between 1945 and 1954 stand as the most impressive pieces of Catholic political theology ever written by a North American theologian. The incisive essays on Catholicism and the First Amendment in Murray's book, *We Hold These Truths: Catholic Reflections on the American Proposition*, are as compelling today as they were on the eve of the Council. Through these and other works, Murray probed the outlaw idea that social freedom and religious truth could theologically coexist in Roman Catholicism. His effort unearthed insights enabling the Church to officially endorse, for the first time in its history, the human right to religious freedom and the institutional separation of church and state.

In this effort, Murray did more than probe an idea. He educed meaning for the universal Church from an American story he lived. Emboldened by that story's virtues of inner strength and hard work, Murray conveyed an insight that came to him by *living* the story's prized values of social freedom and religious truth. One could say that the Murray family's own version of *The Uprooted*—and the versions of countless other American Catholic families since the eighteenth century—figured into the conciliar teaching of *Dignitatis Humanae* as surely as Pope Gelasius I's *Duo Sunt.*

While Murray worked creatively from the heart of one American story, another pressed upon him. This latter story told not of European oppression, transatlantic voyage, and hard-won immigrant achievement, but of the difficult experiences that followed: generational conflict over the exercise of freedom and the disappearance of long-standing religious customs and rituals. This was the second American story, a saga of contentious arguments and vanishing traditions.

It is a truism that every generation challenges its forbearers. But with their progeny's freedom energized by notions of personal autonomy and individual rights, immigrant parents faced the defiance of their youth in the 1950s and 1960s, well in excess of the age-old cliché.

Some young adults may have occasionally restrained their impatience and briefly humored their immigrant parents and grandparents, but as the postwar years unfolded, the perceived relevance of an elder's advice for living in fast-paced America waned. Even first generation, American-born parents were suspect; hadn't they already co-opted their freedom by thoroughly "buying into the system"? And when these obsolete elders wondered whether their offspring had gone utterly mad, *Time* magazine assured them in 1966 that America's youth was "Man of the Year."

For Catholics, only slight reprieve from such domestic conflict was gained by going to church. There too, everything appeared different. Latin mass, meatless Fridays, Saturday confession, family rosary, parish novenas—all seemed to vanish quickly after the American bishops began implementing Vatican II's liturgical reforms in 1965. Some pastors strove mightily to explain these changes as a return of the liturgy to its historical roots. But who ever thought the liturgy was historical? Hadn't everyone been taught that Roman Catholic mass and devotions were timeless?

No wonder *Fiddler on the Roof* was the Broadway hit of 1964 and one of the most popular American musicals of all time. Tevye's conflict with his daughters over their freely chosen marriage partners and his pain over the dissolution of his beloved traditions were tropes millions of Americans experienced in their everyday lives. If only for a moment, it was good to be blithe—to laugh and cry with Tevye over these common anxieties; just as it was good to hope that one could—like the fiddler—bring life back in balance, after most of one's house had fallen down and only a thin roof-edge remained to stand on.

Murray possessed the fiddler's hope as he worked within this second American story. Though he well understood these tensions in his society and his church, Murray caught sight of a deep value in the new freedoms and truths they expressed.

In a 1965 commencement speech at St. John's University in Collegeville, Minnesota, Murray claimed that "for all its dangers, freedom remains the first truth about man." "For long centuries" in the Roman Catholic Church, he continued, this was a "forgotten truth." Now, at the close of Vatican II, Murray hoped that the "new age which the Church is entering" would be an "Age of Renewal of this truth."[3] The conciliar text *Dignitatis Humanae* provided, in his view, groundwork "for the articulation of a full theology of Christian freedom."[4]

Arguments will always accompany freedom, not only the divisive arguments between generations one wishes to reduce, but also the constructive arguments between citizens that signal a healthy democracy. In *We Hold These Truths*, Murray stressed a point oft-repeated in his writings: civilization depends on "men locked together in argument" and good argument depends on shared truths.[5] Because we "hold certain truths," wrote Murray, "we can argue about them."[6] From these observations, Murray derived his counterintuitive insight: real disagreement—as distinct from a shouting match—"is not an easy thing to reach."[7]

Yet, neither our access nor our construal of these necessary truths is static; truths are situated, like freedom, in history. As painful as the abrupt liturgical changes were to his co-religionists, Murray felt American Catholics needed to realize the historicity of these ritual truths. This was not unlike Murray's earlier claim about the truths Americans needed to share regarding their democracy: these truths have a "growing end" requiring constant discovery through a process in "large part reserved to experience."[8]

Murray called this view of truth the "deeper significance" of *Dignitatis Humanae*, a document he considered "permeated by historical consciousness." The truth about religious freedom articulated there was not a conclusion drawn from "Christian dogma"; "the connection" he said, "is rather more historical."[9] Murray believed the whole Church needed to recognize the centrality of history and freedom for the discovery and growth of truth.

If the first American story helped draw out Murray's convictions on the right to religious freedom and the separation of church and state, this second story of contentious arguments and vanished traditions incubated Murray's courageous reflections on the meaning of freedom for human life and the historicity of truth. However, while his conclusions from the first American story reached closure in the conciliar teaching of the Roman Catholic Church, Murray's conclusions from the second story did not and have not reached such closure. What freedom's vitality and truth's historicity mean for Catholics remain much debated questions in the Church. To be both a respected member of that church and a theologian committed to Murray's legacy on freedom and truth, one is perched today, like the fiddler, on a precarious edge.

While Murray honored the play of freedom and the development of truth in human life, there were limits. He appreciated Lord Acton's remark that freedom is "not the power of doing what we like, but the right of being able to do what we ought."[10] Nor did Murray think truth simply an unalloyed product of human perception. Rather, truths make discrete claims on human intelligence from the "structure of reality."[11]

On both points, Murray found himself in profound tension with a third American story: the saga of American commercialization. Murray lived within the "golden era" of American capitalism, a time of the greatest rise in economic production and consumption the world had ever known. No force in American culture more effectively severed the relationships Murray saw between morality and freedom and between reality and truth than the rampant commercialization marking this post-World War II period.

As American consumerism grew, more and more people located their experience of freedom in the act of consumer choice. The power to choose what one liked became, despite Lord Acton's warning, most American's everyday experience of freedom. But this freedom:

> is the "freedom" to be out of the loop of the discussion that went into making the consumer good what it is; we pay to acquire that debate in commoditized form, already finalized. . . . we pay to avoid the burden of critical thought so that we may relax in our purchases.[12]

For many Americans in this amplified commercial environment, exercising one's will through buying became the most meaningful act of self-definition. One's "truth" became more what one owned, than what one was or did. Paralleling freedom's new association with satisfying one's *likes*, truth seemed more linked to one's *perceptions* than to any "structure of reality."

Murray's grief over this American story surfaced in many of his writings. His frequent association of commercialism with "barbarianism" connected his grief to Arnold Toynbee's "decline of Western civilization" thesis. In a memorable line from *We Hold These Truths,* Murray wrote: "The barbarian need not appear in bearskins with a club in hand. He may wear a Brooks Brothers suit and carry a ballpoint pen with which to write his advertising copy."[13] How painful these lines he must have had to write; just twelve years earlier Murray had imagined the children of Catholic immigrants someday in the "humble outward garbs" of business suits acting as forces for a moral "renovation of the world."[14]

Murray keenly perceived the damaging impact of commercialization on human freedom. "These forces operate," he observed, "under the device of 'freedom,' but unto the disintegration of the human personality."[15] The paramount disintegrating factor was the privatization of freedom, inducing over time a near-amnesia in American culture over the essential sociality of freedom. The American exemplar subtly changed from the morally engaged, town hall citizen to the morally vacuous, marketplace consumer. Highlighting this point, Murray shifted from the language of barbarism to the language of idiocy:

> The real enemy within the gates of the city is not the Communist, but the idiot. . . . going back to the primitive Greek usage; the "idiot" meant, first of all, the private person. . . . the man who does not possess a public philosophy, the man who is not the master of the knowledge and the skills that underlie the life of the civilized city . . . He is the man who is ignorant of the meaning of the word 'civility.'[16]

Truth was also a victim in this process. When the "marketplace of ideas" literally becomes the economic marketplace, "there is the consequent dissolution of the idea of truth itself to the point where no assertion may claim more that the status of sheer opinion."[17] Whereas the impact of highly commercialized markets on commodities is product diversity, the effect on ideas, now "opinions," is just the opposite. "American culture," decried Murray, "is uniform, and it is tending always to become more and more unitary and uniform." He continued: The threat today is "cultural uniformity and the menace it holds to the distinctiveness of personality and to the distinctiveness of the religious community within contemporary homogenized culture."[18]

Murray feared that not only the replacement of religious faith by a secular faith in commercialism, but also the commercialization of religious faith itself. In both cases, a "substitute" faith "would undertake to take the place of the traditional religious faith that has historically given substance to the civilization we call Western."[19] The result would be a loss of real identity for Americans and America. Said Murray:

> The complete loss of one's identity is, with all propriety of theological definition, hell. In diminished forms it is insanity. And it

would not be well for the American giant to go lumbering about the world today, lost and mad.[20]

Unlike the first American story, the saga of commercialism did not educe insights from Murray that changed institutions. Akin to the ideas he generated out of the second American story, the thoughts triggered in Murray by the commercialization of America have not found closure. But here too, there is a difference. One imagines Murray intellectually thriving today in a Catholic university where the meanings of freedom's vitality and truth's historicity for human life and the life of his Church remain lively questions. In relation to the third story of American commercialization, however, one can only imagine Murray further demoralized were he alive today.

When Murray began his career, "consumption" was a disease; by the end of his life, consumption was a celebrated pastime. Today, it is a lifestyle. If, as Murray argued, an inverse relationship exists between commercialization and the human experience of authentic freedom and real truth, then the American giant is still lumbering, lost, and mad.

Murray experienced three American stories: the Catholic immigrant narrative, the tale of generational conflict, and the saga of commercialization. Though his intellectual footings were in ancient and medieval philosophy and not in narrative theory, each of the stories Murray lived shaped his perceptions of freedom and truth in vital ways.[21] American society and the Roman Catholic Church benefited from these rich perceptions—the story about which members of both institutions would greatly benefit by rereading today.

7. Memories of "Uncle Jack": A Nephew Remembers John Courtney Murray

Mark Williams

In mid-April 2005, while attending a Georgetown-sponsored Ignatian retreat in western Maryland, I realized that the former Woodstock College was nearby. It is where my uncle, John Courtney Murray, S.J., lived and taught for many years, and where he is now buried. The Woodstock's buildings and campus were sold to the State of Maryland in the early 1970's. It is now the Maryland Job Corps Center, but the Jesuit cemetery, which lies at the edge of the property, remains intact and accessible. And so, late on a warm and sunny spring afternoon, I spent an hour at the simple gravesite of the man who was both a loving presence and important influence in my life.

The memories flooded back, not in any organized way, but as a disparate collection of mental pictures, remarks, and anecdotes. Still, the mental pictures remain clear, the remarks are well remembered, and the anecdotes still bring a smile. As the son of the late Katherine Murray Williams, the younger sister of John Courtney Murray, I have some vivid memories of "Uncle Jack."

My earliest and most enduring memory is of his smile, bestowed from on high—he was 6′4″ but seemed taller—when my older sister Robin, my younger brother David, and I were still very young. It was a warm and loving smile that lit up his face, and it was totally at odds with the stern countenance that appeared on the 1960 cover of *Time* magazine. Over time I came to realize that the smile reflected a mirthfulness and lightness of spirit that was as much a part of his person as his truly extraordinary mind. His voice was distinctively modulated, and he spoke slowly and carefully, seeming never at a loss for articulate expression. However, while his words in my presence were always gentle and friendly, I have reason to believe he could be sharp-tongued when he felt the occasion demanded or permitted. While famously tolerant of the contrary beliefs and opinions of others, Uncle Jack was nonetheless disinclined to mince words or suffer fools lightly and, on occasion, he borrowed with attribution George Bernard Shaw's prideful claim never to have insulted anyone by accident. He could also be snappish, as when, for example, he would fondly say, "One can learn from students, but not much."

My early memories of Uncle Jack revolve around his visits, usually at Thanksgiving and Christmas, to our home in Jamaica, New York, not far from where he and his sisters, Elizabeth (Bess) and Katherine (Kay), themselves grew up. He was totally at ease during those visits, and I later realized he rather enjoyed not being the center of attention. In fact, I remember quite well his enthusiastic participation in loud and highly competitive table hockey and indoor bocci contests involving the whole family.

Given Uncle Jack's commitment to religious pluralism, it is only fitting that my mother should have decided to marry a Baptist, something taboo for a Catholic in the thirties. When my parents married in 1933, the antipathy of the Catholic Church to mixed marriages was such that Uncle Jack was not allowed to perform the ceremony in my mother's parish church, even "outside the rail." Rather, the ceremony had to be held in my grandmother's apartment and, even then, only with diocesan approval. The Church's semiofficial position in those days, famously declaimed in later years by the widely publicized Father Feeney, was *extra ecclesiam nulla salus*, "outside the Church there is no salvation." Happily, Uncle Jack played a key role in changing all that.

He loved a good joke or funny story, the more sophisticated the better, and he periodically passed along real-life observations that reflected his dry sense of humor. Asked about the beer served at Woodstock, which was brewed on-site, he noted: "It's perfect. If it were any better, we wouldn't serve it. If it were any worse, they wouldn't drink it." And following a trip to Hollywood in the late fifties (possibly to consult, but I'm not sure), he shared with the family his conclusion that: "All the lies they tell about what goes on out there are true!" Another time, describing Henry Luce's golf game, he observed: "Harry's got a terrible swing, but he can *will* the ball 200 yards down the fairway."

Speaking of golf, Uncle Jack loved the game, and he played whenever circumstances allowed, which was not often, with my father, my brother, and myself. Like the rest of his manner, his swing was graceful and unhurried, and he could score in the eighties, despite having to play with borrowed clubs that were invariably too short, and having to compensate for a foreshortened right leg, the result of a clubfoot. This lifelong condition led almost inevitably to a chronic back problem that plagued him throughout the last twenty-five years of his life and, on occasion, became almost disabling. On the day of my marriage in December 1964, his back was so painful that he could not genuflect and could barely bow at the altar. However, he never even alluded to what must have been excruciating pain, lest it cloud a day that belonged to others.

As for Uncle Jack's other leisure-time activities, I remember that his reading was not confined to the works of fourteenth century mystics. On the contrary, he was quite addicted to Agatha Christie mystery novels, traded them regularly with my sister Robin, and was reluctant to get on a plane without one. This brings to mind one of Uncle Jack's idiosyncrasies: an aversion to being alone in airports. I was working at a law firm in Los Angeles in the summer of 1961, when Uncle Jack was traveling to Asia and had a long layover in San Diego. At his gentle request (he certainly was not insistent, but I got the message), I drove the two hours from Los Angeles to San Diego to keep him company in the airport lounge.

Over the years, I remember him expressing two convictions that, to my mind at least, sum him up as a priest and a man. On the first occasion he was counseling and seeking to reassure a family member who was facing a spiritual crisis. I remember his words: "I don't know whether hell exists, but if it does, it's a lot more difficult to get there than people believe." I'm sure this statement doesn't surprise those who knew how much more focused Uncle Jack was on God's embracing love and mercy than on His "terrible swift sword." And I have little doubt that Cardinal Ottaviani would have found such a sentiment quite inappropriate.

On another occasion, this truly brilliant man exhorted: "Courage, Mark, it's far more important than intelligence." I don't remember him elaborating on the subject, but I took him to mean that we will ultimately be measured, as human beings and Christians, by what we do, not by what we think or what we think about doing. It's an insight that fits comfortably with the "Serenity Prayer," to which he introduced me, and which has been an important guide in my life: "God, grant me Serenity to accept the things I cannot change, Courage to change the things I can, and Wisdom to know the difference."

Uncle Jack directly influenced my choices of high school and college, both of which were obviously predestined to be Jesuit institutions. First, he gently nudged me toward his alma mater, Xavier High School, the Jesuit military academy in New York City where he had found his own vocation. Although my daily commute was well over two hours, I treasure the education and formation I received at Xavier, and recall the feeling of pride as Uncle Jack delivered the commencement address in 1955.

Then it was on to Georgetown, again at his urging, even though my original plan had been to accept an academic scholarship to Holy Cross. In the second semester of my freshman year, just a year after Uncle Jack had been "silenced" by Rome for his views on Church-State relations, Georgetown awarded him an honorary Doctor of Laws degree. The citation, which he gave to me and which remains a precious possession, reads in part:

> Indefatigably, in all media of communication—in writing, on the speaker's platform and at the professional rostrum—he has sought to discover and to expound the orderly relation which should ideally exist between the powers of the [Church-State] diarchy, whose source is the wisdom of Divine Providence, whose arena is in the depths of individual conscience, whose objectives are defined in the unity and integrity of human personality. As a churchman, he properly asserts the primacy and transcendence of the spiritual; with equal vigor, this loyal upholder of civil society defends the autonomy of the temporal order. Above all, as a Christian humanist, his prime concern is the protection and enhancement of human dignity, the progressive approach to that peace which is the fruit of justice, that liberty which is the tranquility of order.

I have always believed that the Georgetown University degree had special significance for Uncle Jack. It was a university he greatly respected for its declared admiration for his work, even in the face of Vatican disapproval.

Three years later, I was selected by my class to deliver the Cohonguroton Address, the traditional Georgetown valedictory, the night before commencement. As I began to draft the address, I had one of my first "Be careful what you pray for" experiences, as I could find neither the inspiration nor the energy to compose anything sensible, much less memorable. As it turned out, I was coming down with a rather serious case of mononucleosis that landed me in Georgetown Hospital two hours after the graduation ceremony. With time running out, and my panic increasing, I called Uncle Jack for help and, at his suggestion, drove up to Woodstock. Sensing my distress and fatigue, Uncle Jack promptly put aside his other, far more important writing, and provided input and assistance I would not have sought, and certainly would not have received, from anyone else. Although it was I who ultimately delivered the 1959 Cohonguroton Address, one passage is distinctly John Courtney Murray:

> Since history began, the leading minds and spirits of the human race have been struggling to civilize the world in which men must live, and to make it less a wilderness, less a place of savagery and barbarism. But the task is never finished; and at every moment it is threatened with destruction. "Our generation," said Christopher Dawson, "has been forced to realize how fragile and unsubstantial are the barriers that separate civilization from the forces of destruction. We have learned that barbarism is not a picturesque myth or a half-forgotten memory of a long-paused stage of history, but an ugly underlying reality, which may erupt with shattering force whenever the moral authority of a civilization loses its control.

The words seem sadly prophetic as I reflect on events over the past several years in the United States, the Middle East, and elsewhere around the world.

Politically, Uncle Jack declared unequivocally that he stood at the "extreme center," his way of expressing disdain for ideologues of either left or the right, with their attendant biases, agendas, and labels. For him, truth was the only goal, and fact, reason, and principles were the only roads to follow. Unsurprisingly, that approach sometimes put him at cross-purposes with politicians who hoped he would tailor his views to support their positions. For example, at the request of the Johnson administration, Uncle Jack traveled to Vietnam in late 1966 to examine various war-related issues and, presumably, report favorably on U.S. policy and strategy. Instead, he concluded that the U.S. could never win the war.

According to his friend and longtime colleague, Father Walter Burghardt, Uncle Jack was quite dispirited after his "silencing" by Rome in 1954. Remarkably, however, and perhaps reflecting his (prophetic) conviction that the cause of religious freedom would ultimately prevail, he seemed more bemused than offended at being excluded from the first session of the Second Vatican Council. Indeed, he was mischievously explicit in correcting anyone who was under the mistaken impression that he had not been invited: "Oh, but you see, I *was* invited, and then I was *disinvited*. The distinction is crucial." I don't believe he ever doubted he would eventually get to Rome, and that is exactly what happened. The rest is history, wonderful history.

Uncle Jack's death from a heart attack in August 1967 was sudden but sadly, not totally unexpected. He had been hospitalized for cardiac insufficiency back in 1953, suffered his first heart attack in 1958 (I remember driving up from Georgetown to visit him in a Baltimore hospital), and suffered another heart attack in early 1962. Ironically, his 1962 heart attack occurred while he was visiting Jamaica Hospital, where his sister Bess, to whom he was utterly devoted, lay dying. To his great sadness, he remained hospitalized during the period of her death and burial.

For the last six years of his life, throughout the stress and crushing workload associated with Vatican II, he suffered frequently severe angina pain that required him to take digitalis and nitroglycerin (but, unfortunately, did not dissuade him from cigarette smoking). However, I never heard a word of complaint.

I have always believed that Uncle Jack recognized physical signs that death was approaching, and that he went to considerable lengths to visit my mother on August 16, 1967, because he felt it might be their last time together. The visit involved a long cab ride from Rye, New York, in Westchester County, where he had been visiting friends, to my mother's apartment in Queens. Following the visit, he started another lengthy cab ride into New York City, but died only a few minutes into the journey.

The Funeral Mass for Uncle Jack was held at the Church of St. Ignatius Loyola in New York City on August 21, 1967. Fittingly, the sermon was delivered by his dear friend, Walter Burghardt, S.J., perhaps the finest homilist the Catholic Church in America has produced. Rereading the sermon recently, I was again struck by Father Burghardt's eloquent overview of Uncle Jack's legacy:

> Unborn millions will never know how much their freedom is tied to this man whose pen was a powerful protest, a dramatic march, against injustice and inequality, whose research sparked and terminated in the ringing affirmation of an ecumenical council: "The right to religious freedom has its foundation" not in the Church, not in society or state, not even in objective truth, but "in the very dignity of the human person." Unborn millions will never know how much the civilized dialogue they take for granted between Christian and Christian, between Christian and Jew, between Christian and unbeliever, was made possible by this man whose life was a civilized conversation. Untold Catholics will never sense that they live so gracefully in this dear land because John Murray showed so persuasively that the American proposition is quite congenial to the Catholic reality.

On August 21, 1967, Uncle Jack returned to his beloved Woodstock and was buried with his Jesuit brothers in the simple cemetery where I now stood. His headstone is no different from any of theirs, however different his life may have been. But that is as he would have wanted it—a final recognition that, when all is said and done, we are all the same in God's eyes. I'm honored and grateful to have known him.

8. Murray on Loving One's Enemies

Leon Hooper, S.J.

John Courtney Murray never wrote much about loving one's enemies, though he did have a clearly identifiable enemies list. Many on that list he adopted from his ecclesial tradition, and some he developed on his own or, at least, gave them his own spin. In what follows I discuss four such enemies and then spell out how Murray—in using and abusing, rejecting and developing his tradition—gave a new social nuance to the usually personalistic understandings of the command to love one's enemies.

These enemies are: first, America itself; second, Catholic University of America staff and Roman Catholics of similar mind; third, Protestants universally but only in limited aspect; and, fourth, atheists of any and all aspects. I will discuss Murray's "big hate" toward each of his enemies (a phrase he himself used, as discussed below) and how his own tradition often encouraged those hates, while also it encouraged him to something that looks—painfully even—like bearing a social cross and loving one's tribal enemies.

The First Enemy: Americanism

America, or at least Americanism (all those New World attitudes that Leo XIII condemned in his 1899 encyclical *Testem Benevolentiae Nostrae* [Concerning New Opinions, Virtue, Nature and Grace, with

Regard to Americanism]) was Murray's first enemy. After returning to Woodstock College in 1939 from his Roman studies for a Gregorian STD (doctorate of sacred theology), he could, even in the face of the rise of fascism and the outbreak of war in Europe, claim that

> It would appear that our American culture, as it exists, is actually the quintessence of all that is decadent in the culture of the Western Christian world. It would seem to be erected on the triple denial that has corrupted Western culture at its roots, the denial of metaphysical reality, of the primacy of the spiritual over the material, of the social over the individual.

He applauded European desires to escape the individualism and isolation that characterized much of Anglo-American culture and asserted that fascism was offering a needed "communitarian" alternative to our own decadence, even though he admitted that fascism was an inadequate form of communitarianism. Of course, Catholicism offered an more adequate form of communitarianism.

Murray eventually moved beyond this America, this America he and his church scorned, to another America. In his eventual discussion of the historical emergence of religious freedom, he would find in the Anglo-American political tradition traces of God's intentions, even for Catholics and institutional Catholicism. Still, before he was forced in that direction, his own tradition began to move him to an appreciation of moral agency well beyond anything tolerated in fascist societies.

Such a correction showed up first in his dissertation on the German theologian Matthias Joseph Scheeben.[1] Scheeben had tried to carve out a Thomistic-based theology for the laity. Murray appreciated Scheeben's attempt to understand all human cognitional and emotive operations (including, in the case of the laity, practical reasoning) as capable of being taken up by the very cognitional and emotive powers of an incarnate God, under Athanasius's theme of whatever has not been taken up into the Godhead has not been redeemed. In an intricate faculty-psychological dissecting of knowing and valuing, Sheeben (with admittedly Murray's help) developed a basis for a laity-in-the-world closeness to God that veers toward the hypostatic, built as it is on the metaphor of the beatific vision—defined as a participation in Christ's view of his Father—in which we even now participate. God and humans united in the very internal unity of Christ Jesus.

To help in that union, though, Murray had to confront two elements that Scheeben placed in the way of lay social action, namely, the fundamental paternalism of Scheeben's own understanding of the divine/human relationship, and his subsequent reduction of all human action to blind, if loving, obedience. To correct for what Murray called Scheeben's "big hate toward liberalism" that is, toward anything Gallic or Anglo, Murray suggested that the primary governing metaphor for lay action must be other than Scheeben's supplied metaphor of the Ten Commandments. Murray countered—with the help of Newman—that one might more adequately understand the sacrifice of intellect, which all agreed is required by faith, as more akin to moving into uncharted territory, than to blind obedience to a clear demand. "Obedience of faith is not precisely that of Moses receiving the Laws on Sinai, but rather that of Abraham going out from country and hearth and kin, into the land that God would show him, but of which he had as yet no vision."

Murray then tried to move Scheeben's graced agent toward someone capable of deciding and acting on the strength of his or her own creative insights (certainly a quality needed in post-war reconstruction). But note that Murray's notion of grace, while redeeming individual human acts of understanding, willing, and even feeling, is at best poised to, but not yet capable of, disclosing God's actions in social realities and in human history. Only after turning away from faculty psychology to movements of social history in his later religious freedom discussions would Murray's eyes be open to the social aspects of love for enemies.

The Second Enemy: Catholic University of America

Murray did not begin by picking a fight with Catholic University of America's Joseph Fenton, Francis Connell, or Paul Hanley Furfey, though his public voice was eventually silenced when he did attack them and their sponsor, Alfredo Cardinal Ottaviani, on Catholic University's premises. Why and how he turned them, if not all Catholics, into enemies is important for understanding his own loving.

Murray began his search for an active God with a distinction between theory and action, initially in addressing the question of who among Catholics should participate in post-World War II reconstruction and how they should so participate. He insisted that the task of reconstruction was so vast that Catholic laity were obliged to work directly with Protestants and other believers. (I will return to Protestants themselves and to nonbelievers in the next two sections.)

The argument, mostly with the faculty at Catholic University of America, focused on the choice between, on the one hand, parallel centers of action segregated from each other by denominational boundaries—joined perhaps only at the highest leadership levels of each—and, on the other hand, interfaith, action-oriented groups religiously mixed together from top to bottom. Murray endorsed the latter—full integration top to bottom. His justification for these interfaith organizations, where the faith of Catholics could be challenged, rested on three premises: (1) that only through such mixed groups could the work get done (a practical argument that the international common good required it); (2) that the work would be primarily in the realm of the temporal, not the eternal; and (3) that it would be "work," that is, it would be at the level of action and practical intelligence, not at the level of theory and theology. He appealed to Pius XI's insistence concerning Catholic Action that the clergy stay out of the realm proper to the laity. In this cognitional division of labor, priest/theologians should work at redeeming human *theoretical* intelligence, while the laity worked at redeeming the temporal order through the semiautonomous functioning of *practical* reasoning. Granted that such a sharp distinction made the social construction that the laity were to perform look suspiciously like the technical reasoning that Europeans condemned in Americanism; and granted that bishops were still supposed to judge the moral qualities of lay action and, therefore, could interfere as bishops, though not as priests, in the lay sphere. Nonetheless, this action/theory distinction worked fairly well for Murray. He could in principle allow lay autonomy in social reconstruction, while keeping them theologically safe.

That is, it worked fairly well until he tried to use it to establish a coherent argument to support a Catholic affirmation of civic religious liberty. In his first attempt to dispel Protestant suspicions of Catholic eagerness to coercively suppress heretical voices, Murray tried to use an argument that distinguished between natural and revealed knowledge as theory, on the one hand, and as action—practical applications based twinly on natural and theological theory—on the other. The argument was so porous that Murray abandoned the two further articles he had promised in support of religious freedom, and turned to an area that he had previously spurned, namely, the realm of the temporal, the on-the-ground historical action between church and state. From this work he eventually had to admit that there was a new theoretical understanding of human social nature that emerged outside the church, to which the church must be attentive. In his vocabulary of the time, natural law theory could, and empirically did, develop in its own right, independently of the Roman Catholic Church.

One principle of that earliest argument for religious freedom, however, did make it into his later arguments, namely, his assertion that that which is true in the natural order would not be reversed by revelation, because the God of nature cannot be in contradiction with the God of revelation. We should note the strong lexical relationship here, even in Murray's prehistorical arguments. Nature has its own autonomy that can make claims against that which is claimed in the name of revelation. Further, once Murray cast his natural law argument into the historical flow, with the possibility that *new* theoretical insights can and will emerge (in natural knowing, though not until the council in theological knowing), the challenge to Roman Catholic self-understanding, including its understanding of its own unique role within the order of grace, was firmly in place.

Of course Murray could counterclaim that all he was talking about was the temporal order, not the world of eternal life, so the Church should not be alarmed that its own claims to the fullness of redeeming truth were being challenged. And he did so counterclaim, genuinely and sometimes disingenuously. But those in Rome and at Catholic University were smart enough to know that a rose by any other name is still a rose and can smell the same. Especially given the lexical relationship Murray continued to accord now to emerging natural and supernatural truths, he was in fact granting, at the least, two independent sources of divine "revelation" that could not easily be subordinated in either direction over time. In principle natural truth could legitimately challenge and transform religiously based claims, just as, in principle, religiously based claims could transform natural (temporal) claims. Genuinely, in the vocabulary of Pope Gelasius I: "Two there are, oh Emperor." Two sources of moral authority in this world.

At the end of the decade during which Catholic University helped silence him, Murray would scan over the entire Catholic American scene and cry out: "Faith supposes reason as grace supposes nature. If the genuine powers of reason are destroyed or undermined, the true notion of Christian faith suffers the same fate." And again, "not even religion will supply the lack if reason fails in its functions: for religion cannot form a civilization" if it forgo public reasoning. Murray had discovered that Catholics could manage or mismanage their own mission and faith by what, for want of a better name, could be called the style of their public reasoning, styles operative in both the ecclesial and secular orders. Argument in both orders could encourage moral participation or destroy the possibility of participation, encourage mature agency or encourage infantilism, demanding faithfulness to much the same rules of discourse.

The Third Enemy: Protestants at Large

Again, Murray inherited a strong dislike of America's materialism, hedonism, and individualism. In that aforementioned 1940 address, he asked: Who can we blame for our being the "quintessence of all that is decadent in the culture of the Western Christian world?" And he did have a sure answer. Surprisingly, it was not social atheism, neither of the Dewey pragmatic variety, nor of the Soviet Marxist variety, nor even fascism in its various 1940 forms. He continued his address:

> In terms of three qualities of the Puritan soul, its anti-intellectualism and anti-humanism, its this-worldly morality, its intense individualism, you will, I think, find a major . . . explanation of the transformation of early American ideals of democracy. They were dehumanized, deintellectualized, moralized, clothed with fierce emotion and [thereby justified the] unregulated activity of the individual in the field that absorbed him—business, economic life. Thus American culture became doubly material: material in its body, its economic order and material in its soul—emotional individualism.

While this 1940 address is quite early in Murray's academic life, it does reflect the tradition within which Rome and Woodstock formed him—influenced probably by Christopher Dawson in his attitudes toward Calvinism and by the early Jacques Maritain in his understanding of Americanism. This disdain of the heretical was in line with a paper Murray wrote as a student in 1933 in which he claimed, as he would up to 1962, that no *theological* conversation with heretics was possible, that the best we can do is discuss natural law and natural theism. Some of Murray's funniest, if harshest, public writing and speaking took aim at Protestants. In an *American Mercury* exchange with the Protestant Russell Bowie, Murray suggested that "hostility to the Catholic Church is profoundly lodged in the Protestant collective unconscious, in consequence perhaps of some natal trauma."[2] Repeatedly Murray claimed that any misunderstanding between Catholics and Protestants was based on the Protestant inability to function other than as solely a religion of protest, for being purely on the defensive (quoting Tillich), as knowing only what it is against, not what it is or should be for.

After the Council, on the other hand, a very confident Murray did claim that we were now entering an age in which theological reflection must begin and end in ecumenism. We new theologians must talk to theologians across the faith spectrum if we are to learn anything new about our God, or they anything about their God. In a 1965 merciless bringing of Lonergan coals to a Lutheran Newcastle, one can feel Murray's uneasiness with speaking theologically with Lutherans. Indeed he obviously desired to share that uneasiness with his new Lutheran colleagues. But talk he did, theologically, with the heretics.

So, once again, Murray moved from his inherited tradition with the help of that very tradition, but also with the help of something outside that tradition, to something quite new.

The Fourth Enemy: The Atheist of Any Stripe

Murray did judge fairly early that Catholics and other believers must and could in principle collaborate, as long as they stayed within natural law and nature's God. At no point prior to Vatican II, however, could he find any principled grounds on which a Catholic could collaborate with an atheist. In his early Catholic Action arguments, he insisted that it was clear to whom Pius XII's call to post-war reconstruction was directed: to all who believe in God—and only to them. By 1959 Murray could admit that America's public arguments had to be open to four groups: Catholics, Protestants, Jews and secularists.

However, he offered only pragmatic, lesser-of-two-evils defenses of secularistic or atheistic participation. In Murray's discussion of the East Communist threat to the Christian West, he described Cold War strategies solely in term of sheer power. The East operated under the norm of "maximum security: minimum risk." The West should counter with "maximum risk" and "minimum security." Their own survival is the only value that the East can understand, and the only way we will get their attention. In all else they stand counter to all for which the West stands, not least the rule of law. At the 1962 suggestion that John XXIII was opening a dialogue with Marxists, Murray countered that John must be talking about nineteenth-century secularists. That he could not have meant Marxists and that generally what John in *Pacem in terris* had to say about East/West relations could be of little help. Those who turned even from nature's God offered no ground for any mutual understanding, much less mutual action.

By 1965 Murray participated in Christian/Marxist dialogues, albeit painfully and reluctantly. As reported in the *National Catholic Reporter*, he left the meetings talking about how much Christians and Marxists do not understand each other, and despairingly suggested that fruitful, mutually intelligible conversations are far in the future.

Yet, despite his own reluctance, what was it that brought Murray into those dialogues? Beyond simply the spirit of the times, Murray finally moved into a principled dialogue on the basis of what he had claimed from the beginning of his life was a special concern to the Catholic faith—the integral functioning of human reasoning. It was human reasoning in the secular order, as eventually understood in Lonergan's terms of historical consciousness, that had allowed Murray to talk theologically with Protestants.

So now it was also another understanding of the structures of human consciousness that allowed him, in his 1964 *The Problem of God*, to enter into a dialectical argument with atheists of both the existentialist and Marxist varieties.[3] To ground that conversation, he suggested that all human knowing, but especially the human knowing of God, is grounded in two human cognitional drives: the drive toward knowing (*gnosis*) and the drive toward the transcendent (*agnosis*). He then suggested that Marxists have locked on human knowing (*gnosis*), claiming to fully understand, while existentialists claim the fundamental unintelligibility of human existence (*agnosis*). Then he asks: is not human existence more humane when humans remain dialectically suspended but constantly moving between affirmation and negation?

To this day I don't know where Murray picked up the idea of a permanent internal dialect within human consciousness, this *gnosis/agnosis* consciousness, though I suspect it was from Schillebeeckx.[4] In these days we have rhetorical analyses that describe mystical discourse functioning very similarly to the dialectic that Murray advanced. But I do know that what he now had gave him the principled grounding he needed to admit the right of atheists to public voice, that his allowing such voices was not simply a matter of the lesser of two evils. And, again, by noticing that atheists could claim more than they knew or that they could claim less than that to which they are open, Murray could and did then talk about his own Church claiming more than it knew or being closed to that to which it ought to be open, to empirically itself having fallen off that dynamic dialectic. At this point in his life all the languages of the cross and of grace began entering his many discussions. He could talk with Anglicans about the sinfulness of his own Church, about Luther's *simul justus et peccator* predicated of the church as an institution, not just of individual Catholics here and there. Murray could also talk about the unbelief of Christians, that unbelief that allows nonbelievers to give up on the very notion of God, nonbelievers who are themselves demonstrably more open to God's future than are self-proclaimed believers.

Over his lifetime Murray moved from an antagonism to most things American to an affirmation that, at least in one significant sense, God was working to redeem humanity through American agency. He got there by expanding his Catholic notion that God has taken up all human reality and was bringing it to completion, not to absolute negation. Further, he moved from a notion that the Roman Church lived the fullness of God's hopes for humanity to a much more nuanced understanding of how Catholics, other believers, and even nonbelievers all stand, individually and institutionally, in need of moving into God's new future, all as under the call of the same God. Again, he moved from an insistence that Protestants and Catholics could only work together in the realm of nature and nature's God to an insistence that future knowledge of God must be ecumenically generated. He got there mostly by the experience of the council, but also with the help of Lonergan notions of emerging intelligibility. And he moved from only lesser-of-two-evils arguments against suppressing atheistic voices to an insistence that both Catholics and atheists exist, collapse under, and transcend their own limits by a permanent dialectic at the heart of each.

Each of these moves was a social cross that Murray found he had to bear; each tore at a Catholic tribalism that placed a priori limits on God's action. He bore each of these crosses sometimes gracefully, sometimes clumsily, but he did manage (for the most part) to adopt forms of loving that do match many of our contemporary discussions of the cross of the Christ. By fate and by grace he did not allow his religion to spare him the pain of effectively loving his enemies or spare him of the need to turn over to them his second, though maybe not his first, cloak. And he learned much from the doing. Now, in this age of easy terrorist destruction, perhaps we are again poised to learn something new of God's wishes for us. Perhaps now we should ask a Murrayesque type question: can we any longer afford claims to the fullness of truth that do not allow to others a similar fullness, and can we, within most notions of following the Christ, claim the full possession of God while granting to others only a partial presence of fully saving grace? Where do the signs of our times point? To what God?

Murray struggled toward an ecumenism, very much within the Ignatian ideal of working with God as God works to transform his world. We now struggle toward interfaith discussions, hopefully under the notion of working with our God as God is suggesting, even in the violence and terrorist brutality we experience. The limits we ourselves place on the good and the godly must be negated, allowing good to be seen wherever it can emerge (which type of negation the mystical writers tell us is distinctively Catholic). Perhaps we can no longer afford the soothing luxuries of the egoist, nor those of the tribalist. Perhaps that is what God is saying. If so, Murray can still be helpful as we move into God's future.

9. Murray: Faithful to Tradition in Context

Thomas Hughson, S.J.

Catholics and other Christians most likely know John Courtney Murray as a protagonist in the production of the Declaration on Religious Freedom at the Second Vatican Council, published almost forty years ago. Its significance for the public life of Catholicism in religiously pluralist societies remains hard to overestimate. Social ethics, fundamental theology, practical theology, public theology, and communications are theological specialties that also have found substance in his writings.

Murray's thought on the twin topics that preoccupied so much of his reflection, Church-state relations and religious liberty, might seem defined by ties to his native land, the United States, and its charter documents to which he appealed, the Declaration of Independence, the Constitution, and the Bill of Rights. Still, the Catholic breadth of his vision is indicated by his study at the Gregorian University in Rome in the late 1930s while a young Jesuit, his academic sojourn in Germany, his dissertation on Matthias Scheeben's doctrine on faith in 1937, his continual reading of history, his attention to World War II and international affairs, his participation in post-World War II assistance to German reconstruction, his career-long interest in ecumenical and interreligious cooperation for the social common good, and his awareness of limits and defects in the culture of the United States.

In the 1940s and into the 1950s some public Protestant doubt circulated on why and how deeply their Catholic fellow citizens endorsed what many regarded as a signal novelty and essential institution in the democratic structures of the United States—the First Amendment guarantee of free exercise and of the nonestablishment of religion. No doubts accompanied the Protestant observation that Catholics in practice supported nonestablishment and religious freedom. The question remained, was that practice principled? Or was it an expedient adjustment to national facts Catholics wished were otherwise, and which they might seek to change if they became numerous enough? Might Catholics be harboring reservations about the First Amendment clauses out of a deeper preference for an established Catholicism that papal teaching recommended as best? This was a question about Catholic thought, principle, and theory, not about practice. It was an impertinent question for families whose children had perished in military service under an oath to uphold the Constitution, but it needed an answer, and an answer in the realm of theory.

In response, starting in the mid-1940s, Murray launched an almost career-long inquiry into religious freedom and Church-state relations. The two topics are indissociable. Religious freedom in any society flourishes or does not according to the political organization of society; the state possesses a monopoly on legitimate use of coercive force in society, and the government exercises it. Religious freedom depends for protection, or suffers abuse, depending on the manner and scope of that governmental exercise of power.

Unfortunately, Catholics in the United States were not lacking a few writers who championed the thesis/hypothesis theory propounded as Catholic doctrine by, among others, Vatican Secretary of the Holy Office Alfredo Cardinal Ottaviani. His view lifted up national establishment of the Catholic Church as the ideal or thesis, and relegated anything else, such as the United States arrangement, to the inferior status of being merely a hypothesis.

By the time Pope John XXIII convoked Vatican II, Murray had become the foremost American Catholic theorist on religious liberty. Murray had entered into controversy in national public life in defense of government aid to Catholic schools as well as by arguing for recovery of a "public philosophy" of natural law truths and values. Before the 1960 presidential election, the Kennedy campaign staff consulted him on Church-state relations prior to a famous speech Kennedy delivered to ministers in Houston, Texas, which was intended to help set aside fears that a Catholic in the White House would mean a pope telephoning instructions to guide presidential decisions. A short time after Kennedy's victory, on December 12, 1960, *Time* magazine featured Murray on its cover.

At Vatican II, Murray was appointed "first scribe" in the commission charged with producing a text on religious liberty. This gave him an important role in shaping the document without his being the single architect. The final document promulgated on December 7, 1965, above the signatures of Paul VI and the assembled bishops, had undergone significant change since its inception. In the commission Murray had steadily argued through five drafts that religious liberty was best understood as primarily a political and legal reality that owed its existence to modern consciousness and institutions, not directly to Church initiatives. Affirming religious liberty by declaring official Catholic approval of an already familiar idea, practice, and set of institutions was a belated aggiornamento, not a groundbreaking development. Modesty, even a little chagrin not triumphalism, was appropriate in view of post-Tridentine Church-state relationships in the area of religious liberty.

Murray had long held that prior centuries, during which the gospel exercised a leavening influence in western political self-understandings and practices, provided a basis for a modern consciousness of human dignity and the legal institutions designed to protect its realization in practice. Well versed in the historical record of protracted conflicts between Church authorities and political leaders from Constantine on, he also pointed out repeated assertions of papal independence in judgment and ministry. The mustard seed of post-Constantinian papal defense of the *libertas ecclesiae* (freedom of the Church) became a tree of faith sheltering both civil society and the eventual emergence of demands for individual freedom in religion.

That tree had sometimes been shaken, as with Innocent III, who crowded out political authority on the premise that all temporal as well as spiritual power passed from Jesus to Peter to popes, and on that foundation he believed that popes rightly seated and unseated emperors and kings. The ancient dualism of Pope Gelasius had not been forgotten, however. In A.D. 494, Gelasius wrote to Emperor Anastasios I: "Two there are, august Emperor, but which this world is ruled on the title of original and sovereign right—the consecrated authority of the priesthood and the royal power." Recalling this vision was Leo XIII's achievement and to develop it was Murray's continuing task. This dualism was, Murray agreed, the major impact of Christianity on political life, and applied Jesus' God/Caesar difference.

On the basis of this diarchy, Murray recognized the legitimacy of royal claims to independence from ecclesiastical jurisdiction in political judgment and action. His views increasingly followed Thomas Aquinas and John of Paris on the natural law, temporal purposes of the political structures in any society. He came to disagree with Robert Bellarmine's proposal that in religious emergencies, not as a regular matter, a pope could temporarily exercise authority over a political area for a good spiritual end. This limit purified the exercise of apostolic jurisdiction without infringing on the duty to teach the gospel. Contrarily, even if requested by a pope or bishop on behalf of a society's spiritual welfare, any governmental repression of heresies precisely as religious doctrines and practices overstepped the bounds of political authority, though a state always had a duty toward public order, safety, and civil morality.

Murray assimilated the nineteenth-century papacy's critique of the supremacy of the individual reason (continental liberalism), especially when writ large as a nation-state's supreme authority in all zones of social existence (totalitarianism). Consequently he contrasted the Anglo-American tradition of constitutional government (which he considered unknown to Leo XIII), including the United States constitutional provisions of nonestablishment and religious liberty, to continental state absolutism (which Leo knew from the French Revolution and its aftermath). He argued that medieval recognition that the consent of the governed belonged to the legitimacy of political authority passed to the founding of the United States, not through the Catholic nations of continental Europe, but through England, where the Magna Carta in 1215 initiated a long train of curtailments to monarchical power. The concept of a divine right, absolute monarch in Europe was a bad idea with demonstrably negative consequences. Governance under a constitution was a much better political idea because governmental exercise of power was submitted to the rule of known public law. It was more congruent with Gelasian dualism than was, for example, *l'état c'est moi*.

Murray focused to a surprising extent on what today would be called political culture and civil society, not solely on laws, structures, and the technical procedures of democracy. In fact, the theoretical and operational priority of society over the state was both a cardinal emphasis in Catholic social teaching and was the hallmark of resistance to totalitarianism of the right or left. Simply put, the state and government existed for the good of society and the people, not the other way around. States and governments, however, have a momentum of their own that tends to reverse this. Nor do I think Murray would have expected that a democracy would spring up like a mushroom, in Russia for example, if only a stone of oppressive state fascism were removed. A functional civil society is a more substantial prerequisite for democracy than a warehouse filled with voting booths.

Moreover, Murray's understanding of civil society and political culture was thoroughly historical. He stated that, "the Bill of Rights is not a piece of eighteenth-century rationalist theory; it is far more the product of Christian history." Behind it lay not John Locke's books so much as a lengthy British progress toward the commonly accepted "rights of an Englishman." And underpinning that progress were people who had learned their human dignity "in the school of Christian faith," and a political culture that developed and applied the principle of the consent of the governed under a rule of law.

In that light, free exercise of religion is a public, social condition dependent on a state respecting the limits of its authority, which is to say that this authority is nonexistent in regard to religion. Historical arrival at this position depends on a prior affirmation of human dignity and on some manner of religion-state dualism. On the dualist premise, political governance for Christians—and perhaps unlike Church or religious authority in a non-Christian religion—has no authority from the Creator to define or decide religious belief, practice, or institutional existence, though it must see to public safety, order, and morality. In the founding of the United States, for example, it was not the religion clauses in the First Amendment of the Bill of Rights that anchored protection for liberty of religion. The clauses simply made explicit the civil liberties of individuals in a limited state with enumerated powers. Authority to establish religion or prevent its free exercise was not on the list of powers. The Constitution already, before the Bill of Rights, had eliminated establishment and assured free exercise.

Keeping in mind the formative English history behind the Constitution leads us to a realization that some form of widespread education accessible to a people, rather than simply elections, is the first step in forming a democratic state. In trying to support democracies around the world, Western powers may look too much to elections, written laws, and a willingness to compromise, while scanting the essential roles of education, political culture, and formation in human dignity. Likewise, human rights monitors attending to freedom of religion hopefully attend carefully to a people's whole everyday way of life and their culture rather than only to written statutes. De facto conditions, not simply de jure documentation, need to weigh heavily in any plans to form or support democracy. Murray emphasized that the founding of the United States was not according to a preconceived, doctrinaire plan.

An alternative perspective argued within the Vatican II preparatory commission focused on individual human rights. This view of the human and civil right to religious liberty revolves around individual human rights, and around the freedom of individual conscience, or in the Catholic version, the dignity of the human person that grounds the "rights of man." Once the conciliar text embraced the principle, it had to balance it with a teaching that the innate obligation to the truth, not arbitrary personal preference, formed personal freedom of conscience and religion. Murray fell ill and was hospitalized during the final rewrite of the document. So in the final text the "individual" argument assumed a larger role than it would have if Murray had been active. He saluted its publication with two cheers, not three.

Murray upheld, of course, freedom of conscience and the dignity of the person as essential to civil society. Christian freedom was something more. It had a communal aspect, and sprang from the new human situation due to Christ, the gospel, and the Holy Spirit. It flourished insofar as Christians opened themselves to the leading of God, and issued in zeal for the gospel. It also pertained to life inside the Church. After the Council, Murray commented that Vatican II moved the Church out of a post-Tridentine configuration in regard to Christian freedom. Four centuries of understandable pastoral reaction to rejections of ecclesiastical authority, first by the Reformation and then by the Enlightenment, amounted to hypertrophy of the principle of authority, with a correlative atrophy of the principle of freedom in the Church. Conciliar renewal reaffirmed Christian freedom.

But in civil society Murray thought protection for free exercise of religion came first and foremost from circumscribing state authority within due bounds, not from asserting individual freedoms. The text voted by the bishops and signed by Pope Paul VI, nonetheless, offers more common ground with Protestant understandings of religious freedom, and so better serves the ecumenical goal of the Council. Murray's approach remains a sign of Catholic understanding that social and political dimensions are internal to personal liberty, not added on from outside to a purely individual or private reality.

Two Dramas

Was the contest between alternative views of religious liberty within the drafting commission the central drama of Murray's theological career? Probably not. True, all his previous research and reflection indeed came into play—the stakes were high, the differences real, the arguments sharp. But the commission was, after all, collaborative if strenuous. Any conflict was subordinate to a common purpose. There were, however, two conflicts in Murray's life as a theologian that do qualify as major dramas. Both arose from the fact that Catholicism in the United States has had a quality of originality that American Protestants and European Catholics alike had a hard time locating. Drama involves a main character contending with inescapable tensions, an apex of conflict, and a denouement.

The Protestant/Catholic drama in the United States was a set of tensions between an immigrant Catholicism gaining its place after World War II and a culturally regnant Protestant ethos gradually coming to terms with religious pluralism. Many Protestants still saw Catholics in the United States as the local presence of European Catholicism. They had read Leo XIII's fulminations against religious liberty and Church-state separation, had observed Vatican policy in making Church-state concordats, and saw how Spain was taken by Rome to exemplify the establishment wanted by the Church. Murray's extensive writing on Church-state matters was a prolonged demonstration that the Church's actions, policies, and theories in Church-state relations had historically contingent elements. Some in the Church, highly placed at that, mistook post-Reformation, post-wars of religion alliances with confessional states as an immediate consequence of Catholic faith, treating Spain as if universally normative. Catholicism in the United States had never wanted establishment. Doubts about American Catholics were unfounded. His interest was in citizens of all religions cooperating for the common good and for the intellectual empowerment of Catholics to pick up their share of active citizenship in a religiously pluralist democracy.

Murray's best-known book, the preconciliar *We Hold These Truths: Catholic Reflections on the American Proposition* (1960) capped a theoretical explanation of how and why Catholics consented to the American experiment in full fidelity to Catholic principles.[1] At the basis was a theory of Church-state relations summed up in four principles. The first principle was the irreducible difference in origin, activity, and end of Church and state. The second principle was the effective spiritual primacy of the Church and faith in relations with the political order. The third principle was the integrity of the political order and its independence from ecclesiastical jurisdiction. The fourth principle affirmed the immanent finality of Church and state to some manner of harmony for the sake of those who belong to both simultaneously. Much of Murray's work concentrated on the third principle, which he took to be a valid modern differentiation between sacred and secular. He understood this to be true to Catholic tradition on Church and state and more particularly to Leo XIII's development of it.

The election of John F. Kennedy in 1960 seemed to have settled in practice what Murray had demonstrated in theory. It drew the Protestant/Catholic drama in the United States to its last act. The Catholic faith, the outcome of the election showed, did not preclude a Catholic citizen from becoming president. Kennedy's executive prowess showed it did not entail submission to the authority of the pope as temporal ruler, as if American Catholics were subjects in the former papal states. Finally, though, it was the 1965 Declaration on Ecumenism that removed the underlying premise for the post-Reformation, Protestant/Catholic drama in every nation, at least from the Catholic side. The older premise, that Protestant and Catholic were first of all antagonists over Christian truth, became awareness that what we have in common is greater than what divides us. The ecumenical movement, among Protestants who accept ecumenism, the Orthodox, and Catholics, has resolved the Protestant/Catholic drama in which Murray played a part. Subsequently, the 2004 debate over another Catholic citizen's electoral campaign in the United States advises that the Protestant/Catholic drama has ceded to "culture wars" within the Catholic Church, as well as among Protestant and Orthodox Americans. Murray's theory of civil dialogue has much to offer this condition too.

There was a second drama in Murray's theological life. Another set of tensions sprang up between Murray and the dominant school of thought on Church-state relations that had representatives in Rome and in the United States. This was a tradition/modernity conflict. It played out through conflict, resolution, and denouement in Murray's relations with the Vatican. His book *We Hold These Truths* followed painful tension with Alfredo Cardinal Ottaviani, Vatican Secretary of the Holy Office (now the Congregation for the Doctrine of the Faith), who published and acted on a Church-state theory of tolerant establishment where a predominantly Catholic population made this feasible, as it did in Spain. The tragic climax was the silencing of Murray by his religious superiors on the Church-state topic in 1954. Behind this lay a background of European Catholic difficulty in grasping that Catholics in the United States, a mission country, were actually Catholic but inculturated in a different way. Many in Catholic Europe had seen the United States as a Protestant nation, American Catholics as quasi-Protestant, and the pairing of religious liberty with nonestablishment as contrary to Catholic tradition.

In response, Murray pointed to the historical contingency of the post-Reformation confessional state in order to remove its ostensible status as an arrangement that Catholic doctrines demanded as a necessary consequence of their truth. What the state owed the Church was not establishment but protection of its citizens' religious liberty, so the Church could flourish from its own native energies apart from state coercion. Murray distinguished Anglo-American constitutionalism from what Leo XIII had learned about and condemned in democracy carried by the French Revolution and its aftermath.

A lesser-known book by Murray, *The Problem of Religious Freedom*, made the case at Vatican II that conciliar development beyond Leo's gravamen against religious liberty and Church-state separation was possible because in historical context Leo inveighed only against certain kinds of nineteenth-century, continental instantiations of these, not all possible versions.[2] That Murray's view on this carried the day, that he was a *peritus* at Vatican II in the first place, that he had a significant hand in drafting the Decree on Religious Liberty, and that he received a special blessing from Paul VI, resolved the conflict with Ottaviani. Notable is the fact that Leo XIII, Catholic social teaching after him, Murray, and Vatican II, all have taken their bearing on political life from Aquinas rather than Augustine's *City of God.* This poses a challenge to neo-Augustinian social theologies.

Concluding Reflection

In a monarchy or nondemocratic state, relations between Church and state occur insofar as legitimate authorities representing each "perfect society" meet and conduct business together. Church and state convened in meetings, or in relationships carried out according to formal, legal arrangements between popes and emperors, popes and kings, bishops and princes, clergy and magistrates. Leo brought forward recognition that such relationships were not for the sake of authorities themselves, or only for the dignity of the offices they occupied, but above all for the sake of peoples beneath them. The *civis idem et christianus*, the citizen (or subject) who was both under state and Church authority, had duties to fulfill in both societies. If Church and state authorities were at odds to the extent that they commanded opposite acts, the effect was to introduce division into the consciousness of Christians who owed obedience to both. This interior conflict was contrary to the peaceful conscience that the New Testament commended as the condition in which followers of Christ could conduct their lives of faith under God's supreme authority in Christ, visibly represented by those succeeding the apostles, while also obeying legitimate political authority.

Pius XII took this a step further by identifying the person as the source, agent, and end of all societal processes. This meant, and it was carried through most fully in a democratic state, that Church-state relations were not only for the sake of the people who dutifully received decisions made above their heads and then harmonized them. Rather, the relations passed through the people. Ordinary people were involved in and were agents in those relations. Murray clarified it as follows: In a democracy the first officer is the citizen, not the elected or appointed official. The citizen is the state's representative in relating to the Church. Whom does that citizen encounter as representative of the Church? That same person himself or herself as baptized believer, the one person who is both believer and citizen is the meeting point.

A nonestablishment regime does not recognize the religious authority of a bishop, pope, or any Church authority as having jurisdiction over any part of the political order. So the conduct of Church-state relations devolves to the believer/citizen. In them, in their consciences, Church and state meet and seek a harmonious relationship. Conscience becomes the meeting hall. The Church represented by the person-as-believer and the state represented by the person-as-citizen are in continual, usually quiet session.

It follows, I suggest, that ecclesiastical authority cannot intervene in a Catholic citizen's conscience by laying upon it a command to perform or act on a particular political judgment. That prudential judgment, rather, is an irreplaceable function of the believer's own conscience, which also has the obligation to form itself according to Catholic faith and morality. To be sure, apostolic authority has every right to fulfill a duty to preach and teach the gospel in its implications for public life and for the political order of society. This might lead to making public judgments on the immorality of specific public policies or their administration. That is one thing; it is another thing to try to exercise ecclesiastical jurisdiction over the person's politically prudential judgment. That is, to attempt direct exercise of ecclesiastical authority over something political in nature, namely, the proper act of an informed citizen. That turns the ecclesiastical act into an act of a political nature. No less than commanding a government official to repress a heresy, this violates the hard-won differentiation between the temporal and the spiritual and runs against the spiritual mission of the Church. Equally a state, its government and officials have no basis and no authority to command that an act of religious nature be performed by citizens, whether the act be internal like personal prayer or belief that God has chosen one's nation for the mission of spreading democracy, or external-like attendance at worship or professing that the unborn are nonhuman.

Leo XIII and Murray's fourth principle, of a finality in Church and state to a mode of harmony that permits peaceful consciences, does not mean peace at any price. Nor does it imply that believers are to treat their faith and their political views as if on par. Nothing suggests anything other than that faith and discipleship are an all-encompassing principle of interpretation, not to be subordinated to political convictions. Harmony presupposes and includes the exercise of political prudence and practical reason. So harmony does not result from what some seem to think is the proper path—a unilateral, rapidly executed jump from faith to prudential decisions on specific laws or policies without an intervening deliberation. To move from a biblical passage, a traditional theme, a papal teaching, a personal spirituality to a political decision without passing through analysis, discussion, reading, and reflection precisely on the political level, is to bypass the virtue of prudence, rather than to stand for the demands of faith. This would be practical fideism.

Consciences, not legislatures or Vatican halls, are host to the most intimate, durable, and influential Church/state relationships. This was how Murray envisioned the dignity and role of conscience in regard to Church and the political order, not so much as a demand for freedom, but as the arena wherein the gospel meets and guides political life.

Consequently, he placed a good deal of value in Church authorities exercising the power of the Church to influence society indirectly by helping the faithful to form their consciences in light of Catholic faith and morality. Direct influence by means of prelates inserting their influence into chambers of law above the heads of believer-citizens, or seeking to steer democratic processes by commanding a political act, runs contrary to the Church/state difference. Strictly speaking, though Murray did not draw this conclusion explicitly, it seems that pope, bishop, or clergy would have no basis for commanding believers to vote this way or that, to take this or that political action. However, the indirect influence of apostolic authority on society by educative formation of consciences is an obligation. Catholics have a correlative duty to learn and to act on the implications of their faith for the temporal order of society, including its morality. Murray insisted, and took his cue from Pope Pius XII on this, that the moral order and legal orders were distinct, that the passage from the moral order to the legal order depended greatly on historical, cultural, social context and conditions; that social peace was of such value that in a pluralist society, it could demand restraint from seeking a direct passage from the moral order to the legal order in a given matter.

It has turned out that practical and theoretical tensions around the second and fourth principles in Catholic Church-state theory have outlived Murray, making him a character in a plot without a climax, resolution, and denouement. He participated in the larger historical drama arising from tensions between Catholicism and American political life. His basic position is now less taken for granted as a direction for future development, unfortunately. Problems attendant upon some modes of episcopal presence in American public life would have been averted or ameliorated were Murray better known to today's prelates. Critiques that reject rather than criticize and develop his contribution seem to have lost confidence in the potential for social change in democracy, or to have reverted to an Augustinian political theology in the name of authentic Catholicity. Whatever the cause, the fact is that Murray's contribution has not connected with many bishops. Critical appropriation and development of his Church-state thought is needed.

In light of a theology of religious pluralism today, it can be added that in some analogous way the Church/state difference pertains to and supports the spiritual integrity of any religion as well as affirms its independence from jurisdiction of any political authority.

Karl Rahner

10. On Reading Rahner in a New Century

Leo J. O'Donovan, S.J.

Having studied with Karl Rahner at the height of his influence, and after teaching and writing about him for many years now, I have come to feel increasingly indebted to him not only as a theologian of stature, but as a pastor of my soul. Difficult as it is to say something meaningful about an author whose bibliography famously includes more than four thousand titles, in this essay I want especially to explain why I think him a vital companion for us all in the coming years of a troubled world. I shall first offer a brief overview of his life and major themes and then give special attention to five key issues for interpreting his thought.

The Gift of Life

Karl Rahner was born on March 5, 1904, the fourth of seven children. "I come from a Catholic, middle-class family," he said on the occasion of his seventy-fifth birthday. "My father [Karl Rahner] was a *gymnasium* professor in Pfullendorf, Emmendingen, and, for the longest time, Freiburg im Breisgau. My mother [Luise Trescher] was a simple but very intelligent and devout woman."[1] In 1922 he followed his brother Hugo (1900–68) into the Society of Jesus. After studying philosophy for three years (1924–27), he taught Latin and Greek and then pursued four years of theological studies in Valkenburg, Holland (1929–33), with ordination to the priesthood in 1932. During this time he became closely acquainted with the fathers of the Church, the medieval theologians, and the great mystics. Originally destined by his order to teach the history of philosophy, he spent two years at the University of Freiburg (1934–36), where he attended seminars led by Martin Heidegger and wrote a doctoral dissertation under Martin Honecker that proved foundational for his later thought: *Geist in Welt: Zur Metaphysik der endlichen Erkenntnis bei Thomas von Aquin* (*Spirit in the World: On the Metaphysics of Thomas Aquinas's Final Discovery*) analyzing the transcendence of the human spirit in the world as always dependent on imagination (*conversio ad phantasmata*).[2]

Professor Honecker had questions about the thesis, but Rahner was never to respond to them, having returned in June 1936 to Innsbruck, where he was promoted to Doctor of Theology that year and, in 1937, received a cumulative *Habilitation* for previously published essays. In his first year at Innsbruck, he gave a major course on grace, delivered a lecture series in Salzburg on the philosophy of religion, and published classic meditations on prayer in the contemporary world.[3] The Nazis closed the faculty in July 1938, and for the next six years, Rahner worked first at the Pastoral Institute in Vienna and then at a parish in Bavaria. After the war, he taught at Pullach, a Jesuit house of studies near Munich, then returned to Innsbruck in 1948 and became an Ordinary Professor the following year.

At Innsbruck, Rahner was responsible principally for courses on grace and the sacrament of penance, topics that shaped his thought for the rest of his life. Rooted in the experience of grace as God's mysterious self-communication, his thought broke new ground in a whole range of areas: the biblical understanding of God, current problems in Christology, nature and grace, the human condition after original sin, human dignity and freedom, the meaning of church membership, existential ethics, and the pastoral situation of the Church. His major essays from this time on were gathered in a multivolume collection, *Schriften zur Theologie* (1954–1984).[4]

A theologian of grace and reconciliation, Rahner engaged in extensive positive research, as is clear in *Schriften* XI (1973), which collects his historical essays on penance in the early church. But the special creativity of his writing showed itself in his efforts to correlate the circumstances of particular experience with the permanent "existentials" (or enduring structures) of the human condition. This interrelation of historical and transcendental dimensions was evident as well in the prodigious editorial labors that began in his early Innsbruck years and continued with the publication of four editions of Denzinger's *Enchiridion Symbolorum* (*Handbook on the Creed*,1952–57) and seven editions of *Der Glaube der Kirche in den Urkunden der Lehrverkündigung* (*The Doctrine of Church in the Original Proclamation of the Disciples*,1948–65).

In this period Rahner was also coeditor of the second edition of the *Lexikon für Theologie und Kirche* (*Lexicon for Theology and Church*, 1957–65) and a leading figure in the preparation and course of the Second Vatican Council, despite efforts at first to disqualify his participation. His retrieval and renewal of tradition in light of contemporary perspectives had previously been achieved largely through pressing particular questions against the background of scholastic theology. Now he drew out the consequences of these studies and began to speak more programmatically of a theological anthropology encompassing the history of a world whose call to union with God ("the supernatural existential") evokes transcendental reflection on the structural possibilities for salvation. In powerful essays on mystery, incarnation, theology of symbol, and the hermeneutics of eschatological assertions, collected in *Schriften* IV (1960), Rahner developed his analogy of transcendence so as to face questions posed by evolutionary science, the great world religions, and utopian views of the future. Other major essays in *Schriften* V (1962) present the scope of the divine salvific will in more comprehensive terms and argue for the coextension of salvation history and the history of the world. Corresponding to the council's ecclesiological focus, *Schriften* VI (1966) collects papers presenting a dialogue with secularized, pluralistic society and seeking to express the Christian Church's new self-understanding in it. After publishing a collection of essays in pastoral theology, *Sendung und Gnade* (*Mission and Grace*, 1959), he gathered a new collection of essays in spirituality (*Schriften* VII, 1967) and in 1962, cooperated in drafting a plan for the *Handbuch der Pastoraltheologie* (*Handbook on Pastoral Theology*), which subsequently appeared in five volumes (1964–72), with Rahner as an editor and contributor of 500 pages from his pen.

In 1964 Rahner succeeded Romano Guardini in the chair of Christian *Weltanschauung* (worldview) at the University of Munich. When it became apparent that he would not be allowed to direct doctoral students in theology (as he had been promised), in 1971 he accepted a call to the University of Münster, where he taught until his retirement. In these first years of Vatican II's reception within Catholicism, criticism of Rahner's thought grew in various quarters. Concerned with fidelity to tradition and to Christian symbolism, some writers, such as Hans Urs von Balthasar, accused him of anthropological reductionism. Others, especially his former student Johann Baptist Metz, drew back from what they considered an individualistic, idealistic existentialism. Rahner took the second critique more seriously, giving new emphasis to Christianity's historical concreteness and social responsibility. Renewing the dialectic of unity-in-difference, with which he had from the beginning sought to understand time in its openness to eternity, he also addressed basic conciliar themes with a deepened sense of faith's constructive participation in its secular context. In *Schriften* VIII, IX, and X (1967, 1970, 1972), he called for a new understanding of Jesus of Nazareth as the human way to God ("Christology from below")[5] and for church reform toward a declericalized, more democratic, and socially critical community of service. Meanwhile, he had undertaken additional editorial responsibilities for the four volumes of *Sacramentum Mundi* (*Sacrament of the World*, 1967–69) and for the journal *Concilium*, inaugurated in 1965.

During the first years of Rahner's retirement in Munich, his major project was the preparation of his *Grundkurs des Glaubens* (*Foundations of Christian Faith*, 1976–78), an introduction to the idea of Christianity. While not intended as a complete systematic theology, the book presents many of his basic positions on the central topics of Christian doctrine and has commonly been seen as a summation of his thought.[6]

In the last years of his life, Rahner continued to lecture and write vigorously. Four further volumes of *Schriften* were published (XIII, XIV, XV, XVI: 1978, 1980, 1983, 1984); two while he was still living in Munich; two more after his final retirement to Innsbruck in 1981. They were accompanied by numerous smaller works and several anthologies, two of which, *Rechenschaft des Glaubens*, 1979 (*The Content of Faith*, 1992) and *Praxis des Glaubens*, 1982 (*The Practice of Faith*, 1983), may also serve as general introductions to his thought. These later years are again of a piece with his whole career and include familiar themes as well as considerable repetition. Nevertheless, some significant developments occur here, too: consolidation of a historical

Christology, proposal of a "universal pneumatology" that might precede Christology, pleas for ecumenical seriousness, and arguments for a truly world church. One sees, also, a deepening concern for the mounting relativism and skepticism he felt in the world. The writings of this last phase show, finally, how thoroughly dialectical his thought was, seeking to mediate between opposed positions in doctrine or morals, speaking of the fruitful tension between permanent polarities of historical existence, and, above all, offering an understanding of the relation between continuity and discontinuity through the passage of time.[7]

In the rest of this essay, I intend to analyze more closely five pivotal interpretive issues in Karl Rahner's thought: his understanding of human knowledge; the priority he gives to love and freedom; his understanding of the fundamental interrelatedness of God, self, and community; his importance for a new understanding of Christian praxis; and, finally, the dialectical method he commends to us individually and as a community. Taken together, these questions are decisive in reading Rahner as a theologian for the twenty-first century.

Before the Mystery

In his later years Rahner frequently polemicized against the reduction of human reason to its technical and instrumental use, as presupposed for the most part by natural science. He likewise rejected the notion that clear concepts and precise definitions are the highest ideal of knowledge. The most important experiences and ideas in human life, he countered, are analogous ones, shot through with mystery. Indeed, the most important experience of all, the presence of God in human life, is ultimate mystery, beyond comprehensive grasp by human agents. The incomprehensible, inexhaustible, limitless reality of the presence we call "God" is not a term we have yet succeeded in understanding entirely, but rather an ultimate of intelligibility inviting us to accept and embrace it unconditionally.

Already in his profound 1959 essay "On the Concept of Mystery in Catholic Theology," Rahner had noted that the First Vatican Council took for granted an understanding of human reason derived largely from eighteenth- and nineteenth-century science. But what if, in a deeper understanding, reason is our capacity to learn about matters that cannot finally be defined—love, fidelity, trust, for example—and, indeed, about the divine heart of the world that surely cannot be defined?

> What if there is an "unknowing," a knowing unknowing with respect to itself and what is not [fully] known, which when compared with [other] knowledge, that is, with any knowledge not really aware of itself, is not a pure negation, not simply an empty absence, but [rather] a positive characteristic of a relationship between one subject and another? What if it is essential and constitutive of true knowledge [knowledge in its deepest, fullest sense], of its growth, self-awareness and lucidity, to know by knowing also that it does not know, to know itself orientated from the start to the incomprehensible and inexpressible, to recognize more and more that only in this way can it truly be itself and not come to a halt at some regrettable limit? [8]

Eighteen years later, in a powerful essay on "The Human Question of Meaning before the Absolute Mystery of God," Rahner again addresses the theme. (Here, think not only of a person before God but of one's own sense of deep personal love, acts of surpassing sacrifice, artistic fecundity.) "Reason," he says, "must be understood more fundamentally as precisely the capacity of the incomprehensible, as the capacity of being seized by what is always insurmountable, not essentially as the power of comprehending, of gaining mastery and subordinating something to oneself."

> Reason must be understood (to use Aquinas's terminology) as the capacity of *excessus*, as going out into the inaccessible. If reason is not understood from the very outset as the capacity of incomprehensibility, of unfathomable mystery, as perception of the ineffable, then all subsequent talk of the incomprehensibility of God comes too late, falls on deaf ears, and can be understood only as an intimation of what happens to remain of objectivity, of what has not yet been processed by all-consuming reason but will sooner or perhaps later be so processed.[9]

This explicit critique of modernity (and of the Catholic Church's response to modernity) may qualify Rahner, to the surprise of some, as a postmodern and even liberation theologian.[10]

Understanding Love

As early as the seventh and eighth chapters of *Hearers of the Word* (1963), Rahner understood knowledge as ordained to fulfillment in love. There, in an undeniably dense phenomenology and with appeal to the creative freedom of God, he speaks of love as "the light of knowledge" and of knowledge as "the luminous radiance of love." Human beings cannot fail to pose the question of the meaning of their lives. Similarly, they cannot fail to take a position with regard to seeking that meaning. Moreover, whatever they learn about life shapes the context in which they will *choose* their *own* lives. Drawing on his 1934 study of Bonaventure and the notion of ecstatic reason, and seeking to conceive knowing and loving in a unified, dynamic way, Rahner refuses to choose between an intellectualism that emphasizes the transcendental of truth and a voluntarism that emphasizes the good. Instead he sees the two transcendentals—and the human process by which they are realized—as mutually related to one another, indeed as indwelling each other: "In the heart of knowledge stands love, from which knowledge itself lives."[11] Here the commonplace misunderstanding that we can choose only what we first understand yields to the experientially more accurate sense that inquiry is always *motivated*, that it is the inquiry of a subject who has concerns, commitments, and convictions. "Thus will and knowledge can only be understood in a relationship of reciprocal priority with one another, not one of linear sequence."[12]

In this view, truth is itself transformative: a creative power that establishes correspondences and harmonies in reality *because* it expresses itself faithfully, that is to say, is self-revealing fidelity. The notion recurs repeatedly: in essays on the meaning of God in the New Testament, the nature of religion today, the uniqueness of Christ, and the universality of salvation. It is perhaps most prominent in Rahner's treatment of the central and summarizing doctrine of the Trinity.

It is well known that Rahner wanted "to make the doctrine of the Trinity fruitful for practical Christian living."[13] He begins by proposing a harmony between human truth and God's Word and conceives human truth as a mediating moment in all human experience. Truth in general may thus stand as an analogy for God's Word; just as later he will analyze the relation between the spirit of human love and God's Spirit. Asking how we should understand truth and how it can represent the origin of the offer of God's grace through the course of human history, he answers that truth "is first the truth which we *do*, the deed in which we firmly posit ourself for ourself for others, the deed which waits to see how it will be received."[14] Truth is the word that waits to see how it will be received, that wishes to be accepted, that can bear fruit only if it is welcomed. *We* are the truth of lives that only love can guarantee. Here again, knowledge is only momentarily an end in itself; it must always be guided by love, just as, in strictly Trinitarian terms, Christian believers can accept God's Word only if they are guided by the Spirit of God (compare 1 Cor 12:3; John 14:26, 16:12).

The process of our self-constitution through enlightened choice is not normally linear but recursive, a matter of gradually establishing what we reasonably care for, and thus shaping a moral character through which we make further choices. Deep within us, the human *longing* for God and for a more humane world is the spring driving us toward all we come to understand of either. Thus, gradually, we take our stand in the world around us—for good or ill.

> But this implies that the concrete transcendence of the concrete human being towards God also bears as an inner moment within itself a free decision. The free decision is not simply a result of knowledge, but also already constitutes the knowledge. But this means that the deepest truth is also the freest. The truth of the knowledge of God in the way in which someone understands the person's God is always also carried by the order of the person's love or by its disorder.[15]

Here Rahner is probing the deeper unity of intelligence and freedom within the human spirit transcendent in the world. His thought from its very beginnings, I believe, struggled to forge a genuinely historical conception of God's grace redeeming the world, something his commentators often overlook. They typically applaud his anthropology—as even postmodern, or at least as restoring a future to tradition. Or they criticize it—as individualistic, reductionistic, or ideological. His actual concern with dynamic history, however, becomes even clearer when one considers the place of Christian praxis in his thought.

God, Self, Community

Before turning to that point, however, I pose a simple, if mysterious question: of *whom* really, in all the previous discussion, is Rahner speaking? Very often, as in *Spirit in the World* or any number even of his pastoral essays, the theme seems to be the relation between the individual human subject and the Holy Mystery of God. How do we come to understand, what does our freedom amount to, what can we hope for as individuals; these seem to be his concern. But I do not believe that interpretation does justice to his thought.

Rather than considering individuality a primordial anthropological given, Rahner had in fact a profoundly social conception of humanity. Though less developed in his earlier writings, even there the theme is present: "We are human beings only within humanity."[16] Later, he spoke powerfully in all but Augustinian terms of the "whole Christ" and the incompleteness of his resurrection until all members of the human family are gathered home. Without entering into detailed development of his thinking, let me summarize here what I take to be his basic position.

A truly social conception of humanity in its universal solidarity might stem from several sources: humanity's common creation and call to redemption, the promise of the Kingdom of God for all, ethical thought on our mutual, unconditional responsibility for one another. Rahner typically draws the theme from biblical teaching on the unity of love of God and love of neighbor.[17] Against the extrinsicist, objectivistic, ahistorical neo-scholasticism in which he was educated, he grounds our sociality not psychologically, sociologically, or ethically, but ontologically, at the very core of who we are together as human subjects.

In a crucial essay of 1971 on "Experiencing Oneself and Experiencing God," Rahner probes the theological implications of human subjectivity, which is always directed transcendentally beyond itself toward reality without limit; religiously, we call this the "Holy Mystery of God" which is, at the same time, always historically (or categorically) engaged with the particularities of its own experience. In this attraction through time toward the mystery of God, we become increasingly aware of ourselves as responsible subjects. "The transcendentality of the human being in knowledge and freedom towards absolute being, toward the absolute future, toward the unattainable Mystery, toward the final ground of the possibility of absolute love and responsibility and thus of genuine human intercommunion . . . is also the condition of possibility for the subject to experience itself strictly *as* a subject and in *this* sense as always already objectified."[18]

But, continues Rahner: "the true and living, concrete experience of life, which is identical with the concrete experience of the self, has a structure with respect to its 'objects' in which not everything has the same and equally valid importance." It is primarily the experience of "a shared world" (*Mitwelt*):

> In the knowledge and freedom of concretely enacted lives, the I is always related to a Thou, is just as primordially with the Thou as the I, is always only by meeting the other person able to experience itself as once distinct from and identified with that person. The primordial objectivity of the experience of the self occurs necessarily in the subjectivity of meeting another person in dialogue, in trusting and loving encounter. We experience ourselves insofar as we experience the other person, not the other thing.[19]

Clearly this is a radical interpretation of human interconnectedness. "Our experience of ourselves," says Rahner, "occurs in unity with the experience of others. If we have the latter, then we have the former. [But] whoever does not find the neighbor is also not truly present to himself, is not a true and concrete subject who can identify himself with himself, but at best an abstract philosophical subject and a human being who has lost himself."[20] With explicit reference to the unity of love of God and neighbor, he continues:

> In the unity of the experience of God and the experience of one's self, on the one hand, and in the unity of the experience of the self and encounter with the neighbor, on the other hand, we see that these three experiences are fundamentally one experience with three aspects which mutually condition each other. But that means, reciprocally, that the unity of the love of God and neighbor is only conceivable if we presuppose the unity of the experience of God and of the self. What first appears as a purely philosophically formulated and indirectly grounded unity of the experience of the self and of God is also an implication of the fundamental Christian statement on the unity of the love of neighbor and of God.[21]

Professor Francis Fiorenza of Harvard rightly argues that Karl Rahner's insistence on the fundamental unity of the love of God and the love of neighbor is a significant contribution to contemporary theology.[22] Clearly, it is of paramount importance for all theologies of liberation.[23]

The analysis I have just summarized shows, I believe, *how* Rahner grounds and justifies that position—not psychologically, sociologically, or even morally, but through a religiously motivated ontology.

The Primacy of Praxis

Thus far we have seen Rahner arguing that human experience necessarily has, whether acknowledged or not, a fundamentally religious and intercommunicative (or social) structure. He also understands human knowledge and love as intimately interrelated in empowering human beings in community to shape their lives and destiny together freely. A further perspective important in reading Rahner is his elevation of the practical: church teaching must be subordinated to church praxis, and theology should be conceived, not as a primarily theoretical, but as a practical discipline.[24]

Rahner often couched his emphasis on lived experience—his deep insight into the accumulating determination of our shared lives through time—in abstract, Thomistic terms. But he was concerned with the actual historical responses of a humanity for whom God had acted through Christ and still acts through the Spirit. In *Encounters with Silence* (1938), as a young theologian, he had spoken passionately of the true wisdom of experienced love. In an interview for his seventieth birthday he said, "Behind everything I did stood a very immediate, pastoral and spiritual interest."[25]

We have noted his commitment to the development of an integrated pastoral theology. He could not refuse requests for counsel from any religiously troubled correspondent. But he was a theologian of praxis most fundamentally because he believed that, in our shared, fallible, selfish, but wondrous freedom, we are called to share in the justice and generosity of God's own freedom. From the very beginning, he understood Christian faith not simply as knowledge about God, but as trust in the saving grace of God. Revelation is not information about God, but God's own self-disclosure to us. Jesus is not a messenger with unexpected news, but a mediator of all-encompassing, divine grace. The Spirit is not a universal instinct, but a transforming power. And the church is not meant to be a self-sufficient institution, but a sacrament, an effective sign of salvation for all of us poor, wayward human beings.

Because of his emphasis on the process of *free* human lives empowered by mutually related moments of knowledge and love, Karl Rahner held that our knowledge is trust in our action, not in prior speculation:

> Theology is directed toward living out hope and love, in which there is a moment of knowledge, which is not possible without them. This is not contradicted by the fact that praxis served by theology also includes an intention of disinterested knowledge that seeks "*sapere res prout sunt*" ["to know things just as they are"]. But such knowledge can only be attained in the actual deed of hope and love. Orthodoxy and orthopraxis mutually condition each other in a primordial nameless unity, which is only well known, if at all, through praxis. And this is because all [religious] knowledge is valid only as saving action, when it has fulfilled itself in love and *thus* remains as theory.[26]

This view has fundamental significance for the role of theology and theologians in the Church. In his groundbreaking *A Theology of Liberation* (1973), Gustavo Gutiérrez defined theology as critical reflection on the praxis of the church in light of the revealed word of God.[27] Several years earlier, Karl Rahner had made a similar point: "Theology is only of interest," he wrote, "when it is reflection—in a critical way, of course—on the faith of a church which acts freely on the basis of its faith."[28] Revising Thomas's classical definition of theology's formal object as *Deus sub ratione Deitatis*,"the God underlying the things of God," he proposed instead "God in God's self-communication"—not only as the object of theology but, at the same time, as "the subjective principle of the faith that carries theology forward."[29] Theology is meant not so much to inform the Christian life, if you will, but to empower it, precisely by seeking always to bring its hearers before the Word. "Theological speech does not simply speak about the mystery [of God]. It does that correctly only when it serves as something like a guide to bring us before the mystery."[30]

In this view, Christianity lives truly when human subjects—intimately bound up with and belonging to one another—respond freely to the mysterious presence of a gracious and forgiving God, the Holy Mystery who calls us to full communion with the divine life itself, in Word and Spirit *and* with one another. The sorrows of life: sickness, suffering, natural disasters, and finally death; and the horrors of injustice: slavery, racism, subjugation of women, the Holocaust, outrageous economic inequities, and the threat of nuclear devastation challenge the credibility of this gospel, perhaps challenging it now more than ever. But the gospel lives on. Or, better still, it is lived still by men and women whose witness is undeniable and whose holiness, as Karl Rahner says, constitutes the Church's real hierarchy of truth.

The Dialectic of Freedom

How are we to think about and live our lives? This is my final point: Karl Rahner's approach to the dialectic of our thought and of our lives. Rahner is commonly considered a transcendental Thomist, someone who retrieved the Thomistic heritage through the perspective of modern transcendental thought. He did, indeed, conceive human life as a transcendental dynamism beyond all particular experiences, toward what one might call the ultimate experience of God. This conception led him to ask, consistently, *how it is possible* and *how we can think* of a wholly transcendent God communicating with a finite creation. At the same time, however, he was just as consistently a historical Thomist: He argued, as we have seen, that men and women move toward God and each other *only through* the limited particularities of their historical experiences. And, thus, he has been presented as employing, not simply a transcendental, but a twofold method, in which transcendental reflection and historical research each indispensably require the other.[31]

While Rahner uses the term "dialectic" often, and increasingly in his later writings, he does not give it extended analysis. (Nor do any of his interpreters give it a really promising place—although, curiously, several rather negative critics do.[32]) Often "dialectic" indicates Rahner's method of developing a position located midway between two contrary extremes. Frequently it was the way he spoke of unity-in-difference, whether epistemologically or ontologically. Still more often, "dialectic" refers to the fruitful tension between permanent polarities of historical existence in its various forms (for instance, psychologically, between freedom and necessity; socially, between the individual and society; religiously, between law and righteousness; ecclesiastically, between theology and teaching authority). Most basically, however, "dialectic" is his way of conceiving identity in history, acknowledging both continuity and discontinuity through the passage of time and recognizing that finite reality must change in order to remain itself.

Approaching dialectic as historical process, his usage in context clearly relates him to both Hegel and Marx. At the same time, it distinguishes him sharply from their views of that process as a necessary movement. In several prominent passages, he gives a somewhat more extended treatment of the relation between analogy and dialectic. *Foundations of Christian Faith*, for example, argues that analogy is not a hybrid between univocal and equivocal language but the appropriate way to speak about God: "Whenever we make [our] original, transcendental orientation to God explicit and thematic, we have to speak about God by means of secondary and categorical concepts which are contraries within the realm of the categorical." God is, for example, unfathomable, infinite reality and yet is "more interior to us than we are to ourselves." And so we must say "on the one hand . . . but also, on the other hand." And yet, what we say directs us to truth. God is good, said Thomas, but so eminently good that we must deny that God is good as a finite being is good, and say rather, that God is goodness itself.

Such "dialectical, bipolar statements . . . can never be conceptually synthesized into a higher synthesis."[33] They represent "a tension which we ourselves as spiritual subjects originally *are* in our self-realization, and which we can designate by the traditional term 'analogy' if we understand what this word means in its original sense," namely our own existence "in and through our being grounded in this holy mystery which always surpasses us."[34] The dynamism of transcendence is itself analogous, a process of correspondence between divine origin and finite response. And if one wishes to emphasize the process of its realization, then the term dialectic seems appropriate: referring, first, to language that must always say both Yes and then No before saying the fuller Yes; and referring, secondly and even more basically, to the process of self-transcendence *beyond* recognized limits towards the higher, humanly speaking unattainable goal of God. The process is ongoing, and even if it cannot of itself reach its own resolution (*synthesis* or final union with God), it does, at the invitation of grace, move truly toward it. As "the analogous statement signifies what is most basic and original in our knowledge," so the dialectical process pursues what is most valuable in our lives.[35]

In Rahner's texts, then, one finds the term "dialectical" in many senses: "annulling or canceling"; "interaction, mutual (reciprocal) conditioning"; and, in its most basic, ontological sense, transformation or fulfillment through an action reversed or negated in some way, but then fulfilled at a higher level. For Rahner, the human world is freely called through time toward God's own life in such a way that eternal value is concretely at issue in all the struggles of life. Through the passage of time, with its achievements and its losses, we become the persons and societies whom God has created as a body ready for holy anointing. Not rational necessity, but the mystery of creative love grounds this process, both in time and in eternity, and no understanding of events within it arises without being called to be transformed into love. The love that unifies time transcends all reasons for living in time. But it also engenders new reasons for living and is thus the innermost dynamic of redemptive passage through time.

Dialectic is thus a rule of language and a counsel on how to hope to understand historical process (and, in that sense, a method). But it is, still more, a summary term for the actual process of reality, indicating how historical actions can have purpose and a goal. It addresses the *fuller* reality of certain events. Dialectic is not only logical and methodological but, if you will, ontological. And so, in reading Karl Rahner, it helps to ask not only, "What is he talking about here? What is his argument?" but also "How is he suggesting that my life and our lives together can be larger, more real, more genuinely responsible for each other—and even more full of God?"

"Take and Receive"

Let me close with a final reflection that may serve also as a clue for understanding Karl Rahner most personally and productively. In the 1970s, Rahner began to reflect more explicitly on how Ignatius of Loyola (1491–1556), founder of the Society of Jesus, had influenced his life and theology. Every year of his life as a Jesuit, Rahner made a retreat based on Ignatius's *Spiritual Exercises* and personally conducted them some fifty times. He also published two books based on the retreats he gave. How could Ignatius have failed to shape the thought of this obedient son of his order?

Authors such as Klaus Fischer, Harvey Egan, and Philip Endean have contributed greatly to our understanding of the Ignatian horizon in Rahner's thought.[36] Less attention has been paid, however, to the specific influence of the *Exercises* themselves, in their inner dynamic. Let me briefly summarize their structure to explain my point.

As a text, the *Spiritual Exercises* is a manual to guide retreat directors. As lived by retreatants, it comprises "all the formal ways we have of making contact with God, such as meditation, contemplation, vocal prayer, devotions, examination of conscience, and so on."[37] The intention is to help a person become more *free*—free of all that constrains our becoming ourselves, and free also to respond to whatever way of life to which a gracious God may call us. There is a distinctive dynamic to the process. "Ignatius emphasizes that the kind of book he is writing is one focused, not on content matter, but rather on movement, development or growth, especially as these words apply to insights and affections. The word *dynamics* also refers to the Ignatian order or arrangement. . . . [as well as to] the idea of a power or power source." Most basically, it applies "to the overall makeup of the *Exercises*."[38]

In the first series of meditations, or "First Week," retreatants consider the contrast between their human sinfulness and the gifts of a loving, forgiving God. (This contrast comes after a foundational experience of being creatures of a gracious God.) After a pivotal meditation on how much the authority of Christ surpasses that of any earthly ruler, a "Second Week" comprises prayer on the life of Jesus, seeking (the grace) to know and love him and thus to be able to labor and serve *with* him. Here several exercises (a meditation on "Two Standards" and a consideration of "Three Kinds of Humility") heighten the contrast between serving oneself and serving the gospel.

Ignatius suggests the end of this period as an appropriate time for retreatants who face a choice about their life's direction to make that critical decision (the election, or choice). Then, in a "Third Week," or series of exercises praying over the passion, retreatants test and confirm their choice of companionship with Jesus and seek the grace of compassion, of being with and staying with Jesus in his redemptive suffering. A "Fourth Week" of prayer follows, seeking to enter the joy of the Resurrection and to receive the grace of Christ's consoling presence. A final "Contemplation to Attain God's Way of Loving" recapitulates the search for God in all things that has motivated the previous exercises. In effect, it asks as well whether there can be any limit to our response to a God so limitlessly generous.

Commentators regularly note that the *Spiritual Exercises* offer clearly directed movement, a dynamic of grace building upon grace from one stage of prayer to another. There is also a reciprocal interdependence between such key texts as the introductory Principle and Foundation, the Call of Christ the King, and the Contemplation to Attain God's Way of Loving. But other writers, and principally Gaston

Fessard, S. J., have gone further, arguing that a *real* (ontological) dialectic is intrinsic to the *Exercises*.[39] As Edouard Pousset, an astute commentator on Fessard, says: The *Exercises* "unfold a unique act of freedom, which is all man's [sic] and all God's. All is done by me, and all is from God, who is more myself than I am."[40]

The Ignatian retreat, in other words, invites the retreatant to experience a change in who the retreatant *is*, moving from an inauthentic to an authentic humanity—a humanity accepted as Jesus accepted his—and surrendering that humanity to God, in trust that this surrender is the way to true life. Anthropologically, the exercises center on an understanding of reflective human freedom called to develop in union with God's freedom. Theologically, the process begins and ends in God's grace.

This pattern markedly parallels Karl Rahner's understanding of our shared human freedom before God. For him, human freedom is not the capacity to make ever-different choices and decisions in our lives. It is, rather, a capacity to decide who we will be in a final way and, as he became increasingly concerned with the political dimensions of theology, who we will be together.[41] The fundamental dialectic of freedom in his thought may be summarized as: the discovery, through the grace of God, of one's true self, followed by the donation of that self to God and one's neighbors (in *one* love that alone is salvific), with the hope of then receiving the gift of one's true self, and our true selves together—ultimately, in the communion of saints. I say "followed" and "then," but the terms, while apparently linear, should be understood as indicating not only the sequence but the interdependence of the moments of genuine human time. The process is not a onetime event, nor is it susceptible of final synthesis. But neither is it a matter of separate moments, for it is the real, living freedom of fellow human beings, responsible for one another and to God, to accept in an enduring, indeed eternal way the full promise of their humanity.

The paradigm, though I do not recall a text where Rahner explicitly notes this, is the *kenosis* (self-emptying) of Christ as described by St. Paul in the hymn of Philippians 2:5–11. To intimate the dynamics of this experience of self-domination, Rahner strained language to its limits, ringing changes on a range of words at once ordinary and poetic. He spoke of our giving ourselves to God (*sich ubergeben*), of surrendering ourselves (*sich hingeben*), of giving or risking ourselves away (*sich weggeben, sich wegwagen*), of denying ourselves (*sich verleugnen*), of no longer really disposing of ourselves (*nicht mehr uber sich selbst verfugen*), of letting oneself go (*sich loslassen*), of no longer belonging to oneself (*nicht mehr sich selbst gehören*). And he spoke of the moment when "*alles und wir selbst wie in eine unendliche Ferne von uns weg geruckt ist*" (when everything including our very selves is torn away from us as if into an infinite distance).[42]

This is not a language simply for private devotion. It is a language honed for life—based, I believe, on very personal experience, schooled in a great tradition of philosophical and theological reflection, and pointing in a direction that can give hope even for a bitterly begun century. And it sounds, of course, like nothing so much as the final prayer recommended at the end of the *Spiritual Exercises* by Ignatius of Loyola in order to help the retreatant seek the fullest possible love of God by making "this offering of myself": "Take, Lord, and receive, all my liberty, my memory, my understanding and my entire will. Whatever I have or hold, you have given it to me. I surrender it wholly to be governed according to your will. Give me only your love and your grace. With these I am rich enough and ask for nothing more."[43]

11. Karl Rahner's Theological Life

Harvey D. Egan, S.J.

"Strengthened by the Church's sacrament and accompanied by the prayers of his Jesuit brothers, shortly after completing his eightieth year, Father Karl Rahner has gone home to God. He had loved the Church and his religious order and spent himself in their service." So read part of the official Jesuit announcement of the death of Father Karl Rahner, S.J., on March 30, 1984. With his death, the Catholic Church lost one of her most loyal sons. Although well known for his controversial reinterpretations of the Christian tradition and for his criticisms of much in the Church's practical life, Rahner always spoke from deep within the Church as one who had never lost sight of the total Christian vision. His unanswered questions have provided fresh points of departure for a host of other thinkers.

Add to this his significant impact upon the Second Vatican Council, his fourteen honorary doctoral degrees, and the large number of doctoral students he directed, and one can see how aptly he has been called "the quiet mover of the Roman Catholic Church" and "the Father of the Catholic Church in the twentieth century." Yet Rahner referred to himself as someone who was "not particularly industrious," who "went to bed early," and was a "poor sinner." "All I want to be, even in this work [of theology]," he said, "is a human being, a Christian, and, as well as I can, a priest of the Church."[1]

Although Thomas Aquinas, Heidegger, Kant, Hegel and Joseph Maréchal undoubtedly influenced his thinking, Rahner contended that the great Christian mystics and saints, as well as the Jesuit spirituality he prayed and lived, had a much greater significance for his theological work. For him the saints were theological sources. He saw clearly that the faith of the theologian, as well as the living faith of the contemporary Church, were both crucial to the theological enterprise. From him I learned that theology could be distinguished, but never separated from living faith, hope, and love. Theology must flow out of and then lead back into the prayer of silent surrender to the Mystery of God's love for us in the crucified and risen Christ—and must do so without dissolving theology's necessarily critical function. The theologian must have compassion for the human and worship God with his whole person, knowing when to "kneel his mind" before the incomprehensible God, whose love became manifestly irreversible in Christ's life, death, and resurrection.

Central to Rahner's thinking is the notion that what is at the core of every person's deepest experience, what haunts every human heart, is a God whose mystery, light, and love have embraced the total person. God works in every person's life as the One to whom we say our inmost yes or no. We may deny this, ignore it, or repress it, but deep down we know that God is in love with us, and we are all at least secretly in love with one another. Therefore, one of theology's most important functions is "mystagogical": it must lead persons into their own deepest mystery by awakening, deepening, and explicating what every person already lives. It must challenge persons to grasp the real meaning of their freedom as total response to or rejection of God's self-offer to us, which demands total human authenticity. And because God has conquered the human heart through the pierced and risen heart of Jesus Christ, Rahner stated the hope that all will be saved.

In fact, Rahner contended that the most important achievement of the Second Vatican Council was its optimistic attitude toward salvation, its implicit recognition of "anonymous Christianity." This means that even the agnostic or atheist "who courageously accepts life . . . has already accepted God. For anyone who really accepts himself accepts . . . the One who has decided to fill his infinite emptiness (which is the mystery of the human person) with his own infinite fullness (which is the mystery of God)."

That he has been designated "Doctor Mysticus," the doctor of twentieth-century mystical theology, is indeed fitting. Much of Rahner's theology can be called "mystical" because it takes seriously the experience, albeit often hidden or repressed, of God's self-communication. The experience of God forms the undertow, or that basal spiritual metabolism, of daily life. Because this is so, no one can escape being a theologian. So, Rahner chided academicians for ducking the key question of human existence: "Is life absurd?" Rahner addresses the question and answers it in the negative, for: "the human person is a being who does not live absurdly because he loves and hopes, and because God, the holy mystery, is infinitely receptive and accepting of him." In view of this, much of Rahner's theology may be called "mystical" because it attempts to compress, to simplify, and to concentrate all Christian beliefs and practices by indicating how they evoke the experience of God's loving self-communication to us in the crucified and risen Christ. Even the agnostic or atheist who loves in courageous fidelity to the demands of everyday life lives the "mysticism of daily life."

For Rahner, moreover, "all life is a subject of theological reflection." Impelled by his "Ignatian mysticism of joy in the world" and of "finding God in all things," Rahner's theology also contains a movement of "unfolding" the mystery of God's suffering, and victorious love for us in Christ into every dimension of human life. Has any other contemporary theologian written a "theology of everyday things"—a theology of work, getting about, sitting down, seeing, laughing, eating, sleeping, and the like? Nothing here below is profane for those who know how to see. And if his theology of mystical compression often involves anfractuous dialectics dealing with questions such as the Trinity, the Incarnation, the problem of evil, and so on, his theology of unfolding can be as lovely as advising an unwed mother in her darkest hour to look into the face of her newborn child for light.

Perhaps the secret of Rahner's appeal is his synthesis of two elements: critical respect for the Christian tradition, and unusual sensitivity to the questions and problems of contemporary life. He never overlooked how difficult Christian faith is for a twentieth-century person. But he could and did say to his contemporaries not only, "I am also someone who has been tempted by atheism," but also, "There is nothing more self-evident to me than God's existence." Therefore, Rahner would accept nothing less from theology than speaking about God—not just so-called God-talk—while breathing the air of unbelief.

Moreover, Rahner never doubted the ability of Christianity's tradition to indicate what was necessary for authentic contemporary living. Because of his ability to discover the Tradition in the traditions, Rahner was able to revitalize even some of the oldest "fossils" of Christian creeds, dogmas, and beliefs into living realities. How do the old "keys" of faith fit the various contemporary "locks" to release human authenticity? Rahner also demanded that theology be a science of conversion, faith, and prayer that deepens the way people live their faith, hope, and love. He not only explained critically and precisely what the Christian faith is, not only gave reasons to believe it, he also sought to unite people with it.

In so many ways, therefore, Rahner's theology is preeminently pastoral. Perhaps it was his pastoral work in war-ravaged Europe during and after the Second World War that gave him his spontaneous inclination toward the pastoral care of individuals and the concerns of a Church in "diaspora." In fact, many of his writings are essays written for particular occasions or in response to questions as they arose, not the overly systematic and encyclopedic approach considered typical of German theologians his age. One of the most absurd statements I ever read about Rahner's theology contended that there was nothing priestly, kerygmatic, or pastoral about it. It should be said of him that his theology is supremely pastoral and its major focus: "Salus animarium suprema lex" (salvation of souls is the supreme law).

Prodded by the insights of Johann Baptist Metz, one of his former students, Rahner, moving in the direction of liberation and political theology, developed his well-known thesis that love of neighbor is love of God. If we really believe in the Gospel, how will we treat others and transform society? What is the Church, and what should it be doing in this regard? For Rahner, the social-political ramifications of the Gospel need particular emphasis today.

During an interview a few days before his eightieth birthday, a journalist asked Rahner his views on old age. Rahner replied that a person should never stop thinking, and that if God gives one strength to write in old age, one should receive it as a gift. Rahner saw old age as a chance to sum up one's entire life, to get oneself together before the final Mystery. And when the journalist persisted in questioning him about the fear of death, Rahner replied: "I have the right as a man, a Christian, and a theologian to be afraid of this dark event. . . . I hope to have the strength to surrender lovingly into the great Mystery of God's love which embraces it."

I first met Father Rahner in 1969 when he graciously accepted the invitation to concelebrate my first Mass with me and to spend the day with my family and friends. During my four years of doctoral studies under his direction, I found him to be at once brilliant, creative, traditional, original, provocative, balanced, and healing. His personality was stamped by a passion for hard work, detail, precision, and an impatience with mental laziness, "whoring after relevance," and bureaucratic incompetence. However, most impressive of all were his childlike curiosity and the simplicity, holiness, and priestliness of his Jesuit and theological life.

Father Rahner had an uncanny ability when it came to finding money, food, clothing, and shelter for the needy and downtrodden when they sought him out. He possessed the knack, too, of shanghaiing others into assisting him with his practical works of charity. One of the things I remember most vividly is how we two went grocery shopping in a large supermarket and drove two hours to take the food we bought to a widow and to find her a place to live. One of Rahner's last public acts after the celebration of his eightieth birthday was to appeal for funds to purchase a motorbike for a missionary in Africa.

The countless ways in which he brought meaning, comfort, light, relief, and healing to so many persons prompted one distinguished German author to call Rahner a "most effective psychotherapist." For example, I know how priestly and generous with his time Rahner was to a young Jesuit friend who was leaving the priesthood. This same friend in a recent letter told me that when he began his doctoral studies, he was astonished to find that Rahner spoke and lectured the same way that he wrote. He was also surprised to find Rahner, the spiritual director, as a very holy, simple disciple of St. Ignatius. When he wrote to Rahner to apprise him of his decision to leave the Society of Jesus—a decision made in the context of the Ignatian thirty-day retreat—Rahner wrote: "I want you to know that I have no wish to comment on a decision made during the time of the great exercises. Best wishes and blessings."

Students who understood very little of Rahner's lectures told me that they attended because they "felt better" about themselves in his presence. "This is a professor to whom I can confess," one said. Not many years before his death, Rahner often spent several hours of his intensely busy day helping a young German psychiatrist to recover some of the memory he had lost in a serious auto accident.

When Rahner died on March 5, 1984, I had no desire to attend the funeral and memorials because of work commitments. I also knew that these events would be very well attended. However, an ever-increasing desire to return to Germany and Austria began to haunt me. Even my dreams became filled with Rahner episodes. It soon became apparent that a Rahner pilgrimage was necessary for my own peace of mind. So in the summer of 1984 I went to Germany and Austria with the great desire to talk with people who were with Rahner when he was dying, to visit some of his old haunts and his family in Freiburg, to reestablish contact with various Rahner scholars, to use his archives at Innsbruck, and to pray at his crypt in the Jesuit church in Innsbruck. All those with whom I spoke attested repeatedly to one thing about Rahner: the awesome way in which his spirit shone forth in faith, courage, and intelligence right up to the very evening he died.

Since 1960 I have been reading and rereading Rahner's entire corpus. I have likewise been giving courses and seminars on his thought since 1973. It continues to impress me just how apposite his theology is even in this seeming age of postmodernity. Some of my students have said that Rahner makes even the most obscure Christian dogmas meaningful, that he brings to intelligible articulation the living catechism of the heart to so many contemporary people—and not only to Christians. And I fully agree, for I have long contended that theology cannot be separated from the theologian, that theology is ultimately the person who theologizes. Hence, I always ask myself whenever I read theology: "What kind of person wrote this?"

When asked on his eightieth birthday what he wished to bequeath as his last will and testament, Rahner pointed unhesitatingly to the essay: "Ignatius of Loyola Speaks to a Modern Jesuit."[2] In this spiritual gem, Rahner put himself in Ignatius's place to speak to contemporary Jesuits. Not only did he call this masterpiece his last will and testament, but he also considered it a summary of his theology in general and of how he tried to live it. He wrote:

> You know that I wanted 'to help souls'. . . . therefore to say something about God, his grace, and about Jesus Christ, the crucified and risen one, so that their freedom would be redeemed in God's freedom . . . I [am] convinced that . . . I experienced God directly

and I wish to communicate this experience to others, as well as I can. . . . I mean only that I experienced God, the ineffable and unfathomable one, the silent yet near one, in his trinitarian bestowal upon me. I experienced God also and especially beyond all images—who when he thus approaches in his grace cannot be confused in any way with anything else. . . . I have experienced God himself, not human words about him . . . .This experience is truly grace, but for that reason it is nonetheless essentially refused to no one. . . . One thing remains certain: a person can experience God's very own self . . .

But now I must speak about Jesus. Did what I say before sound as if I had forgotten Jesus and his blessed Name? I have not forgotten him. He was intimately present in everything I said before, even if the words I addressed to you . . . could not say everything at once. I say *Jesus*. . . .

I never had a problem—or at most the one of loving and being a true disciple—finding in a unique way God in Jesus and Jesus in God. And I mean Jesus as he really and truly is in flesh and blood, such that love alone—not hairsplitting reason—can say in what way he should be imitated if one is his disciple. It is from being able to narrate Jesus' story that one has then narrated the history of the eternal, incomprehensible God, without dissolving this history into theory . . .

Since my conversion I knew Jesus to be God's unconditional loving condescension to the world and to me, the love in which the incomprehensibility of pure mystery is totally present and through which a person attains his or her perfection. Jesus' singularity, the necessity of seeking him in a limited treasury of events and words with the intention of finding in this limited reality the infinite and ineffable mystery—this never bothered me . . .

There is no Christianity which can bypass Jesus to find the incomprehensible God. God has willed that legions find Him because they seek Jesus—even though they do not know Jesus' Name, and even though they plunge into death sharing with Jesus the experience of abandonment by God without benefit of knowing how to name this fate or how to name the One with whom they share it. God has permitted this darkness of finitude and guilt in the world only because God has made it His own in Jesus.

> This is Jesus I thought about, loved, and desired to follow. And this was the way in which I found the real, living God without having made Him a figment of my own unbridled speculation. A person gets beyond such speculation only by dying a real death throughout life. But this death is real only if the person, resigned with Jesus, accepts in it the abandonment by God. This is the ultimate "wayless" mysticism. In so speaking I know that I have not clarified the mystery of the unity of history and God. But it is in Jesus who surrendered to God in his crucifixion and received God in his resurrection that this unity is definitively present. It is in Jesus that this unity can be accepted in faith, hope, and love.

Thus spoke the father of my theological life and of my heart.

Finally, I have often emphasized that Rahner's theology begins and ends in prayer. That Rahner began his writing career, for all practical purposes, with a book on prayer, *Encounters with Silence*, and ended it with *Prayers for a Lifetime* emphasizes this point. In fact, explicit prayers and penetrating reflection on prayer punctuated his entire theological life. Even many essays in his meaty *Theological Investigations* often end by shading into prayer. Thus, Rahner stands in a long line of great Christian theologians who were likewise great teachers of prayer. In view of everything above, and especially this final point, I wish to conclude by calling Rahner the Teacher of Prayer for the twentieth and twenty-first centuries. So, is it any wonder that often, since his death, I have found myself praying not only for Rahner but to Rahner: *Father of my theological life and of my heart, may you be plunged more deeply into the Mystery of God, be enlightened by his crucified and risen Son, and burn with the love of the Holy Spirit. Help us to live in daily humdrum love with courage, to look upon the Crucified, and to be ready to die into the holy Incomprehensibility of God when it is our time. Meet with us daily in the Eucharist. Amen.*

12. Karl Rahner: Pastoral Theologian

George E. Griener, S.J.

Karl Rahner is one of the most influential Roman Catholic theologians of the twentieth century. The international impact of Rahner's project, surprising even to some of his close colleagues, irritating to some of his critics, is a phenomenon not yet fully explained by the criteria of academic theology. It also needs to be explored as a historical-cultural event.

Rahner published for sixty years, in a wide variety of genres. He was continually nuancing and rearticulating his thought. In this necessarily selective presentation, I want to say something about the man, his work, his context, and look at a few central ideas. I will begin by capturing the mood of Rahner, his life and work, by citing an excerpt from his *Encounters with Silence*:

> O God, it is good to forget. The best part of most of the things I once knew is precisely the fact that they could be forgotten. Without protest, they have sunk gently and peacefully out of sight. . . . Truly, my God, mere knowing is nothing. . . . How can we approach the heart of all things, the true heart of reality? Not by knowledge alone, but by the full flower of knowledge, love . . .
>
> May you alone enlighten me, you alone speak to me. . . . Then you will be the final Word, the only one that remains, the one we shall never forget. Then at last, everything will be quiet in death; then I shall have finished with all my learning and suffering. Then

> will begin the great silence, in which no other sound will be heard but you, O Word, resounding from eternity to eternity. . . . I will understand what You have been saying to me all along, namely, You. Yourself.[1]

This was Rahner at the ripe old age of thirty-four, already revealing themes that would shape his theology.

Rahner was considered to be a taciturn individual, certainly in talking about himself. He once noted, in typical self-deprecating fashion: "I really didn't lead a life: I worked, I wrote, I lectured, did my duty, tried to earn my bread. In the banal humdrum of the everyday, I tried to serve God. *Fertig!* [Period!]"

Yet, Rahner never left you in doubt about where his heart was. In many ways, he wore it on his sleeve: He would point out with pride the house in Messkirch where "his teacher," Martin Heidegger, had lived. He would guide you through baroque abbey churches nestled in the Bavarian Alps; they were his delight. On his desk he kept a photo of the stained glass window of San Francisco's Grace Cathedral. Dedicated in 1967, it depicted Karl Barth, Paul Tillich, and Karl Rahner as doctors of the contemporary Church. In interviews published under the title *Faith in a Wintery Season,* he expressed profound disappointment over the unrealized hopes of Vatican II. He felt that a cold wind had blown into the church from the East; according to the Rahner "weather channel," the cold front moved in on October 16, 1978. He published an open protest letter accusing Munich's Archbishop, Joseph Ratzinger, of having lied about his role in blocking the appointment of Rahner's student and close collaborator, Johann Baptist Metz, to a post at the University of Munich.

In order to do theology, Rahner said, we need the courage to ask, to inquire, to be unsatisfied with pat answers, "to think with the heart, not with the heart that one is supposed to have, but with the heart that one actually possesses." This admonition is in his groundbreaking essay published on the 1500th anniversary of the Council of Chalcedon: *Chalcedon, End or Beginning?*[2] The "heart" would become a major theme in his theological project.[3]

Rahner wore his passion and his heartfelt experience on his sleeve, and he wore his experience of God there, too. His first published article, composed when he was a twenty-year-old Jesuit novice, was on prayer.[4] Praying is about all Jesuit novices did in those days. Prayer, however, was a theme to which Rahner would frequently return. He was once described as first and foremost someone who prayed—thoughtfully.

His published prayers, especially his 1938 collection, *Encounters with Silence*, were among the most popular and accessible, moving and widely appreciated, republished more than a dozen times, and translated into as many languages. They led us past the scholar and the academician into the heart of a fellow human being who stood before the unspeakable mystery of God in awe and confusion, in wonder and pain.

Rahner didn't just *write* theology; he fostered theological reflection by others, collaborated with them, labored to make academic resources available. He was general editor of the second edition of *Lexikon fur Theologie und Kirche*; he read and edited each of its 30,000 entries. He edited the five-volume *Handbuch der Pastoraltheologie*, the six-volume *Sacramentum Mundi*, and was cofounding editor of a series of modern theological investigations, *Questiones Disputatae*. The series, now running to over two hundred titles, continues a medieval practice of open, public discussion of disputed theological issues, something harder and harder to do today.

He researched the history of the sacrament of penance; discussed theories of evolution with scientists; coauthored a book on sin and guilt with a psychologist; answered questions posed to him by college students at the University of Vienna; preached and directed retreats; and enjoyed whiskey sours.

I think of Rahner here as a pastoral theologian of the Church, very conscious of the peculiar context of German Catholicism in the early twentieth century. There was, after all, a cultural context.

Rahner's theological project is often understood somewhat narrowly to be a response to Immanuel Kant. Kant certainly became the philosophical icon of the Enlightenment. What was unfolding in the modern period, however, was a vast sea change in the social, intellectual, and cultural life of the continent. Rahner saw himself as a theologian of a Church trying to locate itself and find a voice in a new world, especially a new Germany.

The Reformation had divided Germany into two distinct cultures—one Protestant, the other Catholic. Catholics, little more than a third of the population, lived in predominantly agricultural areas, outside the mainstream of the industrial revolution. They were marginalized in the intellectual, political, and cultural life of the country. Catholic teachers and students were underrepresented in German schools and universities. There were few recognized Catholic poets, novelists, or playwrights writing in German.[5] Only in music and architecture did they hold their own.

From outside, the *Imperial Decree of Secularization* in 1803 had shaken the German Catholic Church in a manner unprecedented in its history.[6] A score of major Catholic dioceses, two-score imperial abbeys, another score of Catholic universities, and hundreds of local monasteries were summarily dissolved and Church property seized by the state.[7] Secularization set in motion a transformation of the relationship between the Catholic Church and the larger society.

Secularization was a two-edged sword. Many of the reforms that the Council of Trent had attempted, but had been unable to implement in Germany, were suddenly forced on the Church in the nineteenth century. Moreover, reorganization of the university system in Germany, as well as changes in the German political structure, opened opportunities that were closed before: concordats established Catholic theology faculties at several German state universities, including the initially productive faculty at the University of Tübingen.

But there was also an inside to the story; German Catholics were divided on how to react to the rapidly changing world around them. The Jesuits had been suppressed in 1773, and when they returned to the ecclesial stage in 1814, they allied themselves with the most reactionary political and conservative theological currents in the Church. The Vatican had launched a series of attacks on modernity and on those Catholics who entered into academic discussion with it. The German Jesuit journal, *Stimmen der Zeit*, was founded explicitly to propagate the decrees of the First Vatican Council.

So allied were the Jesuits with the Vatican in public opinion that when Bismarck declared the *Kulturkampf* (culture war) on the Church in 1871, one of the consequences were the Jesuit Laws, which deprived the order of legal status and of the right to exist within most of Germany.[8] The laws didn't fully expire until 1917, thirty-five years later, with the end of World War I.

There were ambitious nineteenth-century attempts at redressing this situation: the early contributions of the Tübingen School of theology; the formation in 1876 by Georg von Hertling of the very orthodox Gorres-Gesellschaft to promote Catholic scholarship, and a late century progressive movement known as Reform Catholicism. Wurzburg theologian Herman Schell[9], and historians Franz Xaver Kraus[10] and Albert Ehrhard,[11] pleaded for reform and a changed relationship of the Church toward modern society.

Reform Catholics, however, did not see Jesuits as allies; they had connived in putting Herman Schell on the Index of Forbidden Books in 1898 and spurned 1903 overtures by Karl Muth to join lay Catholics in the establishment of the progressive Catholic cultural journal, *Hochland.* Anti-Jesuit sentiment, which came not only from the German Protestant community but from reform-minded Catholics as well, lingered into the twentieth century.

Rahner would insist that the theological enterprise had to be scholarly. The scholarly or *wissenschaftliche* character of theology had been at issue throughout the nineteenth century. One thinks of Schleiermacher[12] and Tübingen's von Drey in the early 1800s.

But by the end of the nineteenth century *Wissenschaft* had also become a hotly politicized issue, assuming a high profile in the controversial appointment of a young Catholic historian, Peter Spahn, to the University of Straßburg in 1901. It triggered a heated political discussion, which engaged such prominent scholars as Adolf Harnack and Theodor Mommsen.[13]

Could Catholic scholarship hold its own in an academic world where the dominant scholarly culture was Protestant? Do Catholics belong at public, state-supported universities? As a result of the controversy, several Prussian universities amended their statutes to bar the appointment of Catholics to the faculty.[14] Pius X's 1907 condemnation of modernism did little to assuage German Protestant suspicion of Roman Catholic scholarship.

The First World War undercut cultural Protestantism of the late nineteenth and early twentieth century, but German Catholicism, at least at the grass roots level, came through the conflict with a vitality which has been appreciated only recently, and noted by Professor Margaret Anderson at the University of California, Berkeley.[15]

Internal Catholic differences over approaches to modernity were not resolved, however. Catholics struggled to articulate the relevance or utility of Christianity in a society grown even further secular in its *Weltanschauung* during the early decades of the twentieth century.[16]

One thinks of Karl Adam, Arnold Rademacher, Erich Przywara, Max Pribilla, and Romano Guardini.[17] Guardini became the intellectual mentor of a progressive German Catholic youth movement, *Quickborn*. Rahner belonged to *Quickborn* during his teens and had come under the sway of Guardini. Rahner later attributed his interest in and commitment to Church reform to his *Quickborn* years.[18] His lifelong project had its roots in this movement.

Rahner frequently alludes, often in general terms, to the need for a contemporary articulation of the faith. As early as 1943, however, he had written more pointedly about the need for a theology which addressed a modern worldview. He had been commissioned by Vienna's archbishop to respond to a widely circulated critique of the German–speaking church, its theology and liturgy, issued by the archbishop of Freiburg.

Rahner's response is known as the *Vienna Memorandum*. It lay buried for fifty years in the archives of the Archdiocese of Vienna and was finally edited and published in 1994.[19] It contains Rahner's detailed and revealing assessment of the state of liturgy, theology, and philosophy—Catholic and Protestant—in Germany from the beginning of the twentieth century. Rahner sees the German Church facing a truly new historic epoch, the result of enormous political, social, and cultural changes.[20] The challenge presented to the Church by this transformed cultural landscape would remain even if the severe political restrictions, imposed by the Nazi regime then in power, were to be relaxed or to disappear.[21]

It was not enough to rail against the evils of modernity, Rahner argued, or condemn its intellectual currents—it is incumbent to enter into creative dialogue with them and find the good in their positions. This had been the most successful strategy of the Church in previous ages, he noted.

He urged closer integration of the questions of the day with the more rigorous theology of the academy. The integration should both transform academic theology, and demand that it find articulate, balanced, and accessible expressions satisfactory to German Catholics seeking answers to their faith questions. Unless this happens, Rahner worries, the life experience of the present-day Catholic community finds only ad hoc, ad hominem answers to its questions; but more importantly, the tradition itself remains unchanged, because the questions never force the tradition to come to terms with them.[22]

Rahner had once written an essay titled *Forgotten Truths Concerning the Sacrament of Penance*. Over the ages, he argued, the faith community can forget some of its own most valuable insights. On the other hand, if the ongoing experience of the community is not appreciated for what it is—an invaluable resource for self-understanding—then the work of the theologian is all the poorer.

Influences and Sources

The last twenty years of Rahner's research, certainly in the German-speaking world, converge in the assessment that no single-source theory suffices to explain the unique theological construction that Rahner accomplished. There were many influences such as Scholastic Thomism.

In 1879 Leo XIII had reestablished Thomism as the official philosophical and theological framework for coming to terms with the modern world. Karl Lehmann, student and close friend of Rahner's, argues that no other modern Catholic theologian was as deeply rooted in scholastic theology as was Rahner. This is all so evident in his early writings, suffused as they are with scholastic vocabulary. Most readers need a refresher course, if that is what it would be, to maneuver through the thicket of scholastic rhetoric. It is telling that, although most of the German Jesuits of the nineteenth and twentieth centuries were Suárezians; Rahner followed Thomas Aquinas.

Ignatius of Loyola

Ignatius of Loyola, along with Martin Luther, was a religious icon of the emerging modern epoch, a period that John S. Dunne of the University of Notre Dame depicts as characterized by the "breakdown of spiritual mediation." It is an epoch in which the immediate experience of God becomes thematic.[23] For Rahner, attention to the immediate experience of God had become even more critical in a culture which questioned rather than affirmed religious values, which eroded rather than supported religious commitment. In this situation, the Christian would have to become a mystic, with an internalized conviction of God, or not remain Christian at all.

It might seem self-evident that Ignatius of Loyola, the founder of the Society of Jesus, would influence a Jesuit's theology. In Rahner's case it would be more than happenstance; he was closely connected with a movement engaged in critical retrieval of Ignatian spirituality and the dynamics of Ignatius's legacy, the *Spiritual Exercises*.[24] His older brother and collaborator, Hugo Rahner, and one of his mentors, Jesuit Erich Przywara,[25] did close textual and historical study of Ignatian spirituality. The Ignatian motto of "finding God in all things," and the "discernment of spirits," were segues for Rahner's work.

Bonaventure

In his 1938 work, *Encounters with Silence*, Rahner could pray: "God of my life, Incomprehensible, be my life. . . . why have you kindled in me the flame of faith, this dark light which lures us out of the bright security of our little huts into Your night?"[26] Forty years later, in *Foundations of Christian Faith*, Rahner writes: "For a Christian, Christian existence is ultimately the totality of one's existence. This totality opens out into the dark abysses of the wilderness which we call God."[27]

Bonaventure was the first great theologian of the Franciscan order and a contemporary of Thomas Aquinas. Bonaventure enters Rahner's world through Jerome Nadal, one of Ignatius's early collaborators, one who had himself been linked to the great Franciscan. Brothers Hugo and Karl had written on Nadal, and Karl had been fascinated by the theology of the spiritual senses, first in Origen, then in Bonaventure. By the age of thirty he had published on both.[28]

Bonaventure's ecstatic understanding of our experience of God, and his depiction of the grasp of God in the *apex affectus*, or affective high point of the soul, to be the sum and most intimate dimension of the human being, shaped Rahner's depiction of God as unfathomable mystery, unutterable and dark.[29]

The Patristic and Mystical Tradition

Rahner was intensely interested in the patristic and mystical tradition. One of his first major works, published the same year as his classic text, *Spirit in the World*, was a translation and major revision of a French work by M. Viller on asceticism and mysticism in the patristic period.[30] The reworking of the French text was so extensive that Hans Urs von

Balthasar would describe it as practically an original work of Rahner himself.[31]

Joseph Maréchal (1878–1944), Martin Heidegger (1889–1976), Maurice Blondel (1861–1949)

If Loyola and Luther were religious icons of an emerging modernity, Immanuel Kant would become its philosophical icon, especially when attention turned to the subject. Belgian Jesuit Joseph Maréchal provided Lonergan and Rahner with an attempted mediation between Thomas Aquinas and Immanuel Kant on the question of the starting point and possibility of a metaphysics. Rahner's *Spirit in the World*, intended to be his doctoral dissertation but not accepted by his mentor, becomes his own reinterpretation of Aquinas in light of the questions placed by modern philosophy, not only by Kant, but also by Fichte, Hegel, and especially by Martin Heidegger.

Heidegger provides impetus for Rahner's insistence on the question of being, on the concept of the existentials, and on the fundamental historicity of our being in the world.[32] History isn't the calendar in which we log our deeds, rather we experience our own being as woven into the ongoing flow of history; we are never fully who we are to become.

But through Maréchal, Rahner also encountered the work of the French philosopher, Maurice Blondel. In Blondel one finds intimations of a transcendental theology, of an attempt to overcome the extrinsicism of grace, even of the anonymous Christian.[33]

Theological Themes

If you were to ask is there an overriding theme which touches every corner of Karl Rahner's theology, and which has had the broadest and richest influence, the answer would be Rahner's theology of grace as God's self-communication. As we can see now, his creative approach to the question goes back to his first lectures at the University of Innsbruck in the fall of 1937.

Breaking with the tradition of his neoscholastic predecessors, Rahner's first thesis was the universality of the salvific will of God. "There is in God a binding and effective will for the supernatural salvation of all human beings. . . . and this divine salvific will touches us, *attingit nos*, in Christ and in the Church."[34] Rahner's theology of grace is thoroughly Christocentric, for it is in contact with Christ, and participation in the cross of Christ, that this will of God for our salvation becomes a reality in us.

This divine will is absolute, not in binding God of course, but in making an absolute claim on each and every adult human being (*homines adulti*). The "adult" is part of Rahner's thesis. I would like to repeat one of the lines in the prayer I cited earlier:

> Then will begin the great silence, in which no other sound will be heard but you, O Word, resounding from eternity to eternity. . . . I will understand what You have been saying to me all along, namely, You Yourself.[35]

The salvific divine will that touches us in Christ, the Word, is none other than Godself. It is not first and foremost information, even of the hidden truths of God, it is not propositions or dogmas or creed; it is God's self, God's self-communication. God gives God's self in this saving, revealing moment, out of the innermost depths of God's own freedom. Large segments of the tradition had spoken of grace as a created transformation of our inner being; for Rahner, grace is first and foremost God's self, an uncreated reality because it is the advent of God's communication in us.

This raises questions about the goal and purpose of this self-revelation. And about who we are, that we could be recipients, hearers of the Word that is God's self-communication. Let us look at the first question.

Why on Earth Did God Become Human?

A classic articulation of the mainline opinion is probably found in Anselm's influential work, *Cur Deus Homo?* (Why the Incarnation?) Adam and Eve sinned and the human race is unable to extricate itself from sin's burden. To restore the cosmic justice which this violation of God's honor has caused, God becomes one of us in order to redeem us from our sin.

It is always good to seek a second opinion. And there was one. Rupert, Abbot of the Monastery of Deutz, just across the Rhine from Cologne Cathedral, had first floated it. Often called the Franciscan or Scotist interpretation, it held that the goal of the incarnation is the completion of creation itself, a creative act of love most fully expressed.

Incarnation isn't the fallback plan when creation goes awry; it is creation's goal, its final purpose. Creation finds its wholeness and fulfillment in the Christ.

Without ever formally saying so, Rahner seems to espouse this second, Scotist or Franciscan, framework for understanding the mystery of Christ.[36]

> For me, therefore, the true and sole center of Christianity is the real self-communication of God to creation in God's innermost reality and glory. It is to profess the most improbable truth, namely, that God in God's very self with infinite reality and glory, with holiness, freedom, and love can really and without any holding back enter the creatureliness of our existence. Everything else that Christianity offers or demands of us is by comparison only provisional or of secondary importance.[37]

Rahner has made a strategic choice which, he admits, reflects his own personal experience as a Christian. There are consequences; sin and evil, perhaps even conversion, don't have the same high profile they will have in other theological systems. They become subordinate to the prior truth of God's free, unconditional self-communication to a creation already the product of love.

Rahner even mused about a legitimate Christian *apocatástasis,* namely that in the end, God's will for bringing creation to completion trumps all our sin and stupidity, so that all are saved. Already present in his early lectures, however, his focus on God's self-communication in grace becomes the unifying, all-integrating insight of the rest of this theology. With that as his starting point, Rahner works to interpret what it means to be "human beings."

What Are We as Human Beings?

Groucho Marx once quipped he would never join an organization that would have him as a member. Turning the question on its head, we can ask: Who are we that God would become human?

Rahner constructs an anthropology so understood that it is open to being grasped and embraced by the divine. He appeals to modern, transcendental understandings of the human person, understandings which he sees as a legitimate, ultimately Christian product of modern philosophy. Among those he cites are Descartes, Kant, German idealism, and Maurice Blondel.

One classic articulation of his anthropology is explored in Rahner's *Hearer of the Word*. Rahner is ostensibly composing a "philosophy of religion," but as is evident, he composes a philosophical anthropology, a reflection on the "being" of human being. If all metaphysical questions are generalized questions about the nature of being, what is the nature of "being" that appears as "*human* being?"

By the end of his career, Rahner considers "being human" as a modality or manner of being, which one could designate as "freedom." He speaks of it as "transcendental freedom." It is ultimately as "freedom" that we exist as *human* beings, that our modality or way of being is as being "in freedom." It is the "power to decide about oneself, to actualize oneself," not just as regards this or that choice, vanilla over chocolate, Berkeley over Stanford.[38]

In the course of the history of our freedom, a history punctuated by decisions and choices, commitments and aversions, we define and actualize who we are. That freedom reveals itself in the shape and the contours which our choices effect, but it is never directly accessible to our inspection. It only reaches its term in death.

In *Hearer of the Word*, however, Rahner begins by retrieving a tradition which tends to think of the human being as intellect and will, and his philosophical dependence on Maréchal likely leads him to stress the intellectual component.

Every instance of knowing a finite object of our experience contains within itself, along with knowledge of the concrete object, a nonconceptual—Rahner calls it nonthematic—grasp of being itself. It is *we* who grasp and understand; but we grasp and judge *this* concrete object in front of us to be *this* limited and finite reality because our reach to understand goes beyond this concrete object to affirm implicitly the horizon of being itself. We are forever reaching beyond ourselves, beyond the clutter of objects and choices that choke our days to that which alone can fill us. We are forever self-transcending human beings.

I referred earlier to Rahner's popular work *Encounters with Silence*, which could be translated more literally as *Words into the Silence*.[39] When one reads *Hearers of the Word* side by side with *Words into the Silence*—they were composed at the same time—it is difficult to escape the conclusion that Rahner is attempting to link the pastorally articulated religious experience of seeking and yearning for God, with the philosophical, more critical articulation of the possible foundations of hearing a word of revelation.[40] But it is ultimately the voluntary and affective which is given preeminence. "Truly, my God, mere knowing is nothing . . . . How can we approach the heart of all things, the true heart of reality? Not by knowledge alone, but by the full flower of knowledge, love." This is clear in *Foundations of Christian Faith,* where love is given priority in the analysis of human transcendence.[41]

In the historical person of Jesus Christ, this human self-transcending grasp toward the infinite in love finds God's free offer of self-communication united irrevocably. Jesus is the "real symbol" of God's self-communication addressed into our creatureliness—"real symbol" because it is rooted in God's self.

To understand the mystery of Christ as a saving, our understanding must touch us in the depths of our self-understanding as human beings. It cannot remain as a sort of theological icing, a pious accessory, like wearing costume jewelry. It might make us look better, but it wouldn't really transform us, or our self-understanding. The mystery of Christ must reveal to us something about what it is to be *human being.*

So central must be this self-transcending dynamic, which finds realization in being grasped by God, that Rahner borrows the vocabulary of Heidegger to speak of it as an existential of being human, a true, intrinsic and personal component, one might say, of being human.

And because he is adamant to defend its purely gratuitous presence in us, he uses the rather unfortunate phrase, supernatural existential. We find the ultimate completion of ourselves in God's offer of self-communication. Then the finite "infinite" horizon of our knowing and willing are brought to their goal and end. It might have been better to frame this reality in terms of freedom or love, perhaps intimacy.

In an almost lyric exposition of Christology, "Christology in an Evolutionary Framework," Rahner sees all of creation constantly transcending itself (almost as Albert the Great did in the thirteenth century), finding consciousness and voice in us human beings. "This one material cosmos is the single body as it were of a multiple self-presence (us!) of this very cosmos and its orientation towards its absolute and infinite ground."[42]

Grace as God's free self-communication, the human being as potential recipient and hearer of God's Word, fundamentally open to the infinite and historical event of Jesus Christ as the real, personal symbol of that divine self-offer, which has been realized in the creatureliness of our existence: These are fundamental elements in the theology of Karl Rahner.

The Incomprehensibility of God

There is another element, and that is Rahner's insistence on the incomprehensibility and abiding mystery of God. So often we content ourselves, when confronted with some dilemma or conundrum, or with an event that we cannot fathom, with the quip that we'll have to ask God about that when we see God face to face, while now it remains a mystery.

Mystery isn't the curtain concealing the wizard at the control panel, which will be ripped away at death, giving us access to yet another object of knowledge, long concealed during life. Nor is the mystery of God a temporary, transitory characteristic, which will give way to clarity and understanding once we cross the finish line. God will reveal God's self as all the more mysterious when our own freedom has run its course in death.

Rahner had encountered God as ever greater mystery under the influence of Erich Przywara, an early mentor, who recovered the teaching on analogy as pointing to the ever greater dissimilarity between terms of analogy relating to God.[43] Rahner, after teaching extensively throughout his life on God as incomprehensible mystery, returns to the topic in the last public lecture of his career, delivered as part of his eightieth birthday celebration in Freiburg.

Rahner spoke about his experiences as a theologian. He was predictably modest. He argued that he wished that he had been more emphatic in accompanying each and every one of his theological assertions with an affirmation of God's absolute incomprehensibility. This, he argued, should have been not only the preamble to each of his writings, but a recurring companion statement to the unfolding of his theological reflection.

> I want only to confirm the experience that theologians are worthy of the title only when they do not seek to reassure themselves that

> they are providing clear and lucid discourse, but rather when they are experiencing and witnessing, with both terror and bliss, to the analogical back and forth between affirmation and negation before the abyss of God's incomprehensibility. . . . As theologians we devote too much time to talking about this issue and in all our talk we basically forget the very subject of our discourse.[44]

Finally, he noted that he should say something about what is to come. There is a certain poignancy attached to these reflections. Rahner spoke on February 12 and died within weeks of the lecture.

> I admit that it seems to me to be both an agonizing and an always incomplete task for the contemporary theologian to come up with a better model for understanding the notion of eternal life—a model which would exclude these difficulties from the outset.
>
> But how? But how? The angels of death will gather up all that trivia that we call our history from the rooms of our spirit (though, of course, the true essence of our active freedom will remain). The starry ideals with which we have rather presumptuously adorned the higher spheres of our life will have faded away and gone out. Death will have erected a huge, silent void. And we will have silently accepted this state in a spirit of faith and hope as corresponding to our true destiny and being. Our seemingly long life then appears as a single short explosion of our freedom like an extended replay, an explosion in which question is transposed into answer, possibility into reality, time to eternity, potential freedom into exercised freedom.
>
> Then within that immense terror that is death will come a cry of unutterable joy which will reveal that the immense and silent void we experience as death is in reality filled with the primordial mystery we call God. It is filled with God's pure light, with God's all-absorbing and all-giving love. Perhaps there in this incomprehensible mystery we can catch a glimpse of Jesus, the blessed one who appears to us and looks at us. It is in this concrete figure of Jesus that all our legitimate assumptions about the incomprehensibility of the infinite God are divinely surpassed.
>
> I would like to call what I have just said a description of what is to come. Rather I have merely offered, however falteringly and provisionally, an indication of how one might expect what is to

come, namely, by experiencing the descent that is death as already the ascent of what still awaits us. Eighty years is a long time. For each one of us, however, the life span apportioned to us is that brief moment in time which will be what constitutes our ultimate purpose and meaning.[45]

13. Rahner, von Balthasar and the Question of Theological Aesthetics: Preliminary Considerations

James Voiss, S.J.

Introduction

Following the Second Vatican Council, Karl Rahner dominated the Roman Catholic theological landscape. His ideas on grace and human freedom opened horizons for theological inquiry at which preconciliar theologies only hinted. The generation of theologians following Rahner drew heavily on his insights. More recently, another figure has achieved ascendancy. With his massive, *The Glory of the Lord*,[1] Hans Urs von Balthasar has attempted to redraw the map of the theological landscape. What Rahnerians found to be oases of hope, Balthasar has recast as "mirage" and desolation. Many who felt ill at ease with aspects of Rahner's thought have embraced Balthasar's theology as a corrective to perceived excesses in late-modern and post-conciliar theological developments.

The reception of Balthasar's project into theological discussion has frequently resulted in a juxtaposition of Rahner's and Balthasar's theologies. This contrast has legitimate roots. Rahner's and Balthasar's theological approaches differed significantly. Moreover, Balthasar's observation that

> our starting points were actually always different. There is a book by Simmel, titled, *Kant and Goethe*. Rahner has chosen Kant, or

> if you will, Fichte—the transcendental approach. And I have chosen Goethe—as a Germanist. The form [Gestalt], the indissolubly unique, organic, self-unfolding form—I think of Goethe's *Metamorphosis of Plants*—this form which Kant even in his aesthetics could never really imagine.[2]

and his scathing condemnation of some of Rahner's ideas in *The Moment of Christian Witness*, have left a very clear impression that their theologies are irremediably opposed in content, method, and conclusions.[3]

Nevertheless, some voices have emerged calling for a more conciliatory reading of these two great thinkers. For example, Kevin Mongrain has observed that "there are numerous points of agreement between Karl Rahner's transcendental theology and Balthasar's theological aesthetics."[4] I share Mongrain's conviction. However, in what follows, I will take issue with an implied assumption in his statement, an assumption which is common to comparisons made between Rahner and Balthasar. When the juxtaposition between their theologies is based on the contrast between transcendental and aesthetic starting points, the assumption arises that Rahner lacks what Balthasar terms a theological aesthetics.

My purpose will not be to prove that Rahner does have a theological aesthetics. Instead I shall pursue a more modest goal. I shall argue that the implicit assumption that Rahner's theology lacks a theological aesthetics is not as justified as appears to be commonly assumed. Toward that end I shall first present a sketch of Balthasar's project of a theological aesthetics. I will then explore whether Rahner's work really stands as far removed from Balthasar's intentions as is commonly held. Finally, I will suggest further possible lines of exploration that may be useful in the pursuit of common ground between the works of these two great Catholic theologians.

One caveat is in order. The breadth and depth of theological riches found in Rahner's and Balthasar's writings prevent this essay from being anything more than a preliminary foray into the topic. My presentation will necessarily be schematic. Nevertheless, if it prompts further, more detailed exploration of these questions, it will have achieved its purpose.

Balthasar's Project of a Theological Aesthetics

Hans Urs von Balthasar saw his project of a theological aesthetics as a corrective to systemic distortions in the work of his contemporaries.

These distortions had their roots in a flaw in their theological methods.[5] This methodological flaw, in turn, led to a distorted understanding of the nature and purpose of theology itself. Balthasar's argument is complex and multilayered. I will summarize briefly, focusing on those elements necessary for contextualizing the present question.

Balthasar's Critique of Modern Theology

Balthasar's critique of modern theology suggests that it has embraced a Trojan horse carrying three distinct but related forces in its belly. First, by engaging the Kantian problematic, the epistemological limitation that one cannot know the thing in itself, but only our perceptions of it, modern theologians have ceded the ground of objective truth.[6] All that remains is my perception, filtered through the a priori structures of consciousness. Presupposed here is an unbridgeable gap between perception and "objective truth" (the thing-in-itself). In the pursuit of knowledge (truth), the moderns have forsaken the relevance of the form of appearance.

This separation between form and truth leads to the second force in the belly of the Trojan horse: the trivialization of beauty. Moderns no longer recognize beauty as integral to the truth, goodness, and unity of beings. It has become, instead, merely a characteristic of appearance. It is evaluated, not in terms of the truth, goodness, and unity to which it belongs, but in terms of merely subjective taste. As a result, moderns devalue the form in which Being discloses itself. They see form as irrelevant to "objective" knowledge (if such can ever be attained, given the structures of Kant's epistemology).

Third, Balthasar alleges that, because it has devalued the form of beauty, modern reason has instrumentalized truth. Reason has become distorted into a one-sided rationalism which valorizes knowledge as a means of control.[7] These three forces mutually presuppose each other in the modern mind-set.

Theological Consequences

Balthasar maintains that these intellectual developments have disastrous consequences for theologies on which they have left their stamp. His full argument extends over several hundred pages, but three points are crucial for the present question: Balthasar's understanding of the object, the method, and the end of theology.

First, for Balthasar, the main object of theology's inquiry is God as revealed in history.[8] God's self-disclosure has to come to its unsurpassable apex in the historical person, Jesus of Nazareth. Premodern theologians, unaffected by Kantian agnosticism, accepted the unity of the external form and the inner truth. They recognized and affirmed the particularity of the historical Jesus as the Christ of faith. Modern theologians, accepting the rupture between perception and the inaccessible "thing-in-itself," look for a "meaning" behind the external form, thereby making the historical particularity of Jesus of Nazareth as Christ irrelevant.[9] In their neglect of the historical particularity of God's revelation in Christ, Balthasar argues, modern theologians have relativized what is most central to Christian faith.

Second, the theological appropriation of the turn to the subject, when combined with the separation of beauty from truth, has distorted modern theological methodologies. The subject becomes the judge of the true, turning the true into a merely inert object. The mind goes out in pursuit of truth, as a "thing" on which it acts. The self stands over against the true as its judge.[10] Balthasar critiques three implications of this orientation: (1) it makes anthropology the central focus of theology.[11] (2) it makes God and God's self-disclosure in Christ into one "object" among others, subject to human conceptual manipulation; and (3) it generates "epic" theologies which elevate the theologian to a position above God and the cosmos.[12] According to Balthasar, this distorts the proper relationship of the theologian to God.

Third, Balthasar contends that modern theology has lost sight of its proper end. Certainly, modern theologians could subscribe to the dictum that theology is "faith seeking understanding." The issue here is the driving motivation behind the pursuit of understanding. Balthasar sees in the modern project a pursuit of understanding for the sake of mastery and control.[13] It is driven by a pragmatics whose further ends tend toward (merely) intramundane expressions. For example, liberation theologies seek transformation of social structures and just distribution of wealth; feminist theologies advocate changes in the status of women in the church and in the world; and so on. Against these approaches, Balthasar argues that the understanding which forms the proper end of theology is to be measured by "fruitfulness," not by specific pragmatic results. Fruitfulness here means holiness of life, transformation into the dynamics of God's own way of being in the world, as revealed in the historical particularity of Jesus Christ.[14]

The Meaning of "Theological Aesthetics"

If, as Balthasar contends, the problems of modern theology stem from the loss of beauty as a transcendental and the form of its expression, then theology needs an aesthetic grounding. But what kind of aesthetics is required? Some distinction will be helpful here.

First, there are two distinct but related understandings of the term "aesthetics" in Balthasar's writings. One refers to an articulated theory of beauty and how it comes to be recognized. This theoretical articulation is the basis of his multivolume, *The Glory of the Lord: A Theological Aesthetics*. But the articulation of aesthetic theory, particularly in theology, follows upon a more primordial experiential aesthetics: "the perception of faith of the self-authenticating glory of God's utterly free gift of love."[15] This experiential aesthetic appreciation is the foundation for the theoretical reflection. It is that sensitivity which fits one to be able to "see" and be enraptured by the form of beauty as it presents itself. "Seeing the form" signals for Balthasar the experience of being seized by beauty itself in its objective self-presentation.[16] Since form and content are inseparable in the unity of truth, goodness, and beauty, "seeing the form" is essential to grasping the truth of the presentation.

"Seeing" in this context is not merely visual perception. Balthasar uses the term analogically. "Seeing" means grasping the unifying integrity (form) of the true as objective (independent of my merely subjective appreciation). Thus, it is a mental act of *recognitio* which is not reducible to the *cogito* of Descartes or to the critical reason of Kant.[17] An adequate theory of beauty (aesthetics in a theoretical sense) must preserve the objectivity of the form and its integral relation to the truth being disclosed.

Balthasar's understanding of "form" is likewise nuanced. The form perceived is the outward expression of the inner truth—the manifestation which makes the truth present.[18] But the perceived form does not exhaust that truth. Moreover, the form presented is not simply the "object." Context co-constitutes the form of the truth's self-disclosure and is therefore part of the truth presented in the form.[19]

Second, Balthasar distinguishes "theological aesthetics" from "aesthetic theology." Aesthetic theology is the theological application of aesthetic concepts derived from "an inner-worldly theory of beauty."[20] When modern epistemological assumptions regarding the distinction between the thing-in-itself and perception hold sway, the aesthetic element in theology derives in theory and in practice from subjective taste and will be understood in intramundane terms. But when one accepts the radical integrity of form and truth in finite (and infinite!) beings, then aesthetics (aesthetic appreciation) is integral to knowing and obtains an explicit objectification in our reflections.

These two distinctions help to clarify what Balthasar understands by the phrase "theological aesthetics" especially when read against the object, method, and end of theology outlined above. Theology's object is God revealed in time. At the center of God's self-revealing action stands Jesus of Nazareth, the Christ, in all his historical particularity. The form of this revelation is integral to its truth.[21] Theology therefore requires an aesthetics which keeps the form and content of God's revelation united, but which also privileges the form of God's self-disclosure as the criterion of beauty (glory). This implies, further, that the first movement of theology, as faith seeking and understanding, must be contemplative, receptive posture before the form of revelation in its integrity.[22] This form is a manifestation of God's own glory, inviting one into a relationship with God. Theology, therefore, begins with the grace-borne act of "seeing the form," the fundamental act of faith.[23] The theologian must begin from the act of faith, an aesthetic grasp of the truth of the form of revelation itself. Consequently, for Balthasar, theology serves the mission of the Church. Its purpose is to clarify and express the understanding of Christ in ways accessible to the current generation.[24] This should help men and women of today to become enraptured by the beauty (glory) of God revealed in Christ so that they might be transformed (made holy) by their engagement with it. This is the "fruitfulness" for which Balthasar strives.[25]

Balthasar believed that restoring the aesthetic dimension of Being to its proper place in theology would have profound implications. A theological aesthetics would develop its understanding of beauty from the revelation of God's glory in Christ. This, Balthasar believed, would rescue theology from the three forces in the belly of the modern Trojan horse.

Karl Rahner and Theological Aesthetics

The preceding sketch of Balthasar's theological aesthetics brings to light four topoi in his critique of modern theology: (1) epic pretense; (2) the role of "seeing the form" in theological method; (3) the historical particularity of Christ; and (4) the theology's proper end. These topoi are pivotal to any judgment concerning the presence or absence of a theological aesthetics operative in a theologian's work. More to the point, they permeate Balthasar's own critical appraisal of Rahner's method and his harshest critiques of some of Rahner's ideas. They therefore provide a starting point for asking whether Rahner's theology really lacks a theological aesthetics. I shall examine each of these in turn.

Rahner and Epic Pretense

First, Balthasar critiqued modern theological projects for their "epic" pretensions. Their authors give the impression that they view reality from a position above the plane on which God and creation are situated. Such epic theologies reduce God to an object within the framework of an overarching conceptual system. They then reinterpret the significance of revelation in terms of their own a priori presuppositions. German Idealism, as Balthasar sees it, is particularly guilty of "epic pretense."[26]

Rahner's theology is susceptible to the same charge. His transcendental method asks about the conditions for the possibility of such things as revelation, the experience of grace, and the saving act of faith. At times it appears that, taking his transcendental anthropology as a given, he then proceeds to "deduce" what "must be" the case in relationship to God.[27] This gives the impression that Rahner has reduced God to an object of human speculation within an a priori philosophical system. On this evidence, the charge of epic pretense and the conclusion that he lacks a theological aesthetics appear to have merit.

But other aspects of Rahner's thought call any hasty conclusions on this point into question. For example, he expressly criticized the tendency of idealism to reduce Christianity to a merely theoretical construct.[28] He also discussed the limitations of modern philosophy as a resource for theology in terms very similar to Balthasar's.[29] The fact that Rahner made such statements does not prove him innocent of the charge of epic pretense, nor does it demonstrate that he had a theological aesthetics. However, it does make two important points. It indicates that Rahner shared Balthasar's sensibilities regarding epic pretensions in theology (although expressed in different terms), and that he did not see himself as guilty of that particular flaw. This latter point then raises the question: Why not? Why did Rahner not see his own theology as falling into the danger that both he and Balthasar criticized?

Two themes in Rahner's theology suggest a preliminary response. First, epic pretense consists in arrogating to human reason an ability to "rise above" the divine sphere by means of a priori conceptual systems in order to make "objective" pronouncements about it. Rahner's insistence on the *reductio in mysterium Dei* as an integral moment of theology contravenes precisely this intellectual excess.[30] Indeed, Rahner insists that all theological formulations possess a certain relativity of which they must remain aware. God is absolute mystery; our concepts of God are always inadequate. Theological formulations must therefore recall their provisional nature and refer back to the one central mystery, the transcendent God, revealed as God-for-us in Christ.

But secondly, to perform this *reductio in mysterium Dei,* the theologian must stand in relationship to that mystery in a posture of receptivity for that which it bestows.[31] In terms suggesting very strongly a parallel to Balthasar's notion of the enrapturing character of beauty, Rahner writes of the theologian's proper stance toward God as Mystery.

> It is the attitude of trembling and silent adoration which is intended to beget these [theological and doctrinal] statements, and this belongs to that deathly silence in which man's lips are sealed with Christ's in death. It is, therefore, a very difficult task with which theology has to cope in these statements. They must be expressed in words in order that we can arrive at the authentic silence which we need. They must be borne with in patience and hope in respect both of their necessity and of their incommensurability, in which they attempt to utter the ineffable.[32]

This tension between reverent silence and the need to "utter the ineffable" when in the presence of holy mystery is the wellspring of theology. For Rahner, theology arises from encounter with this mystery and returns to it in worship. This encounter is the source of our access to truth.[33]

These points—the relativity of theological formulations, the *reductio in mysterium Dei*, and the posture of relevant worship before the Holy Mystery as the origin and the terminus of theological labor—when given their full weight in Rahner's theological corpus challenge any overly-hasty charge that he is guilty of epic pretense. Indeed, they express methodological sensitivities which point in the direction of an operative theological aesthetics even in the absence of an articulated aesthetic theory.

Seeing the Form

The question of "seeing the form" is perhaps the most crucial for any judgment about Rahner and theological aesthetics. This is that moment in the act of faith that reflexively grasps the unity in the disparate elements of historical revelatory events *as* united in a single form and *as* revelatory (the two aspects belong together). It is the grace-borne act by which a person is seized by the glory of God "visible" in the form. "Seeing the form" is Balthasar's phrase for what is here termed the "operative theological aesthetics" beneath the theoretical. As such, in the absence of a developed theory of beauty in Rahner's theology, "seeing the form" becomes a pivotal issue for the question of theological aesthetics in Rahner's work. Two aspects of this "seeing" will occupy us here: (1) the recognition of the integral unity of "parts" and "whole" in the revelatory event; and (2) the indispensability of the form for the truth of what is revealed.

It is possible to question whether "seeing the form," as understood by Balthasar, plays any role in Rahner's theology. The evidence supporting the charge of epic pretense applies here, too. Does the unifying vision of Christian self-understanding issue from an a priori philosophical structure imposed on the data of revelation or from the form of revelation itself? Can one abstract from the particularity of the form or must one remain subject to it? Balthasar believed Rahner had opted for the former (a priori abstraction) and abandoned the latter (the form of revelation—specifically, the centrality of the form of revelation in Christ) in his methodological orientation.[34]

Three ideas developed by Rahner in his discussion of "anonymous Christians" lend credence to Balthasar's concern: (1) the treatment of grace as a "supernatural existential" offered to human freedom at all times even though not reflexively grasped as such; (2) the conviction that faith is fundamentally a transcendental act of human freedom which can be attained without any reflexive grasp of a "religious object," to say nothing of a distinctively Christian religious object as the whither of faith's act; and (3) the related notion of a transcendental revelation offered to human freedom's assent even though not reflexively grasped as such. These three interrelated themes make a strong case that the form of revelation and "seeing" that form contribute little to Rahner's theology. Indeed, they suggest that Rahner has succumbed to all three of the forces in the belly of the modern Trojan horse.[35]

Nevertheless, there are significant counterindicators that "seeing the form," an operative theological aesthetics—and not an a priori epic construct—is the source of coherence and consistency in Rahner's theological works. First, despite an emphasis on Rahner's philosophical heritage in the early reception of his thought,[36] more recent scholarship has taken a different approach. It argues that Rahner's theology was, perhaps, more powerfully driven by his personal experience of faith than by the philosophical/theological conceptual apparatus with which it was expressed.[37] Indeed, there appears to be a growing consensus that this core experience of faith provides a more coherent account of the *unity* of Rahner's thought than does his sometimes inconsistent use of philosophical categories and concepts. If this emerging perspective holds, it goes a long way toward repudiating charges of epic pretense and toward grounding the affirmation of an operative theological aesthetics in Rahner's work.

Second, Rahner's "The Theology of the Symbol,"a watershed essay in the Rahner corpus, makes explicit the ontological necessity of holding together the expressive form and that which it expresses.[38] Far from postulating the expendability of form, Rahner theologizes from the affirmation of its indispensability. His writings on symbolic reality express in theoretical terms conclusions derived from penetrating reflection on the form of revealed data such as the Trinity and the Incarnation, as well as on fundamental Christian convictions about the sacraments. Rahner's discussion of these themes under the rubric of the theology of the symbol holds for the distinction without separation between the form of expression and that which is expressed.

Third, the discussion of anonymous Christians notwithstanding, Rahner's Christological sensibilities reflect a sensitivity to "seeing the form" in both dimensions named above: the unity of the parts and whole in the revelatory event, and the integrity of the form of expression to the truth it expresses. This shows itself in Rahner's critical posture toward two distinct Christological approaches. On the one hand, Rahner criticized the theology of "the schools" in which dogmatic theologians had narrowed their reflections on the life of Christ to the incarnation and the crucifixion, consigning other aspects of Christ's life to the realm of exegesis or pious devotion.[39] On the other hand, in the post-conciliar period he expressed reservations about popular "Jesus-isms" which made Christ into a mere humanist.[40] Rahner recognized that, while both approaches hold onto positive values, they are deficient because they fail to see how the singular element on which they focus stands in relationship to the larger picture. They fail, in Balthasar's terms, to "see the form."

One could also argue that "seeing the form" is at issue in another disagreement between Rahner and Balthasar: Anselm's satisfaction theory of atonement.[41] Balthasar embraced Anselm's theory; Rahner rejected it. Rahner criticized Anselm's theory, with its exclusive attention to the saving efficacy of the passion, for many reasons, one of which is vitally important to the present point. According to Rahner, Anselm's theory renders the rest of the life of Christ, apart from the passion and the resurrection, irrelevant to our salvation.[42] The theory, therefore, would undermine the integral unity of the form of God's revelation in Christ, a form which reveals God's saving significance of Christ's passion.[43] He does, however, argue that it must be seen within the context of the whole of Christ's life (integral relationship of whole and parts in the form).

These points suggest that Rahner recognized the importance of what Balthasar terms "seeing the form" and that a foundational aspect of theological aesthetics, as developed by Balthasar, may actually be operative in Rahner's theology.

The Historical Particularity of Christ

The third topos, safeguarding the historical particularity of Christ, stands at the intersection of the first two topoi: concern to avoid epic pretense and the importance of "seeing the form." God's self-revelation occurred in history. The form of revelation can only be seen in and through the historical particulars grasped as a unified, revelatory reality. In "seeing the form," the eyes of faith grasp how historical particulars "converge" on the unity of revealed truth. Balthasar elaborates this principle in detail in his reflections on the "Christological constellation," the historical figures surrounding Jesus whose presence co-constitutes the form of the revelation in Christ (Mary, Peter, John, Paul, and James).[44] This reflects his desire to counteract modern epic theologies that abandon the form of revelation.

Rahner's Christology privileges no such detailed analysis of the theological significance of those historical relationships. Moreover, both the discussion of anonymous Christians and Rahner's use of a transcendental framework for expositing his Christology reinforce the impression that the historical particularity of Christ has been eclipsed in Rahner's thought by an epic construct. Nevertheless, the case against Rahner is far from conclusive on this point. Early in his career, Rahner expressed concern about theological trends which might dissolve the particularity of Christ in a "cosmic drama" (in a Hegelian sense, what is here termed epic pretense), thereby robbing the cross of its significance.[45] But is there any other evidence to suggest that he did not lose sight of the historical particularity of Christ? Where would one look? Three preliminary indications bear noting.

First, finding direct evidence of Rahner's engagement with the historical particularity of Christ is problematic. If one begins the search with the transcendental philosophical apparatus of Rahner's writings—which looks for universal rather than particular determinants—it may be doomed from the start. However, if one begins from the assumption that Rahner's experience of faith—his spirituality—is the font from which his theology flows (the philosophical concepts providing channels of expression), then it may be possible to see more clearly how meditation on the historical particularity of Christ stamps Rahner's theology in accord with an operative theological aesthetics. Andreas Batlogg's work points in this direction.[46] Batlogg has explored in great detail the theological significance of the "mysteries of the life of Christ" for Rahner's approach to theology.[47]

Second, neglect of the historical particularity of Christ would be inconsistent with Rahner's own ontology. His discussion of the theology of the symbol, affirming the integral unity of external form and that which it expresses, makes historical particularity constitutive of finite subjectivity. Human persons attain to their nature/essence over the course of a history of freedom. This happens only through finite, particular choices. The same is true for Christ. To attempt to abstract from the particularity of his history of freedom and focus on only one dimension of Christ (even if that one dimension is the Passion—hence Rahner's rejection of the satisfaction theory), would be to distort the meaning of the revelatory event; it would be to fail to "see the form."[48]

Third, we can see evidence of Rahner's concern to preserve the historical particularity of Christ in his insistence on the eternal significance of Christ's humanity for our salvation. He writes: "(t)he 'Christian yesterday, today *and forever*' of Hebrews 13:8 must have a soteriological significance for us. The human reality of Christ must always be the abiding mediation of the immediacy of God to us."[49] In other words, the historical particularity of Jesus is not merely a past tense, revelatory medium. It remains in the present and into the future the medium of our encounter with God.

These points do not prove that Rahner's theology takes sufficient account of the historical particularity of Christ to satisfy Balthasar's concerns. However, they do suggest, minimally, that the place of the historical particularity of Christ in Rahner's thought may be more profound and pervasive than Balthasar believed. Its "absence" cannot be appealed to as evidence against a theological aesthetics in Rahner's thought without further careful study.

The Ends of Theology

The fourth topos is the fruitfulness of theology. Balthasar held that theology should draw others to contemplate the beauty (glory) of God in the form of God's self-disclosure in history. This would then foster holiness-trans-form-ation into the form of Christ in the lives of believers. *Whether* Rahner's theology (or Balthasar's, for that matter) actually *has been* fruitful in this manner is beyond my ability to assess. However, there is considerable evidence that Rahner shared Balthasar's perspective that theology should be fruitful in this way. I shall limit myself to two points.

First, Rahner himself explicitly criticized "a fundamental theology of a traditional kind" because it "very often remains unfruitful for the life of faith."[50] His understanding of this fruitfulness strongly parallels Balthasar's emphasis on the transformation of believers.[51] Rahner saw the promotion of this fruitfulness is the core of the church's own commission.[52]

Second, Rahner observed that "the Christian of the future will be a mystic or he [sic] will not be a Christian at all."[53] Theology's task in the future will therefore include a resolute commitment to fostering and promoting the transformative fruitfulness called for by Balthasar. Rahner's conviction on this point is the background for his insistence that theology must be both mystical and practical in the future[54] and his belief that, in the future, theology must perform a maieutic/mystagogical function in the lives of believers.[55]

Implications and Further Questions

The purpose of this essay has been to question the often implicit assumption that, in contrast to Hans Urs von Balthasar, Karl Rahner's theology lacks a theological aesthetics. I have not argued that Rahner does have a theological aesthetics. I have only pursued the first step, arguing that the evidence against a theological aesthetics in Rahner's work is inconclusive and that there are indications that such an aesthetics may be operatively present. In arguing this point I have emphasized similarities between Rahner's theology and Balthasar's project. This approach has necessarily pushed the (very real) differences between them into the background. But it has also brought to light further themes which will need to be explored in evaluating the relationship between the works of these two great theologians, particularly on the question of theological aesthetics. I will mention three.

First, I have emphasized the aesthetic elements in Rahner's thought in contrast to his use of philosophical categories. Both elements are present. It will be important to examine in greater detail how these two aspects of Rahner's thought actually interpenetrate, and what role his experience of God plays in their integration. Do the philosophical resources control the appropriation of the "form" being seen? Does the experience of seeing the form control the employment of the philosophical apparatus? Or do they somehow mutually condition each other?

Second, it appears from the argument of this essay that Balthasar has read Rahner's theology exclusively through the lens of Rahner's transcendental framework. Emerging trends in Rahner scholarship are calling such a one-sided reading into question. Has Balthasar perhaps failed to "see the form" of Rahner's theology? Has he mistaken the external, philosophical form for the deeper reality it was used to express? As Balthasar knows, although form is integral to the truth expressed, it does not exhaust that which it expresses.

Third, Balthasar's project of a theological aesthetics postulates that the modern subjectivization of beauty and the consequent trivialization of form have distorted theology and obscured our access to the truth. One must therefore approach the true through the enrapturing beauty of the form in which it represents itself. But do all people at all times experience the dynamics of truth and beauty as Balthasar sketches them? Are there some people whose primary access to the enrapturing quality of the form of beauty is through their recognition of the truth as truth? In other words, for the sake of the fruitfulness of theology today, might the exposition of truth within the conceptual categories most accessible to a given population be exactly the "form" most suitable for enrapturing? And if so, then might this recognition provide us with a starting point in the attempt to fashion a rapprochement between Rahner's and Balthasar's theologies on the landscape of the beautiful?

14. Postscript: 1904 Was a Wonderful Year

David Stagaman, S.J.

It was a pleasure to collect and assemble with Mark Bosco these centenary essays on Bernard Lonergan, John Courtney Murray, and Karl Rahner. Reading through them, I was reminded how much these three Jesuit theologians influenced my young Jesuit life both intellectually and spiritually. In my own contribution, the reader will learn where this influence most deeply touched me, especially as someone fully engaged in teaching and research in theology over the last thirty years. To set the context for my remarks, I will begin by examining the contribution of the father of Transcendental Thomism, Joseph Maréchal, for it is his seminal work that connects all three of these theologians. At the end I will discuss briefly another significant Roman Catholic theologian born in 1904, Yves Congar of the Order of Preachers (the Dominicans).

To understand Lonergan, Murray, and Rahner's desire to develop a discourse with modern philosophy, one must appreciate that all of them were influenced by Joseph Maréchal, professor of philosophy at the University of Louvain in the early part of the twentieth century. His major scholarly contribution was the multivolume, *Le point du depart de la metaphysique*, whose fifth volume, *Le thomisme devant la philosophie critique*, confronted how Immanuel Kant's first two Critiques might help us understand Thomas Aquinas for contemporary philosophical reflection.[1] Maréchal was taken with two key similarities between the two thinkers; both of them argued that human thinking was active in knowing the physical world, and each claimed that the human spirit was the key to our knowing reality. Maréchal understood that both Aquinas and Kant asserted that the physical universe was known through sense knowledge and that the mind played an active role in assessing sense data. While Aquinas affirmed that understanding and willing provided our first notion of Being and ultimately directed us to knowledge of God, Kant moved in a similar direction from the categorical imperative to immortality to existence of God.

Here it might be helpful to consider an interpretation of Kant in continental philosophy that differs from the way Kant has often been taught in the United States. During my early Jesuit studies in philosophy, I was taught that Kant philosophized that we can't know things in themselves but only in their appearances (phenomena); we can, however, know the reality of our souls, at least insofar as we are moral actors (the noumenon). During my doctoral studies in Paris, my teachers there presented a slightly different interpretation. Phenomena direct our attention to the fact that physical matter can only be known in its appearances to us (the senses); the noumenon is the realm of the spirit. The distinction is one that notes a difference in the nature of our knowledge of things and our own spiritual activities; the former is mediated knowledge, the latter is immediate. When Kant says we don't know things in themselves, the emphasis is on "in themselves." He is contrasting knowledge of our own spirit, where we penetrate to the depths of our spirits, to our knowledge of the physical world, where such penetration is not possible. If Maréchal knew this interpretation of Kant, then he would more easily have seen analogies between the Kantian Critiques and Aquinas's analysis of understanding and acting. His major revision of Kant was his attempt to incorporate understanding as a factor in noumenal knowledge and our encounter with God not as a postulate of practical knowledge, but as the real existence of God as the driving force in our knowing and loving whose objects in sum are limitless.

Maréchal was influenced by three other figures in making this claim. The first was Johann Gottlieb Fichte, who argued that our intuition of our activities of knowing and loving is driven by an "infinite absolute" which attracts and energizes our mind and will in all its exercises. In other words, God is foundational for all human knowing and willing. The second influence was Maurice Blondel. For Blondel, the human person experiences an innate orientation to God in the concrete choices we make. Reason does play a role, but the will is primary. Finally,

Pierre Rousselot taught Maréchal that an infinite affirmed as real was a priori for all speculative knowledge.[2] Thus, in each person there existed a dynamic orientation to the infinite which was the goal of all understanding.[3] Maréchal takes these positions and incorporates them into his reformulation of Kant's transcendental claims of human knowing.

The traditional name for philosophers and theologians who have been influenced by Maréchal's work is Transcendental Thomists. Much of the theological zeitgeist of mid-twentieth-century Catholic theology was centered on this school of thought. All three of the persons honored in these essays were such, although Lonergan and Rahner are the two most frequently mentioned.

Bernard Lonergan first came to the attention of the English-speaking world of Roman Catholic philosophy and theology when his *Verbum* articles were published in *Theological Studies* in the late 1940s.[4] His thesis in the articles was that the best exposition of understanding and willing in the writings of Aquinas was to be found in his theology of the Trinity. Lonergan saw that for Aquinas, the understanding was the bridge to some insight into the procession of the Son, while the will served as the bridge to a grasp of the procession of the Holy Spirit.

For approximately fifteen years Lonergan taught systematic theology at the Gregorian University in Rome, where the vast majority of future seminary teachers from Canada, Great Britain, Ireland, and the United States pursued their doctorates in Sacred Theology. While not everyone attended Lonergan's courses, his reputation cast a large shadow over the place. These young scholar-priests returned to their seminaries, cast off the manuals that had been their traditional textbooks, and composed their own class notes which were replete with intellectual inquiry. Prooftexts were replaced by a process of questioning that only then led to answers. The seminary wags at the time claimed that faith seeking understanding reassumed its rightful place in the seminary curriculum, and faith seeking memorization became a thing of the past. The impact of Lonergan on English-speaking seminaries in the 1950s and 1960s was immense.

Eventually, *Insight* appeared in 1956 so that students and teachers could refer to a common text.[5] Its subtitle, *A Study of Human Understanding*, well describes the purport of the book. Lonergan sought to delineate a heuristic structure of the knowing process. The book opened with five chapters of case studies, taken from the disciplines of physics and mathematics. Lonergan endeavored to divine how mathematicians and physicists came to know what they did rather than how they taught the reader their disciplines. There followed two chapters on common sense knowledge. These two chapters provided valuable insight into how common sense operates, but their major contribution was by implication: they revealed that Lonergan's primary interest was in speculative knowledge (or, as it sometimes called, discursive knowing). In sum *Insight* contained twenty chapters and revealed a synthetic thinker of enormous capacities.

In my own estimation, *Insight* enlightened us theologians in three principal ways. First of all, Lonergan described judgment as the grasp of the "virtually unconditioned." In judgment we did not attain absolute certainty, but high probability.[6] In this way we were liberated from the traditional demands for Cartesian certainty that had dogged Catholic philosophical and theological endeavors for centuries.

Secondly, the heuristic structure of knowing was reframed as a composite dynamic of experience, understanding, judgment, and willing. In these activities of the human spirit, we gained access to the Aristotelian and Thomist principles of matter, form, act, and the good. Matter was to be found in the empirical residue, that which remained in the senses after understanding had abstracted form. Existence or act became known in judgment. And the Good was presented to the will by intellect and acted upon by the will.

Thirdly, Lonergan described these four relationships between the operations of mind and will and the way beings existed, not as correspondence but as an isomorphism. Isomorphism is the depiction of a parallelism between the operations of mind and will and the ways Being exists. This parallelism implies two consequences: first, the mind moves from experience to insight and on to judgment in the analogous way that things are composed of matter and form which form essences which become realities by the act of existence. Second, what happens when knower and known coincide is that the subject and object come to a true identity, but each in its own way (e.g., understanding yields a concept whereas forms in material things are principles of intelligibility but not conceptual). Correspondence would imply, for instance, that we could, if asked, stipulate how the empirical residue is found in the material principle of a thing. Isomorphism stipulates that our knowing and acting duplicates in its pattern of operations (its own being) how beings as the objects of those operations exist in their metaphysical principles.

In 1972 the long-awaited *Method in Theology* appeared.[7] Its publication had been delayed by a number of illnesses Lonergan had suffered after publishing *Insight*, which he regarded as propaedeutic to his long-range goal of producing *Method*. At first many theologians of my generation were disappointed with the latter book. Where *Insight* had been replete with cases, *Method* was terribly abstract. Its chapter on research was brief and jejeune; it hardly corresponded to the labors of research as we knew them. Then, there were the functional specialties. Were they anything more than experience, understanding, judgment, and will viewed doubly from the perspectives of the subject and the object?

Then we looked again. First we noticed a surprise in the chapter on foundations; it was not a repetition of the familiar fundamental theology, but a profound consideration of the nature of conversion. At the heart of the doing of theology were three types of conversion: being reasonable, being moral, and being religious.[8] If we wanted to do theology, we had to be prepared to change our minds and lives and take our religious commitments with ultimate seriousness. In an earlier chapter on religion, Lonergan had observed that religion is the implantation in us of the loving God, entirely the work of divine grace.[9] Where *Insight* had ended with "falling in love with God" as the end of philosophical inquiry, *Method* began there. No genuine study of doctrines or any authentic systematics was possible without these three conversions. This threesome constituted a crucial act of self-transcendence for doing theology. God's self-communication carries us beyond ourselves as the love of God poured into our hearts and minds by the Holy Spirit which enables us to fall in love with God, our fellows, and the world. The chapter on foundations reveals a mystical element in Lonergan's grasp of theological method. Beyond the encounter of the theologian-subject and the religious object, we need a priori to be grasped by what is known only analogously.

A closer look at Lonergan's functional specialties showed that, while a particular operation might be present, for example, experience in communications, these specialties were rather domains of theology where all four of the operations previously delineated in *Insight* might be applicable. Lonergan was dividing up the theological pie to make sure that we attended to what was proper to that domain and not intrude on what was proper to another.

Method itself was "a normative pattern of recurrent and related operations yielding cumulative and progressive results." Lonergan's approach to theological method was not prescriptive. Rather, he pointed us in the direction of an interdependent set of operations whose end result lay in the future. Theology was historically conditioned and interdisciplinary; it took place in a context of pluralism. Ultimately, theology might be *reductio in unum mysterium*; but the infinite depth of the mystery warns us not to take the result of inquiries as the final word.[10] Lonergan's method was to become essential to all good theological investigation.

Readers familiar with John Courtney Murray's work on religious liberty may wonder about his being placed in the company of Lonergan and Rahner, the two most prominent transcendental Thomists. His former students at Woodstock College tell me that Murray's response to *Insight* was enthusiastic and very much affected his teaching. At the same time three of Lonergan's textbooks at the Gregorian were available in Latin, and Murray was fluent in Latin.[11] His book, *The Problem of God*, demonstrates that his thinking on this problem was influenced by Lonergan's work.[12]

Murray is, of course, best known for his publications on religious liberty, especially as that thought appeared in *We Hold These Truths*.[13] He had taken issue with the theory of church-state relations articulated by Leo XIII; he maintained that Pope Leo's position was not a matter of dogmatic teaching. Further, he argued for a pragmatic approach to this relationship. Thus, Catholics, if they became a majority in a country, were not bound to establish Catholicism as the state religion or place restrictions on the practice of religion by Protestants or others.

His position became enshrined in *The Declaration on Religious Liberty* at the Second Vatican Council.[14] Murray was the principal author of the penultimate and antepenultimate drafts of the document. Health problems prevented his participation in the composition of the final draft which altered his thoughts on the matter but not substantially. The *Declaration* constituted a major break in the tradition of the Church; John Noonan has cited it as one of the clear instances of the development of dogma.[15]

After the council many American Catholics noted that the Vatican II document restricted itself to religious liberty in the public sphere. They had hoped for some treatment of religious liberty within the Church.

While Murray was initially resistant to the idea of pressing the document to provide principles for freedom in the Church, he did turn his attention to intrachurch liberty in his writings just before his untimely death. His thought became instrumental in contemporary discussions about "thinking with the Church."

Murray stated three principles to guide our thinking. The first stated that the moral claim of the baptized person is original; the claims of church jurisdiction are derivative, that is, subordinate to the claims of the individual believer and existing to support those claims. Thus, the conscience of the believer takes precedence over church rules. Religious liberty in the Church renders each of the baptized immune from ecclesiastical coercion, whether physical, psychological, or moral; the individual's conscience is guaranteed freedom from constraint in believing according to one's best light and acting in accord with one's beliefs. Ecclesiastical jurisdiction exists to vindicate and protect the rights of conscience of the baptized; it may, however, set limits to the sphere in which belief and action of the baptized might operate.

The second principle stated that ecclesiastical jurisdiction can intervene only when the public order of the Church is at stake, that is, the sheer coexistence of church members within conditions of elemental church order. This necessity to intervene should not be justified as utility in promoting collaboration among church members or the promotion of fuller participation in church life. Public order of the Church consists in protection of the public peace against serious disturbance, safeguarding public morality against serious violations, and vindication of the rights of all the baptized against trespass. In any intervention, the burden of proof rests on the church official intervening whose authority to do so must be based on the criteria for public order and not his legal entitlement of office. Such intervention always aims at fostering free inquiry and preserving as much freedom in the Church as possible; censorship must always be the exception to the rule. Church officials need to distinguish between minimum requirements of the true faith, requisite behavior, and public order and the plenitude of the faith, morality, and order.

Finally, Murray claimed that every Catholic has a right and duty to confirm his/her conscience to the imperatives of the order of truth and conform his/her external actions with the imperatives of conscience. Catholics are called to responsible agency and personal autonomy so that their search for human meaning is governed by the rules for the order of truth, often pursued in communion with others. Moral worth attaches only to acts done deliberately and freely, even from a moral perspective. No external agency, not even the Church, can bestow moral worth on the acts of an individual. The religious quest requires that the baptized be permitted to act on their own initiative and with responsibility. This requirement is permanent, irradicable, and begets a right to immunity from coercion in matters religious in any juridical order, including church jurisdiction.[16] In these three principles, Murray attempted to frame the conversation about authority in the Church for a new generation.

At this point an avowal is in order. Although I recall with great gratitude my teachers who were disciples of Bernard Lonergan, contact with his intellectualism eventually led me to Ludwig Wittgenstein where my philosophical mind still resides. During my doctoral studies, I also became enamored of the later Martin Heidegger, in particular his influence on the hermeneutics of Hans-Georg Gadamer and Paul Ricoeur. Nonetheless, one Transcendental Thomist, Karl Rahner, continues to exercise a profound influence on my theological thinking. His transcendental analyses do not have much lasting effect on my thinking, but his approach to theological topics reminds me of something Wittgenstein once said about Thomas Aquinas: "I like the way he asks questions."[17]

My first serious encounter with Rahner came through reading some articles on the topic of grace. It struck me that "grace" for Rahner, first of all, refers to God. It tells us the kind of God we have—one who is gracious. Only against this background does he take up his consideration of sanctifying or justifying grace in us even though that type of grace was the starting point in manual theology.[18]

According to Rahner, God is Holy Mystery. As such God is incomprehensible, but the incomprehensible God is present to us through the divine Word and the Holy Spirit, and thus invites our inquiry into Holy Mystery. This noetic striving yields analogous knowledge in which the more we learn, the more we are aware of our ignorance.[19] This knowledge of God is the kind of knowledge we experience when we fall in love. We fall in love with a God who comes near to us and establishes in us self-surrendering trust. In thinking about Rahner's theology (in the strict sense), I am reminded of Martin Buber's phrase that faith is: "the dark gate through which we step into everyday life that is henceforth hallowed."

Holy Mystery is not synonymous with obscurity; rather, it is simplicity beyond the complexity of all the objects we know in our daily lives. As we contemplate the depths of the divine simplicity and its action within us, we attain wisdom enabling us to understand ourselves and others better, that is, more lovingly. Just as growth in knowledge of our loved ones leads not to total comprehension and control but to an apprehension of the mysteriousness of the other, so does our knowledge of God. George Vass comments that, in Rahner's theology, human beings become an adventure.[20] They find themselves caught up in a movement of self-transcendence, a moving beyond their present selves. God is perceived as the nonspecifiable ground and form of all our striving and loving.

This structure of belief occurs in the context of history. We learn through our experience of ourselves as a particular history that this history calls for a conversion that takes us beyond the darkness of our own egotism and the evil in the world around us to a new status in which we relate ourselves to a particular tradition whose narratives and symbols reform all of our experience. We are summoned to a freedom that is a capacity to let go and be led beyond where we started. We are led to accept ourselves as loved and as gift, i.e., as fragile, questionable, and even impenetrable. While to outsiders this letting go and being accepted by God might appear to be a form of slavery, this dependence on God provides us with responsible relationships with ourselves, other people, the physical world, and, finally, with God acting in the depths of our human spirits. In religious terms we have discovered that we are homeless in the social and physical worlds we inhabit unless we are invited to accept ourselves as sons and daughters of the God who graces us.

In the Christian tradition we are led to Jesus Christ, the man from Nazareth who clarifies what it means to be authentically human in one life lived and one death undergone. At once he is God's idea of what the human person is meant to be and the revelation to us of the kind of God who really exists (apprehension of the meaning of each of these aspects of Jesus Christ involves a dialectical tension in which advance in understanding one aspect of him leads inevitably to a richer grasp of the other aspect). The Holy Spirit is the giver of this new life in Christ. The Spirit makes us free to find creativity and beauty in our worlds. Through the Holy Spirit we are opened to the surprise of unexpected attainment of relationship with others and of entrance into a community of friends (the Church). The Spirit likewise alerts us to the fact that this new life does not result from our own effort, but is God at work in us. This life is never an achievement, but always a task, a promise, and a project.[21]

The above rendition of Rahner's theology of grace hints at my understanding of theology as anthropology. The terms do not mean that theology can be reduced to anthropology, even a theological anthropology, or vice versa. Theology as anthropology names a dialectic in which our knowledge of God and our self-knowledge work hand in hand. As we progress in this adventure, there is a certain logic of excess to our belief in God and authentic self-understanding. We are pledged to tasks we might not otherwise consider: the overcoming of injustice, the resolution of conflicts without violence, the re-constitution of our own or others' lives in the face of tragic circumstances, and, perhaps most daunting, the forgiveness of enemies.

Rahner's notion of the supernatural existential plays a major role in my theological thinking.[22] I understand it as both the enduring and universal offer of God's grace and also the assertion that we live in a world where the effects of God's graciousness abound and have a history. In his original article on this topic, Rahner opined that the supernatural existential was his way for talking about the traditional concept of actual grace. By original sin we are surrounded by evil and live in a world where violence, sexism, consumerism, etc. abound. This culture of destructive evil which bends us in certain directions even before we reflect on our options is counteracted by the supernatural existential.

An example might help here. In the university where I teach, I often feel that the undergraduates view the Catholic institution like an academic Wal-Mart. Thus, they register for courses with the same mentality that they pull a box of cereal off a shelf. Since so many seem to be of this mentality, faith seeking understanding and critical thinking about the religious dimension of human experience loom as sheer impossibilities. Yet some of the students "get it." In my experience they are the ones where faith has been nurtured in a family that takes religion seriously (be it Christian or non-Christian) or the ones whose critical faculties have been honed on the stories of the holy women and men who have gone before us.

Two final comments. I teach ecclesiology to both undergraduate and graduate students of theology. Every time the church course is offered,

Rahner's conviction that our thinking about the Church should be dictated by the kind of church we hope for in the future, and not by the church we presently have, makes an ever deeper impression on me.[23] Also, in the lectures that Rahner gave on theological method in Montreal, he made two important points: theological method is an exercise of the practical intellect; and no overarching theological method exists since the various topics theology takes up require different methods.[24] While Karl Rahner does not go this far, I have always been intrigued that we theologians are best described by what Claude Levi-Strauss called the intellectual as *bricoleur*.[25]

Let me end by connecting the dots of these three Jesuits to another important Roman Catholic theologian born in 1904—the French Dominican, Yves Congar. Even before Vatican II was convoked, he was an active ecumenist. He was well versed in the theology of the Orthodox churches. He published books on the events from Gregory the Great onward that lead to the Great Schism between the Roman Church and the Orthodox Church and reflections on that schism 900 years later.[26] During a sojourn in England, he came into contact with Anglicans and published his thoughts on relationships between that communion and his own church.[27] He saw ecumenism as the future of the Church[28] and published a vocabulary to assist all of us who engage in ecumenical dialogues.[29] He was a church historian of the first order, writing about both Thomas Aquinas and Martin Luther.[30] He published a history of theology.[31] His work on the meaning of tradition in the Church and its relation to the many more specific traditions over the past twenty centuries is considered a classic.[32]

Congar attended all the sessions of Vatican II and made major contributions to several of its documents. He composed illuminating accounts of the first and second sessions.[33] He wrote commentaries on several of the conciliar documents: *Lumen Gentium* (the Church); *Gaudium et Spes* (the Church in the Modern World); and *The Declaration on Religious Liberty*; plus the *Decrees on the Pastoral Charge of Bishops*; and the *Apostolate of the Laity*.[34] One of his books explored the distinction between genuine reform and its opposite.[35] He would be of great assistance in the composition of *Lumen Gentium* because he had published extensively on many of its topics: the Church as Mystery; the episcopate, the priesthood, the deaconate, plus the role of laity in the Church.[36]

Besides what has already been mentioned, he explored almost every dimension of ecclesiology. He inquired whether the Church of his time had to face the problem that racism existed in its bosom.[37] I was privileged to be a student in Paris in the spring of 1969 when he gave a set of lectures that became his greatest ecclesiological work, *L'Eglise*.[38] In the lectures he turned our attention to how images had shaped our thinking about the church from Augustine to Vatican II. It remains a tragedy that this work has never been translated into English.

In Congar's later years he published a three-volume work on the Holy Spirit.[39] And, in the early seventies, he proved to all of us that an elderly theologian can learn some new tricks. After a trip to Latin America, he wrote glowingly about the future prospects for the church of basic communities.[40]

Congar, Lonergan, Murray and Rahner—it is amazing that all four were born in the same year, 1904. The year 1904 was to enrich the Roman Catholic Church in so many ways, in particular from 1962 to 1965 when Vatican II convened and eloquently elaborated a map for all the people of God to pursue on the way to the twenty-first century. Truly, 1904 was an *annus mirabilis*.

Contributors

Mark Bosco, S.J., is assistant professor at Loyola University Chicago, holding a joint position in the Departments of Theology and English. His teaching and research interests include theological aesthetics and the Catholic literary tradition. He has written on Graham Greene and Flannery O'Connor, as well as on the theological aesthetics of Hans Urs von Balthasar. His most recent publication was a book-length study, *Graham Greene's Catholic Imagination* (2005). He is contributor and coeditor of *Academic Novels as Satire: Critical Studies of an Emerging Genre* (Edwin Mellen Press, 2007).

Patrick H. Byrne is professor and chairperson of the Department of Philosophy at Boston College and the founder and first director of the Boston College PULSE Program for Service Learning. He is coeditor of *Method: A Journal of Lonergan Studies.* His recent publications include: *The Dialogue Between Science and Religion: What We Have Learned from One Another* (2005); *Analysis and Science in Aristotle* (1997); "The Good Under Construction and the Research Vocation of a Catholic University," in *Catholic Education: A Journal of Inquiry and Practice* (2003). He is currently working on a book on Bernard Lonergan's ethics. His centenary essay on Bernard Lonergan was presented October 8, 2004, as part of the Jesuit Centenary Lecture Series at Seattle University.

Harvey D. Egan, S.J., received his Doctorate of Theology under the direction of Karl Rahner from Westfälische Wilhelms-Universität and is currently professor of Systematic and Mystical Theology at Boston College. His books include: *Christian Mysticism: The Future of a Tradition*; *An Anthology of Christian Mysticism*; and *Karl Rahner: Mystic of Everyday Life*. He is well known for his studies on Christian mysticism and Karl Rahner. His essay on Karl Rahner first appeared in *Budhi: A Journal of Culture and Ideas* (2004).

Donald L. Gelpi, S.J. has been teaching Systematic Theology at the Jesuit School of Theology at Berkeley since 1973. He cofounded the Institute for Spirituality and Worship, a one-year renewal program at the Jesuit School; as well as the John Courtney Murray Group, a research seminar in theological enculturation in the United States. He has authored twenty-four books and numerous articles, including his theological autobiography, *Closer Walk: Confessions of a US Jesuit Yat* (2006). His essay was presented on September 30, 2004, as part of the anniversary celebrations at the Jesuit School of Theology at Berkeley.

George E. Griener, S.J., is associate professor of Systematic Theology at the Graduate Theological Union and the Jesuit School of Theology at Berkeley, where he was formerly academic dean. He took his Doctor of Theology at the Eberhard Karls University in Tübingen, Germany, where he compared Ernest Troeltsch and Hermann Schell on the absoluteness of Christianity. His research interests include eighteenth- and nineteenth-century Roman Catholic theology, Enlightenment Catholicism, and emerging East Asian theologies. His essay was presented October 14, 2004, as part of the anniversary celebrations at the Jesuit School of Theology at Berkeley.

John C. Haughey, S.J., is on a leave of absence from Loyola University Chicago to Woodstock Theological Center at Georgetown University. He is the author or editor of 12 books; has been an appointee to two international ecumenical dialogues by the Vatican's Council on Christian Unity; has held year-long chairs at three universities; and has had a stint as pastor of St. Peter's Church in Charlotte, North Carolina. His current project is a theology of catholicity for Catholic institutions of higher education. His essay on Lonergan was presented March 26, 2004, as part of Loyola University Chicago's Centenary Celebration.

Leon Hooper, S.J., is a fellow at the Woodstock Theological Center. He currently serves as director of the Woodstock Theological Center Library at Georgetown University and as the book review editor for the journal *Theological Studies*. He has written on the links between John Courtney Murray's later arguments supporting civic religious freedom and the Trinitarian systematics that Murray borrowed and adapted from Bernard Lonergan. He is currently working on a comparison of the theological approaches of Murray and Dorothy Day. His essay was delivered at a Centennial Conference at the Catholic Academy, Erbacher Hof, in Mainz, Germany, on February 26, 2005.

Thomas Hughson, S.J., obtained his PhD from the University of St. Michael's College, University of Toronto. He is on the faculty of theology at Marquette University specializing in Systematic Theology in cultural context with a focus on faith/justice, church/state, and ecumenical concerns. His publications have been in these areas, with research relating to Bernard Lonergan's work. He serves as an editorial consultant for *Theological Studies* and as coconvenor of the Society for the Study of Anglicanism in the American Academy of Religion. His centenary essay on John Courtney Murray appeared first in the *The Way* (fall 2005.)

Elizabeth A. Murray is professor and chair of philosophy at Loyola Marymount University, Los Angeles. She is interested in the thought of Lonergan, Kierkegaard, and Sartre. She is coeditor with Mark D. Morelli of *Understanding and Being*, vol. 5 of *Collected Works of Lonergan* (1990) and *The Lonergan Reader* (1995). She is the founder and current president of the Lonergan Philosophical Society. Her centenary essay was presented October 25, 2004, as part of the Georgetown University 2004 Centenary Series.

Leo J. O'Donovan, S.J., is professor of theology and president emeritus of Georgetown University. He is a past president of the Catholic Theological Society of America and has published widely on topics in systematic theology as well as in art criticism. This essay was presented in different versions at many Centenary Celebrations and in a similar published version in the fall 2005 edition of *Theology Today*.

Michael J. Schuck is associate professor of Christian Ethics at Loyola University Chicago and director of Loyola's Joan and Bill Hank Center for the Catholic Intellectual Heritage. His area of specialization is Roman Catholic social thought. He received his PhD from the University of Chicago in 1988 under the direction of James M. Gustafson. He lives in Chicago with his wife, Lojzka; they have three children—Mateja, Aloysius, and Franz. His essay was presented March 26, 2004, as part of Loyola University Chicago's Centenary Celebrations.

David Stagaman, S.J., is professor of theology in the Department of Theology at Loyola University Chicago. He is the author of *Authority in the Church* (1999) and principal editor of *Wittgenstein and Religion*, a bibliography of articles, books, and theses in the twentieth century that relate the philosophy of Wittgenstein to the study of religion and theology (2001).

James Voiss, S.J., a professor at St. Louis University, received his doctorate in Systematic Theology at the University of Notre Dame in 2000. His dissertation examined the foundations for disagreements between Karl Rahner and Hans Urs von Balthasar on questions of structural change in the Church. His research interests focus on the tensions between von Balthasar's and Rahner's approaches to theology and their potential fruitfulness for future theological discussions. His essay appeared in *Luvain Studies* in 2004.

Mark Williams is a graduate of Georgetown University and New York University Law School. He has served on the Alumni Board of Governors at Georgetown, the President's Council at the Jesuit School of Theology at Berkeley, and the Boards of Directors of Jesuit Volunteers International and Nativity Mission. Mr. Williams recently retired from MBNA America Bank, N.A., and now resides in Palm Beach Gardens, FL. His reflections were presented October 25, 2004, as part of the Georgetown University 2004 Centenary Series.

Notes

INTRODUCTION: CENTENARY CELEBRATIONS
Mark Bosco, S.J.

1. John W. O'Malley, "Development, Reforms, and Two Great Reformations: Toward a Historical Assessment of Vatican II," *Theological Studies* 44 (1983): 396; see his most recent work that develops and extends this theme beyond the confines of the Church in *Four Cultures of the West* (Cambridge: Harvard University Press, 2004).

2. Bernard Lonergan, *Insight: A Study of Human Understanding*, vol.3, *Collected Works of Bernard Lonergan*, ed. Frederick E. Crowe and Robert M. Doran (Toronto: University of Toronto Press, 1992); and Lonergan, *Method in Theology* (New York: Herder & Herder, 1972).

3. John Courtney Murray, *We Hold These Truths: Catholic Reflections on the American Proposition* (Kansas City: Sheed and Ward, 1960).

4. Peter McDonough, "Clenched Fist or Open Palm? Five Jesuit Perspectives on Pluralism," *Studies in the Spirituality of Jesuits* 37, no. 2 (Summer 2005): 7.

5. Quoted in Thomas Sheehan, "The Dream of Karl Rahner," *The New York Review of Books*, 4 February 1982, 29:1.

6. Karl Rahner, *Foundations of Christian Faith: An Introduction to the Idea of Christianity*, trans. William V. Dych (New York: Crossroad, 1982).

2. LEARNING TO LIVE WITH LONERGAN
Donald L. Gelpi, S.J.

1. Bernard Lonergan, *Method in Theology* (New York: Herder & Herder, 1972).

2. Bernard Lonergan, *Insight: A Study of Human Understanding*, vol.3, *Collected Works of Bernard Lonergan*, ed. Frederick E. Crowe and Robert M. Doran (Toronto: University of Toronto Press, 1992).

3. Bernhard Häring, *The Law of Christ: Moral Theology for Priests and Laity*, vol. 1, *General Moral Theology,* trans. Edwin G. Kaiser (Westminster, MD.: Newman Press, 1961).

4. H. Richard Niebuhr, *The Responsible Self: An Essay in Christian Moral Philosophy* (New York: Harper and Row, 1978).

5. Paul Tillich, *Systematic Theology* (Chicago: University of Chicago Press, 1967).

6. Donald L. Gelpi, *Endless Seeker: The Religious Quest of Ralph Waldo Emerson* (Lanham, Md.: University Press of America, 1991)*;* and *Varieties of Transcendental Experience: A Study in Constructive Postmodernism* (Collegeville, Minn.: Liturgical Press, 2000).

7. John Dewey, *Logic: The Theory of Inquiry* (New York: H. Holt and Company, 1938).

3. The Passionateness of Being: The Legacy of Bernard Lonergan, S.J.

Patrick H. Byrne

1. Bernard Lonergan, *Insight: A Study of Human Understanding*, vol.3, *Collected Works of Bernard Lonergan*, ed. Frederick E. Crowe and Robert M. Doran (Toronto: University of Toronto Press, 1992), 3:769 (hereafter cited as *Insight*).

2. Bernard Lonergan, "Mission and Spirit," in *A Third Collection: Papers*, ed. Frederick E. Crowe, S.J. (New York: Paulist Press, 1985), 29–30; emphasis added.

3. See for example, Jacques Maritain, *Distinguish to Unite, or, The Degrees of Knowledge* (New York: Charles Scribner's Sons, 1959).

4. While a great many students complained about the passionless aridity and irrelevance of metaphysics during this era, not everyone found it to be so. Philip Gleason provides a moving account of the way that some were inspired by their studies of Thomistic metaphysics during the "Catholic Renaissance" of the 1920s. See his *Contending with Modernity: Catholic Higher Education in the Twentieth Century* (Toronto: University of Toronto Press, 1993), 83–94; 158–75.

5. Aristotle, *Metaphysics*, E.1 (1062a24). This chapter of the *Metaphysics* does indeed set forth the sentences that came to be interpreted as the three degrees of abstraction. Lonergan, however, argued that the abstract interpretation did not do justice to the spirit of Aristotle's thought.

6. For his detailed discussion, see Lonergan, *Topics in Education: The Cincinnati Lectures of 1959 on the Philosophy of Education*, vol. 10, *Collected Works*, 10:83–94, 158–75 (hereafter cited as *Topics*).

7. Lonergan, *Insight*, 377.

8. Ibid., 97–98, 197, 312–13.

9. Ibid., 521.

10. Bernard Lonergan, *Verbum:Word and Idea in Aquinas,* vol. 2, *Collected Works*, 2:55–56, 74–76. See also Lonergan, *Insight,* 421–423.

11. See Bernard Lonergan, "Cognitional Structure," *Collected Works*, 4:205–21.

12. Lonergan, *Topics,* 52, 209.
13. Albert Einstein, *Ideas and Opinions* (New York: Dell, 1954), 220.
14. Ibid., 46–51.
15. Lonergan, *Insight*, 706.
16. Augustine, *Confessions*, I. 1.
17. Remarkably, the passionateness of being is reflected in the dynamism of our evolving universe. See *Insight*, 470–76. Lonergan also remarked that dynamism is an *eros*, a love of the universe itself for the unlimited passionateness of God: "the universe is in love with God." See *Insight*, 721. This passionate dynamism of the universe emerged and became conscious in human beings in the form of our unrestricted questioning desire. See "Mission and Spirit," 29; and *Insight*, 497.
18. Bernard Lonergan, *Method in Theology* (New York: Herder & Herder, 1972), 104–5 (hereafter cited as *Method*).
19. Lonergan, *Method*, 105; this is one of Lonergan's paraphrases. The *New American Bible* translation reads: ". . . the love of God has been poured out in our hearts through the Holy Spirit who has been given to us."
20. Lonergan, *Method*, 278–83.
21. Ibid., 29.
22. Abraham Maslow, *Religion, Values, and Peak-Experiences* (New York: Viking Press, 1970), 22, 84–90.
23. See Frederick E. Crowe, S.J., "Lonergan's Universalist View of Religion," in *Method: Journal of Lonergan Studies* 12 (1994): 147–79.
24. Christopher Dawson, *Dynamics of World History*, ed. John J. Molloy (New York: Sheed and Ward, 1956), 234.
25. See William A. Mathews, *Lonergan's Quest* (Toronto: University of Toronto Press, 2005), 73.
26. Lonergan, *Method*, 282.
27. Lonergan, "*Insight* Revisited," in *A Second Collection*, ed. William F. Ryan, S.J., and Bernard J. Tyrell, S.J. (Philadelphia: Westminster Press, 1974), 268. The main body text of *Insight* was 748 pages in its 1958 edition; it is 770 pages in the 1992 University of Toronto Press edition.
28. Lonergan, "Healing and Creating in History," *Third Collection*, 106.
29. Ibid.
30. Ibid., 106–8.

4. Longergan and the Key to Philosophy
Elizabeth A. Murray

1. Bernard Lonergan, "Lectures on Existentialism," in *Phenomenology and Logic: The Boston College Lectures on Mathematical Logic and Existentialism*, vol. 18, *Collected Works of Bernard Lonergan*, ed. Frederick E. Crowe and Robert M. Doran (Toronto: University of Toronto Press, 1992), 18:284.
2. Bernard Lonergan, *Caring about Meaning: Patterns in the Life of Bernard Lonergan,* ed. P. Lambert, C. Tansey, and C. Going (Montreal: Thomas More Institute, 1982), 219.
3. Ibid., 220.

4. Frederick E. Crowe, *The Lonergan Enterprise* (Cambridge, Mass.: Cowley, 1980), chap. 1.

5. Bernard Lonergan, *Insight: A Study of Human Understanding*, vol. 3, *Collected Works,* 3:768 (hereafter cited as *Insight*).

6. Ibid., 769.

7. Lonergan summarized his introduction to philosophy in the following: "My philosophic development was from Newman to Augustine, from Augustine to Plato, and then I was introduced to Thomism through a Greek, Stephanos Stephanou, who had his philosophic formation under Maréchal. It was in talking with him that I came first to understand St. Thomas, and see that there was something there." Bernard Lonergan, *Understanding and Being*, vol. 5, *Collected Works*, 5:350.

8. Lonergan, *Insight*, pp. 452–53.

9. This quote from Ludwig Wittgenstein appeared in the brochure: "Philosophy Titles, 2004" (McGraw Hill).

10. Lonergan, *Insight*, 452.

11. Bernard Lonergan, "Horizons and Transpositions," in *Philosophical and Theological Papers, 1965–1980*, vol. 17, *Collected Works*, 17:429.

12. Bernard Lonergan, *The Subject* (Milwaukee: Marquette University Press, 1968), 7

13. Elizabeth Murray, "The Unity of the Self as Given," *Method: Journal of Lonergan Studies* 22, no. 1 (Spring 2004): 93–104.

14. Bernard Lonergan, "Cognitional Structure," in *Collection*, vol. 4, *Collected Works*, 4:208–11.

15. Ibid., 209–10.

16. Lonergan, *Understanding and Being*, 3–4.

17. Ibid., 15.

18. Lonergan, "Cognitional Structure," 210.

19. Thomas Keating, *Open Heart, Open Mind: The Contemplative Dimension of the Gospel* (New York: Continuum, 2002), 75.

20. Bernard Lonergan, *Method in Theology* (London: Darton, Longman & Todd, 1972), 81.

21. Ibid., 83.

22. Lonergan, *Understanding and Being*, 18.

23. Lonergan, *Insight*, 582.

24. Elizabeth Morelli [Murray], "The Duality in Sartre's Account of Reflective Consciousness," in *French Existentialism: Consciousness, Ethics and Relations with Others*, edited by James Giles (Amsterdam: Rodopi, 1999), 19–32.

25. Lonergan, *Insight*, 410–11. In an earlier discussion of patterns in chapter 6, he had distinguished just four: the biological, the aesthetic, the intellectual, and the dramatic. This discrepancy is due to the fact that *Insight* is written from a moving viewpoint, which enables Lonergan to introduce reinforcements as the work unfolds.

26. Ibid., 276.

27. Ibid., 206.

28. Ibid., 208.

29. Ibid.

30. Lonergan, *Method*, 242.

31. Lonergan, *Insight*, 205.

32. Lonergan, "Dialectic," in *Method*, 235–66.

33. Robert Doran, S.J., suggested the addition of a fourth conversion, psychological conversion, and Lonergan welcomed the amendment to his account. However, I am not convinced that the phenomenon he describes is a conversion rather than a highly significant development in affective self-appropriation. The "conversion" he describes has no discernible antithetical poles.

34. Lonergan, *Insight*, 15.

35. Lonergan, *Method*, 241.

36. Ibid., 243.

37. Ibid., 285–88.

38. Lonergan, *Insight*, 11–12.

39. Elizabeth Morelli [Murray], "Post-Hegelian Elements in Lonergan's Philosophy of Religion," *Method: Journal of Lonergan Studies* 12, no. 2 (Fall 1994): 215–38.

40. Lonergan, "Lectures on Existentialism," 294.

41. Lonergan, *Insight*, 13.

42. Lonergan, "Lectures on Existentialism," 295.

43. Lonergan, "The Natural Desire to See God," in *Collection*, 90–91. To unpack this statement fully would require a summary of Lonergan's work *Verbum*. I shall just note here that Lonergan, in the work, painstakingly differentiates the act of understanding from the act of formulating that understanding in concepts. Lonergan's assessment of the pressing problem of our age reveals why it is that Lonergan devoted so many years to working out the issues surrounding the nature of human understanding.

44. *Insight*, 415.

45. Ibid., 413.

46. Ibid., 6.

47. Lonergan, "On the Ontological and Psychological Constitution of Christ," unpublished translation by Michael Shields of *de Constitutione Christi Ontologica et Psychologica* (Rome: Gregorian University Press, 1956), sect. 102.

48. Murray, "The Unity of the Self as Given."

49. Lonergan, "Lectures on Existentialism," 291.

5. Lonergan's Jaw
John C. Haughey, S.J.

1. Peter Currie, "Muscling in on Hominid Evolution," *Nature*, March 2004, 373.

2. Bernard Lonergan, *Insight: A Study of Human Understanding*, vol. 3, *Collected Works of Bernard Lonergan*, ed. Frederick E. Crowe and Robert M. Doran (Toronto: University of Toronto Press, 1992), 37.

3. Lonergan, "Dimensions of Meaning," in *The Lonergan Reader*, ed. Mark and Elizabeth Morelli (Toronto: University of Toronto Press 1997), 401.

4. Lonergan, *Method in Theology* (New York: Herder and Herder, 1972), 105.

5. Ibid., 106.

6. Ibid.
7. Ibid.

6. John Courtney Murray's American Stories
Michael J. Schuck

1. John Courtney Murray, "The American Proposition," *Commonweal*, January 20, 1961,433.
2. John Courtney Murray, "The Role of Faith in the Renovation of the World," *Messenger of the Sacred Heart,* March 1948, 17.
3. John Courtney Murray, "Freedom in the Age of Renewal," in *Bridging the Sacred and the Secular: Selected Writings of John Courtney Murray*, ed. J. Leon Hooper, S.J. (Washington, D.C.: Georgetown University Press, 1994), 181–86. Originally this was a commencement speech given by Murray in 1965 at St. John's University in Collegeville, Minnesota.The reprint is also available at http://woodstock.georgetown.edu/library/Murray/0_murraybib.html (accessed November 29, 2006).
4. John Courtney Murray, "Religious Freedom," in *The Documents of Vatican II*, ed. Walter M. Abbot and Joseph Gallagher (New York: America Press, 1966), 695, n. 58.
5. John Courtney Murray, *We Hold These Truths: Catholic Reflections on the American Proposition* (New York: Sheed and Ward, 1960), 6.
6. Ibid., 10.
7. Ibid., 15.
8. Ibid., 10–11.
9. Murray, "Religious Freedom," 689, n. 26.
10. Murray, *We Hold These Truths,* 36.
11. Ibid., 327.
12. Richard Fox and T. J. Lears, ed., *The Culture of Consumption: Critical Essays in American History, 1880–1980* (New York: Pantheon Books, 1983), 67.
13. Murray, *We Hold These Truths,* 12.
14. Murray, "Role of Faith," 17.
15. John Courtney Murray, "The State University in a Pluralist Society," *Catholic Mind*, May–June 1959, 248.
16. John Courtney Murray, "The Return to Tribalism," *Catholic Mind*, January 1962, 6. The sense of increasing moral vacuity in American culture deeply troubled Murray. In "Reversing the Secularist Drift" (*Thought*, March 1949, 38), he wrote: "The realization has struck home to many that in the course of all our furious building we have succeeded in erecting an immense structure that encloses—a vacuum. The intellectual, moral and spiritual vacuities perceptible in many regions of American culture have given rise to the anxious reflection, How shall these hollow emptinesses, within man, within his institutions, be filled?"
17. Murray, "State University," 245.
18. Murray, "Return to Tribalism," 9.
19. Ibid., 7
20. Murray, *We Hold These Truths,* 6.

21. For a compelling recent study of Murray's specific philosophical and theological treatment of freedom and truth, see Hermínio Rico, S.J., *John Paul II and the Legacy of Dignitatis Humanae* (Washington, D.C.: Georgetown University Press, 2002).

8. Murray on Loving One's Enemies
Leon Hooper, S.J.

1. John Courtney Murray, *Matthias Scheeben on Faith: The Doctoral Dissertation of John Courtney Murray*, vol. 29 of *Toronto Series in Theology*, ed. D. Thomas Hughson (Lewiston, N.Y.: The Edwin Mellen Press, 1937).

2. John Courtney Murray, "The Catholic Position: A Reply," *American Mercury*, September 1949, 274–83.

3. John Courtney Murray, *The Problem of God: Yesterday and Today* (New Haven: Yale University Press, 1964).

4. A Dominican theologian, Edward Schillebeeckx was an advisor to the Dutch bishops at the Second Vatican Council in Rome (1962–65).

9. Murray: Faithful to Tradition in Context
Thomas Hughson, S.J.

1. John Courtney Murray, *We Hold These Truths: Catholic Reflections on the American Proposition* (New York: Sheed and Ward, 1960).

2. John Courtney Murray, *The Problem of Religious Freedom* (Westminster, Md.: Newman Press, 1965); appeared originally in *Theological Studies* 25 (December 1964):503–75.

10. On Reading Rahner in a New Century
Leo J. O'Donovan, S. J.

1. Karl Rahner, *Aneiger für die katholische Geistlichkeit* (März 1979) in *Karl Rahner: Gotteserfahrung in Leben und Denken* by Herbert Vorgrimler (Darmstadt: Primus, 2004), 19. An earlier and still useful study by Vorgrimler has been translated into English as *Understanding Karl Rahner: An Introduction to His Life and Thought* (New York: Crossroad, 1986). Invaluable is Karl H. Neufeld, *Die Brüder Rahner: Eine Biographie*, 2nd ed. (Freiburg: Herder, [1994] 2004).

2. Rahner, *Geist in Welt: Zur Metaphysik der endlichen Erkenntnis bei Thomas von Aquin* (Munich: Kosel, 1939). A 2nd edition, revised by J. B. Metz, was published in 1957; translated by William Dych as *Spirit in the World* (London: Sheed and Ward, 1968).

3. On the first lectures on grace, compare Paul Rulands, *Menschsein unter dem An-Spruch der Gnade: Das übernatürliche Existential und der Begriff der natura pura bei Karl Rahner (ITHS 55)* (Innsbruck-Vienna, 2000), 63–96; and Walter Schmolly, "'*Der Heilswille Gottes berührt uns in Christus Jesus und der Kirche': Die erste Gnadenvorlesung,*" in *Der Denkweg Karl Rahners: Quellen-Entwicklungen-Perspektiven*, 2d ed., ed. A. R. Batlogg et al. (Mainz: Grunwald, 2004), 106–43. The Salzburg lectures were published as *Hörer des Wortes* (Munich: Kosel, 1941); translated by Joseph Donceel as

Hearer of the Word (New York: Continuum, 1994). The classic meditations, *Worte ins Schweigen* (Innsbruck: Rauch, 1938), were translated by James Demske as *Encounters with Silence* (Westminster, Md.: Newman, 1960).

4. The *Schriften zur Theologie* (hereafter cited as *S*) have been translated by Cornelius Ernst et al. as *Theological Investigations*, 23 vols. (New York: Crossroad, 1974–92); hereafter cited as *TI*. A wholly new edition of Rahner's writings *Sämtliche Werke*, is currently being published under the editorial direction of Cardinal Karl Lehmann, J. B. Metz, Karl Heinz Neufeld, Albert Raffelt, and Herbert Vorgrimler; 13 of the planned 32 vols. have appeared. For further information, see www.ub-uni-freiburg.de/referate/04/rahner/rahnerma.htm.

5. See also A. R. Batlogg, *Die Mysterien des Lebens Jesu bei Karl Rahner: Zugang zum Christusglauben (ITHS 58)*, 2d ed. (Innsbruck-Vienna, 2003); L. J. O'Donovan, "The Word of the Cross," *Chicago Studies* 25 (1986): 95–110.

6. Karl Rahner, "*Grundkurs des Glaubens*," Translated by William V. Dych as *Foundations of Christian Faith* (New York: Seabury Press, 1978); *S*, XIV: 48–62; *TI*, 19:3–15; also, L. J. O'Donovan, *Religious Studies Review* 5 (1979): 194–9.

7. L. J. O'Donovan, "A Journey into Time: The Legacy of Karl Rahner's Last Years," *Theological Studies* 46 (1985): 621–46; and "A Final Harvest: Karl Rahner's Last Theological Writings," *Religious Studies Review* 11 (1985): 357–61.

8. *S*, IV:57; *TI* 4: 41.

9. *S*, XIII:120; *TI* 16: 256.

10. Compare Philip Endean, S.J., "Has Rahnerian Theology a Future?" in *The Cambridge Companion to Karl Rahner*, ed. Declan Marmion and Mary E. Hines (Cambridge: Cambridge University Press, forthcoming).

11. Rahner, *Hörer des Wortes*, 126; *Hearer of the Word*, 83.

12. Ibid.

13. *S*. XII: 321; *TI* 16: 256.

14. Rahner, *The Trinity* (New York: Herder, 1970), 96.

15. Rahner, *Hörer des Wortes*, 131; *Hearer of the Word*, 83.

16. Ibid., 164; ibid., 111).

17. His two classic essays on the topic are found in *S*, VI: 277–98 *TI* 6: 237–49; and *S*, 5: 494–517 *TI* 5:439–59.

18. *S*, X: 137; *TI* 13:126.

19. Ibid., 138–9; 127.

20. Ibid., 139; 127–8.

21. Ibid., 139; 128.

22. Edouard Pousset, "Method in Theology," in *Cambridge Companion*.

23. See Jon Sobrino, S.J., "*Gedanken über Karl Rahner aus Lateinamerika*," *Stimmen der Zeit* 222 (Spezial 1–204): 43–56.

24. See also Karl Neumann, *Der Praxisbezug der Theologie bei Karl Rahner* (Freiburg: Herder, 1980); L. J. O'Donovan, "Orthopraxis and Theological Method in Karl Rahner," *Proceedings of the Catholic Theological Society of America* 35 (1980): 251–71; written before Neumann's book was published.

25. Karl Rahner, "*Gnade als Mitte menschlicher Existenz*," *Herder Korrespondenz* 28 (1974): 77–92.

26. *Sacramentum Mundi* IV (author's translation).

27. Gustavo Gutiérrez, *A Theology of Liberation: History, Politics, and Salvation,* trans. and ed. by Sister Caridad Inda and John Eagleson (Maryknoll: Orbis, 1973).

28. *S,* IX: 92; *TI* 11: 80.

29. *Sacramentum Mundi* IV: 866 (author's translation).

30. *S,* V: 74; *TI* 5: 60.

31. Compare Anne Carr, *The Theological Method of Karl Rahner* (Missoula, MT: Scholars, 1977).

32. Patrick Burke is a conspicuous example. In *Reinterpreting Rahner: A Critical Study of his Major Themes* (New York: Fordham University Press, 2002) Burke proposes "dialectical analogy" as central to Rahner's thought. But from the very beginning he conceives this quite contrary to Rahner's clear intention. "Man himself [for Rahner]," claims Burke at the start, "is the *schwebende Mitte*, the dynamic oscillating midpoint between God and the categorical world, but also and always a pure static nature," Ibid., 8. A still more unfortunate formulation is found at 230–31.

33. Rahner, *Grundkurs des Glaubens,* 79; Rahner, *Foundations of Christian Faith,* 71.

34. Ibid., 80–1; *Foundations of Christian Faith,* 72–73.

35. Ibid., 80; *Foundations of Christian Faith,* 72.

36. Fischer's magisterial *Der Mensch als Geheimnis: Die Anthropologie Karl Rahners* (Freiburg: Herder, 1974) first addressed the question centrally. See also the fine studies Egan, *The Spiritual Exercises and the Ignatian Mystical Horizon* (Saint Louis: Institute of Jesuit Sources, 1976); and Endean, *Karl Rahner and Ignatian Spirituality* (Oxford: Oxford University Press, 2001).

37. David L. Fleming, S.J., *The Spiritual Exercises of St Ignatius: A Literal Translation and a Contemporary Reading* (Saint Louis: Institute of Jesuit Sources, 1978), 5.

38. Fleming, *Like the Lightning: The Dynamics of the Ignatian Exercises* (Saint Louis: Institute of Jesuit Sources, 2004), 16–7.

39. Influenced especially by Blondel and Hegel, Fessard (1897–1978) viewed Christianity as praxis and held that faith is fulfilled, not only in theory, but in the historical engagement of one's life. In 1956, he published *La Dialectique des Exercises Spirituels de saint Ignace de Loyola* (Paris: Aubier); and ten years later he added a second volume on further aspects of Ignatius's little manual; cf. Michael Schneider, "*Unterscheidung der Geister*": *Die ignatianschen Exerzitien in der Deutung von E. Przywara, K. Rahner und G. Fessard* (Innsbruck: Tyrolia, 1983).

40. Edouard Pousset, *Life in Faith and Freedom: An Essay Presenting Gaston Fessard's Analysis of the Dialectic of the Spiritual Exercises of St. Ignatius* (Saint Louis: Institute of Jesuit Sources, 1980), 23.

41. Cf. Karl Rahner, *Politische Dimensionen des Christentums: Ausgewählte Texte zu Fragen der Zeit,* ed. Herbert Vorgrimler (Munich: Kosel, 1986).

42. Cf. L. J. O'Donovan, "Losing Oneself and Finding God," *America,* 8 November 2004, 12–5.

43. Fleming, *Spiritual Exercises,* 234.

11. Karl Rahner's Theological Life
Harvey D. Egan, S.J.

1. Karl Rahner, "Selbstporträt" *in Forscher und Gelehrte*, ed. W. Ernst Bohm (Stuttgart: Battenberg, 1966), 21.
2. Paul Imhof, S.J.,"Ignatius of Loyola Speaks to a Modern Jesuit," historical introduction to *Ignatius of Loyola* by Karl Rahner, trans. Rosaleen Ockenden (Cleveland: Collins, 1978). The following quotations come from 11–15 and 19–21; translation emended.

12. Karl Rahner: Pastoral Theologian
George E. Griener, S.J.

1. Karl Rahner, *Worte ins Schweigen* (Innsbruck: Felizian Rauch, 1959), 26–33. Translated by James Demske S.J. as *Encounters with Silence* (Westminster: Newman Press, 1962), 27–33.
2. "Allerdings so, daß man den Mut hat, zu fragen, unzufrieden zu sein, mit *dem* Herzen zu denken, das man hat, und nicht nur mit dem, das man angeblich haben sollte," in "Probleme der Christologie von heute," vol 1, *Schriften zur Theologie*, 1:174. *Schriften zur Theologie* have been translated by Cornelius Ernst et al. as *Theological Investigations*, 23 vols. (New York: Crossroad, 1974–92).
3. Andrew Tallon, "The Heart in Rahner's Philosophy of Mysticism," *Theological Studies* 53 (1992): 700–728; and "The experience of grace in relation to Rahner's philosophy of the heart," in *Philosophy and Theology* 7 (1992), 165–83.
4. Karl Rahner, *Von der Not und dem Segen des Gebetes*. (Innsbruck: Felizian Rauch, 1949). Translated by Bruce Gillette as *The Need and the Blessing of Prayer* (Collegeville: Liturgical Press, 1997).
5. Heinz Hurten, "Deutscher Katholizismus am Ende des Kaiserreichs," in *Deutschen Katholiken 1918–1945* (Paderborn: Schoningh, 1992), 13–34.
6. Karl Otmar Frhr. von Aretin, "Die Reichskirche und die Säkulatisation," in *Säkularisation der Reichskirche 1803: Aspekte kirchlichen Umbruchs*, ed. Rolf Decot (Mainz: von Zabern, 2002), 13.
7. Ulrich Ruh, "Der Begriff Säkulatisation und seine Geschichte," in *Säkularisation der Reichskirche*, 1–11.
8. Róisín Healy, *The Jesuit Specter in Imperial Germany,* (Boston-Leiden: Brill Academic Publishers, 2003); Healy traces anti-Jesuitism in Germany, esp. "The Jesuit Law of 1872: Genesis and Implementation, 1870–1890, chap. 2.
9. Herman Schell, *Der Katholicismus als Princip des Fortschritts* (Wurzburg: 1897) and *Die neue Zeit und der alte Glaube: Eine culturgeschichtliche Studie* (Wurzburg: 1898).
10. Franz Xaver Kraus, *Liberaler Katholizismus: Biographisiche und Kirchenhistorische Essays,* edited and commentary by Christoph Weber (Tübingen: M. Niemeyer, 1983); cf. Jorg Haustein, *Liberale-katholische Publizistik im spaten Kaiserreich. "Das Neue Jahrhundert und die Karusgesellschaft* (Gottingen: Vandenhoeck & Ruprecht, 2001).
11. Albert Ehrhard, *Der Katholizismus und das zwanzigste Jahrhundert im Lichte der kirchlichen Entwicklung der Neuzeit* (Stuttgart: Roth, 1902).

12. Hubner, Ingolf, *Wissenschaftbegriff und Theologieverständnis: eine Untersuchung zu Scheiermachers Dialektik.* (Berlin; New York: De Gruyter, 1997).

13. Stefan Rebbenich, *Theodor Mommsen und Adolf Harnack: Wissenschaft und Politik im Berlin des ausgehenden 19. Jahrhunderts: mit einem Anhang, Edition und Kommentierung des Briefwechsels.* (Berlin: De Gruyter, 1997); Christian Nottmeier, *Adolf von Harnack und die deutsche Politik 1890–1930: Eine biographische Studie zum Verhältnis von Potestantismus, Wissenschaft und Politik.* Beiträge zur historischen Theologie. (Tübingen: Mohr Siebeck, 2004).

14. Rosener, 122.

15. Margaret Lavinia Anderson, "Die Grenzen der Säkularisierung. Zur Frage des Katholischen Aufschwungs im Deutschland des 19. Jahrhunderts," in *Säkulariseirung Dechristianisierung, Rechristianisierung im neuzeitlichen Europa. Bilanz und Perspektiven der Forschung*, ed. Hartmut Lehmann (Göttingen: Vandenhoeck & Ruprecht, 1997), 194–222.

16. Thomas Ruster, *Die Verlorene Nutzlichkeit der Religion: Katholizismus und Moderne in der Weimarer Republik* (Paderbron: Schonigh, 1994).

17. Cf. Robert Krieg, *Karl Adam: Catholicism in German Culture* (Notre Dame: University of Notre Dame Press, 1992); as well as his *Romano Guardini: A Precursor of Vatican II* (Notre Dame: Notre Dame University Press, 1997).

18. Neufeld, *Die Brüder Rahner*, 56–57; Krieg, *Romano Guardini*; Heinz Hurten, *Deutschen Katholiken 1918–1945* (Paderborn: Schoningh, 1992), 67–72.

19. Karl Rahner, *Theologische und philosophische Zeitfragen im katholischen deutschen Raum (1943)*, edited by Hubert Wolf (Ostfildern: Schwabenverlag, 1994); appears also in Rahner, *Sämtliche Werke. Band 4.* Horer des Wortes. Schriften zur Religionsphilosophie und Grundlegung der Theologie, edited by Albert Raffelt (Freiburg: Herder, 997), 497–556.

20. Arno Zahlauer, "'Was bisher nicht gegeben war.' Neuheit als Kategorie im Denken Karl Rahners," in *Was den Glauben in Bewegung bringt: Fundamentaltheologie in der Spur Jesu Christi*, edited by Andrea Batlogg, Mariano Delgado, and Roman Siebenrock (Freiburg: Herder, 2004), 50–62.

21. Karl Rahner, *Theologische und philosophische Zeitfragen im katholischen deutschen Raum (1943)*, edited by Hubert Wolr (Ostfildern: Schwabenverlag, 1994), 81; cf. Heinz Hurten, "Kirche im Nationalsozialismus," in *Deutsche Katholiken 1918–1945* (Paderborn: Schoningh, 1992), 342–61, which describes restrictions placed by the Nazi government on political activity of Church officials and clerics.

22. Rahner, *Theologische und Philosophische Zeitfragen*, 102–5.

23. Bernd Jochen Hilberath, *Karl Rahner: Gottgeheimnismensch* (Mainz: Grunewald, 1995), 68; John S. Dunne, *A Search for God in Time and Memory.*

24. Cf. Philip Endean, who appreciates the link between Rahner and Ignatian spirituality, but locates the discussion in a broader Christian tradition. Cf. "Die ignatianische Prägung der Theologie Karl Rahners: Ein Versuch der Präzisierung," in *Karl Rahner in der Diskussion. Erstes und zweites Innsbrucker Karl-Rahner-Symposion: Themen-Referate-Ergebnisse*, edited by R.

Siebenrock (Innsbruck-Vienna: Tryolia Verlag, 2001), 59–73; and more fully in his *Karl Rahner and Ignatian Spirituality* (Oxford University Press, 2001); cf. also Arno Zahlauer, *Karl Rahner und sein 'produktives Vorbild' Ignatius von Loyola* (Innsbruck: Tryolia Verlag, 1996).

25. *Deus semper maior: Theologie der Exerzitien.;* mit Beigabe Theologumenon und Philosophumenon der Gesellschaft Jesu. (Vienna- Munich: Herold, 1964); cf. Michael A. Fahey, foreward to *Erich Przywara, S.J.: His Theology and His World* by Thoman F. O'Meara (Notre Dame: University of Notre Dame Press, 2002).

26. Rahner, *Encounters with Silence*, 10.

27. Rahner, *Foundations of Christian Faith*, 2.

28. Rahner, "The Spiritual Senses according to Origen," in *Theological Investigations*, 16:81–103; "Der Begriff der Ecstasis bei Bonaventura," in *Zeitschrift fur Askeze und Mystik* 9 (1934): 1–19.

29. Stephen Fielding, "Balthasar and Rahner on the Spiritual Senses," *Theological Studies* 57 (1996): 224–241.

30. Viller and Rahner, *Aszese und Mystik in der Väterzeit* (Freburg: Herder, 1939).

31. Hans Urs von Balthasar, *Stimmen der Zeit* 136 (1939): 334; referenced by Karl Neufeld, *Die Brüder Rahner: Eine Biographie* (Freiburg: Herder, 1994), 134.

32. Emerich Coreth, "Philosophische Grundlagen der Theologie Karl Rahners," *Stimmen der Zeit* 212 (1994): 525–536.

33. Albert Raffelt, "Rahner und Blondel," in *Was den Glauben in Bewegung bringt: Fundamentaltheologie in der Spur Jesu Christi*, edited by Andreas Batlogg et. al. (Freiburg: Herder, 2004), 17–33; cf. René Virgoulay, *Le Christ de Maurice Blondel.* Jésus et Jésus-Christ, vol. 86. (Paris: Desclee, 2003).

34. Wally Schmolly, "Der Heilswille Gottes beruhrt uns in Christus Jesus und der Kirche': Die Erste Gnadenvorlesung," in *Der Denkweg Karl Rahners,* 113. "Thesis 1: Existit in Deo voluntas obligans et operosa quoad ominum hominum salutem supernaturalem."

35. *Encounters with Silence*, 33.

36. Robert Kress, *A Rahner Handbook*, 44; Ignacy Bokwa, "Das Verhältnis zwischen Christologie und Anthropologie also Interpretationsmodell der Theologie Karl Rahners," and "Blondels 'anction' von 1893 und Rahners transzendaltaler Ansatz im "Grundkurs," in Roman A Siebenrock, *Karl Rahner ind er Diskussion. Erstes und zweites Innsbrucker Karl-Rahner-Symposion: Themen-Referate-Ergebnisse* (Innsbruck: Tryolia Vergalg, 2001). Albert Raffelt, "Rahner und Blondel," in *Was den Glauben in Bewegung bringt: Fundamentaltheologie in der Spur Jesu Christi. Festschrift fur Karl H. Neufeld, S. J.* Edited by Andreas R. Batlogg, Mariano Delgado, and Roman Siebenrock (Freiburg: Herder, 2004), 17–33.

37. Rahner, *Theological Studies* 61 (2000).

38. Rahner, *Foundation of Christian Faith*, 38.

39. I am grateful to the revealing essay by Rahner's long time collaborator, Karl Heinz Neufeld, presently director of the Rahner Archives, "Worte ins Schweigen. Zum erfahrenen Gottesverständnis Karl Rahners," in *Zeitschrift fur katholische Theologie* 112 (1990): 427–36.

40. Roman Siebenrock, "Gezeichnet vom Geheimnis der Gnade: 'Worte ins Schweigen' als ursprüngliche Gottesrede Karl Rahners," in *Gott finden in allen Dingen: Theologie und Spiritualität*, ed. Christian Kanzian (Wien: Thaur, 1998), 199–217.

41. Rahner, *Foundations of Christian Faith.*

42. Rahner, *Foundations of Christian Faith*, 189.

43. *Analogia entis: Metaphysik.* (München: J. Kösel & F. Pustet, 1932)

44. Rahner, *Theological Studies* 61 (2000).

45. Available, among other locations, in Rahner, *Theological Studies* 61 (2000): 3–15.

13. Rahner, von Balthasar and the Question of Theological Aesthetics: Preliminary Considerations

James Voiss, S.J.

1. Hans Urs von Balthasar, *The Glory of the Lord: A Theological Aesthetics,* 7 vols., (San Francisco: Ignatius Press, 1982–89).

2. Balthasar, "Geist und Feuer: Ein Gespräch mit Hans Urs von Balthasar," *Herder Korrespondenz* 30, no. 2 (1976): 76 (my translation).

3. Balthasar, *The Moment of Christian Witness* (San Francisco: Ignatius Press, 1969) (hereafter cited in text as *MCW*).

4. Kevin Mongrain, *The Systematic Thought of Hans Urs von Balthasar: An Irenaean Retrieval* (New York: Herder & Herder, 2002), 156. As will become clear in what follows, I believe that approaching the potential for common ground by accepting the contrast between Rahner's "transcendental" theology and Balthasar's aesthetics hobbles the discussion from the outset. My argument will suggest—not prove—that the reason for this agreement may be the presence of an operative aesthetic element in Rahner's own theology, an element often overlooked when his theology is too facilely discussed as transcendental.

5. Balthasar presents his concerns regarding trends in contemporary theology in the introduction to *Seeing the Form*, vol. 1, *The Glory of the Lord: A Theological Aesthetics* (San Francisco: Ignatius Press, 1982), 17–27, esp. 17–34 (hereafter cited in the text as *TA* 1). See also his discussion of partial or "catch-phrase" theologies in Balthasar, *Theo-Drama: Theological Dramatic Theory,* vol. 1, Prolegomena (San Francisco: Ignatius Press, 1988), 25–51 (hereafter cited as *TD* 1). These sources signal Balthasar's disaffection with systems of thought which try to impose a priori constructs to control the data of revelation, what will be discussed below as "epic theologies."

6. Balthasar sees this as a consequence of the pursuit of a theological method grounded on the understanding of objectivity appropriate to the natural sciences. See his discussion of the centrality of belief to theological method in Balthasar, *Convergence to the Source of the Christian Mystery* (San Francisco: Ignatius Press, 1983), 51 (hereafter cited as *Convergences*). See also his critique of the Kantian heritage in Balthasar, "Zum Begriff der Person," in *Skizzen zur Theologie,* Bd. 5 (Einsiedeln: Johannes, 1986), 99.

7. Balthasar, *New Elucidations* (San Francisco: Ignatius Press, 1986), 187–88 (hereafter cited as *NE*). Balthasar's argument draws on the use of

gender typologies. He believes that an overly "masculine" dynamic in modernity has led us to instrumentalize the other. These gender typologies, and Balthasar's presentation of Mary as the exemplar of the receptive feminine, are provocative and deserve further attention. However, it will not be possible to explore them here. See Balthasar, *The Office of Peter and the Structure of the Church* (San Francisco: Ignatius Press, 1986), 131–223 (hereafter cited as *OP*); and for detailed presentations of Balthasar's use of gender typologies see Balthasar, *Dramatis Personae:Persons in Christ*, vol. 3, *Theo-Drama: Theological Dramatic Theory* (San Francisco: Ignatius Press, 1992), 263–360 (hereafter cited as *TD* 3).

8. See, for example, Balthasar, *TA* 1:145, 154, 165. This revelatory history has reached its apex in Christ, but is still ongoing in the life of the church. For this reason, Balthasar sees the lives of the saints as an appropriate focus for theological reflection. See Balthasar, *A Short Primer for Unsettled Laymen* (San Francisco: Ignatius Press, 1985), 53–4.

9. Balthasar critiques Bultmann, Schleiermacher, and others for this flaw in *Balthasar, TD* 3:64–68. As will become clear below, this is part of his criticism of Rahner's Christology.

10. See, for example, the critique of modern approaches to truth in Balthasar, *The Truth of the World*, vol. 1, *Theo-Logic: Theological Logical Theory,* trans. Adrian J. Walkert (San Francisco: Ignatius Press, 2000), 28–29, 65–66, (hereafter cited as *ThL* 1); and Balthasar, *TA* 1:18, 174.

11. See, for example, Balthasar, *ThL* 1:262; Balthasar, *Dramatis Personae: Man in God*, vol. 2, *Theo Drama* (1990), 89, (hereafter cited as *TD* 2); and Balthasar, *Theology: The New Covenant,* vol. 7, *Glory of the Lord* (1989), 415 (hereafter cited as *TA* 7).

12. Balthasar contrasts "epic" theologies with "lyric" theologies. The former abstracts from the latter in the pursuit of their formal structures. But lyric theologies have a closer obvious connection to the spiritual experiences that give rise to the assent of faith. See, for example, the discussion in Balthasar, *TD* 1:42. See also Balthasar, *TD* 2:55–57.

13. See his critique of rationalism, Balthasar, *ThL* 1:136; and his reservations about approaching theology.

14. See the discussions of fruitfulness in Balthasar, *Elucidations* (London: SPCK, 1975), 13–14, 61, 174 (hereafter cited as *EL*).

15. Balthasar, *Love Alone: The Way of Revelation* (London: Sheed and Ward, 1968), 9 (hereafter cited as *LA*). See also Balthasar, "Revelation and the Beautiful," in *Word Made Flesh*, vol. 1, *Explorations in Theology* (San Francisco: Ignatius Press, 1989), esp. 107–08.

16. See Balthasar, *TA* 1:119.

17. See Balthasar, *TA* 1:152, on the importance of "aesthetic knowledge" as an integral dimension of knowing.

18. The parallel to the theology of the sacramental mediation of grace should be obvious; the sacrament is a sign which effects that which it signifies.

19. Thus, when writing about Jesus, Balthasar insists on attending to the relationships which are co-constitutive of the form of the revelation in Christ. See his discussion of the "Christological Constellation" in *OP,* 131–82. See also the discussion of "theological persons" in Balthasar, *TD* 3:253–461.

20. Balthasar, *TA* 1:38.

21. This is preeminently true of Christ. See Balthasar, *TA* 1:126–216.

22. Balthasar, *TA* 1:203; and Balthasar, "The Place of Theology," in *Word Made Flesh,* 155. This claim is at the heart of Balthasar's conviction that theology must always begin from obedient receptivity in relationship to the form of God's self-disclosure in history. See Balthasar, *Razing the Bastions* (San Francisco: Ignatius Press, 1993), 14, 50; Balthasar, *LA*, 93, 96; and Balthasar, *Convergences,* 91, 148.

23. Thus, for Balthasar, theology presupposes the act of faith and is, as such, inimical to postures of "scientific objectivity" which would bracket the commitment of faith as their methodological presuppostion. See his discussion of the "eyes of faith" in, for example, Balthasar, *TA* 1:31, 70, 175 and esp. 190; also Balthasar, *TD* 2:87–89; and Balthasar, *TD* 3:63, 77, 419, 507.

24. Balthasar, *NE,* 71; Balthasar, *Truth is Symphonic* (San Francisco: Ignatius Press, 1987), 89; and Balthasar, "Theology and Sanctity," *Explorations in Theology*, 1:198.

25. Balthasar, *EL*, 61, 131–34, esp. 174. This is also the basis for Balthasar's use of the saints as sources for theology. As those who have been transformed by their relationship with God in and through the contemplation of the form of revelation in Christ, they exhibit for later generations continuing fruitfulness of engagement with God. See "Theology and Sanctity," esp. 196.

26. Hegel and Fichte epitomize this way of thinking according to Balthasar. Part of Balthasar's criticism of Rahner is his perception that he has too strongly allied himself with elements of Hegelian and Fichtean epic pretenses. See, Balthasar, *TD* 3:63; *MCW,* 106, 147 for the Hegelian element. For his views on Fichte's influence, see Balthasar, *The Realm of Metaphysics in the Modern Age*, in *Glory of the Lord,* 5:549–57, esp. 551, n.6.

27. See Karl Rahner, "On the Theology of the Incarnation," trans. Kevin Smyth, vol. 4 of *Theological Ivestigations* (London: Darton, Longman & Todd, 1966), 106. Reading Rahner through the lens of his theological method leads almost inevitably to this charge. Rahner's exposition of Christology in terms of his transcendental anthropology, for example, can give the impression that he has "deduced" certain conclusions from an a priori set of premises which control the interpretation of the data (epic pretense). See Karl Rahner, "Dogmatic Reflections on the Knowledge and Self-Consciousness of Christ," in vol. 5, *Theological Investigations*. See also Rahner, "Jesus Christ," in *Foundations of Christian Faith: An Introduction to the Idea of Christianity* (New York: Seabury, 1978), chap. 6, 178–321 (hereafter cited as *FCF.*) That Rahner can be read in this way is undeniable. Such a reading would render conclusive the judgment that Rahner's theology does, indeed, lack what Balthasar advocates as a theological aesthetics. The question here is whether such a way of reading Rahner is adequate.

28. See Rahner, "Christology Within an Evolutionary View of the World," *Theological Investigations*, 5:188.

29. See his criticism of Platonizing tendencies in modern thought in Rahner, "The Eternal Significance of the Humanity of Jesus for Our Relationship with God," trans. Karl-H. Kruger and Boniface Kruger, *Theological Investigations* (New York: Crossroad, 1982), 3:41. For his critique of the tendency of idealism to posit theoretical constructs that diminish the importance of contingent, historical realities, see Rahner, "The Theology of Power," trans.

Kevin Smyth, *Theological Investigations*, 4:405; and "Christology Within an Evolutionary View of the World," 188. On the need for a nuanced appropriation on modern insights and methods, see Rahner, "Theology and Anthropology," trans. Graham Harrisonin, *Theological Investigations* (New York: Seabury), 9:38–39; and Rahner, "Reflections on Methodology in Theology," trans. David Bourke, *Theological Investigations* (New York: Crossroad, 1982), 11:88.

30. See his discussions in Rahner, "Reflections on Methodology in Theology," 101–14. For related discussions see Rahner, "The Concept of Mystery in Catholic Theology," trans. Kevin Smyth, in vol. 4, *Theological Investigations*, esp. 62–63; and Rahner, *FCF*, 430.

31. Rahner, "Reflections on Methodology in Theology," 112.

32. Ibid.

33. See Rahner, "Concept of Mystery" and "The Hiddenness of God," trans. David Moreland, *Theological Investigation* (New York: Crossroad, 1983), 16:62–63, 236–43.

34. Balthasar, "Geist und Feuer," 73; Balthasar, *Test Everything: Hold Fast to What is Good* (San Francisco: Ignatius Press, 1989), 38 (hereafter cited as *TE*).

35. For a detailed analysis and critique of the charge that Rahner has "relativized" Christianity in his discussion of anonymous Christians, see Eamonn Conway, *The Anonymous Christian—a Relativised Christianity?: An Evaluation of Hans Urs von Balthasar's Criticisms of Karl Rahner's Theory of the Anonymous Christian*, Europäische Hochschulschriften, Reihe 23: Theologie, vol. 485 (Frankfurt: Peter Lang, 1993).

36. See Francis Fiorenza, introduction to *Spirit in the World* by Karl Rahner (New York: Herder and Herder, 1968), xix–xlv; Karl Rahner, preface to *Karl Rahner: The Philosophical Foundations,* by Thomas Sheehan (Athens: Ohio University Press, 1987); and George Vaas, *A Theologian in Search of a Philosophy: Understanding Karl Rahner,* vol. 1 (London: Sheed & Ward, 1985).

37. In making their case, many of these new readings of Rahner's theology draw particular attention to the role of Ignatian Spirituality (the spiritual heritage of the Society of Jesus) in shaping Rahner's theology. See Andreas R. Batlogg, *Die Mysterien Des Lebens Jesu bei Karl Rahner: Zugang Zum Christusglauben*, Innsbrucker Theologische Studien 58 (Innsbruck: Tyrolia, 2001), esp. 407–18; Philip Endean, *Karl Rahner and Ignatian Spirituality*, Oxford Theological Monographs (Oxford: Oxford University Press, 2001); and Declan Marmion, *A Spirituality of Everyday Faith: A Theological Investigation of the Notion of Spirituality in Karl Rahner,* Louvain Theological and Pastoral Monographs 23 (Louvain: Peeters, 1998), chap. 2.

38. Rahner, "The Theology of the Symbol," in vol. 4, *Theological Investigations*.

39. Ibid., 123.

40. See Rahner's comments in Karl Rahner, "The Church and Atheism," trans. Hugh M. Riley, vol. 21 of *Theological Investigations* (New York: Crossroad, 1988), 147; and "Brief Observations on Systematic Christology Today" (ibid., 236–37).

41. For Balthasar's appraisal, see *TE*, 38–40.

42. See Rahner, *FCF,* 124; and Rahner, "The One Christ and the Universality of Salvation," *Theological Investigations*, 16:208.

43. See Rahner, "Questions of Controversial Theology on Justification," *Theological Investigations*, 4:201; Rahner, "The One Christ and the Universality of Salvation," 13; Rahner, "The Christian Understanding of Redemption," *Theological Investigations* 21:247. See especially, Rahner, "Some Theses for a Theology of Devotion to the Sacred Heart," *Theological Investigations*, 3:345.

44. Balthasar, *OP,* 136–45, esp. 137 for Balthasar's enumeration of key figures in the Christological constellation.

45. Batlogg, *Die Mysterien des Lebens Jesu bei Karl Rahner: Zugang zum Christusglauben*, 69. It is important to note that Rahner's comments, preserved on a handwritten note from around 1940, is not a repudiation of Balthasar's *Theo-Drama*, but of epic theologies. The first volume of Balthasar's *Theo-Drama* was not published until 1983, some 43 years later.

46. Batlogg, *Die Mysterien des Lebens Jesu*, esp. 58–73, 88–121, 271–347.

47. The works of Declan Marmion and Philip Endean, cited above in n.37, point in a similar direction. However, a detailed genealogy of the impact of particular "mysteries" on specific Rahnerian formulations remains an open project.

48. Rahner's use of the theology of symbol to explain the devotion to the Sacred Heart aims at preserving the integral unity of the whole of the person of Jesus as expressed in the real-symbol of his heart. See Rahner, "Symbol," 245–52; also Rahner, "The Theological Meaning of Devotion to the Sacred Heart," in *Christian in the Market Place* (New York: Sheed and Ward, 1966); and Rahner, "Some Theses for a Theology of Devotion to the Sacred Heart."

49. Rahner, *FCF,* 308 (Rahner's emphasis); also "The Eternal Significance of the Humanity of Jesus for Our Relationship with God" for an extended discussion of this topic.

50. Ibid., 12.

51. See Rahner, "The Significance in Redemptive History of the Individual Member of the Church," in *The Christian Commitment* (New York: Sheed and Ward, 1963), 107; and Rahner, "Paul, Apostle for Today," in *Christian in the Market Place* (New York: Sheed and Ward, 1966), 15–16.

52. Karl Rahner, G*race in Freedom* (New York: Herder and Herder, 1969), 45–47.

53. Rahner, "Theology and Spirituality of Pastoral Work in the Parish," trans. Edward Quinn in vol. 19 of *Theological Investigations* (New York: Crossroad, 1983), 99; also Rahner, "The Spirituality of the Church of the Future," vol. 20, *Theological Investigations* (London: Darton, Longman & Todd, 1981), 149–50.

54. Rahner, "Possible Courses for the Theology of the Future," 13:40–42.

55. Rahner, "The Sacrifice of the Mass and an Ascesis for Youth," *Christian Commitment*, 147. For Rahner's thoughts on theology and living, see Rahner, "A Theology That We Can Live With," 21:99–112. On the importance of theology having a mystagogical dimension, see Rahner, "Art Against the Horizon of Theology and Piety," trans. Joseph Donceel and Hugh M. Riley, *Theological Investigations* (New York: Crossroad, 1992), 23:164.

14. Postscript: 1904 Was a Wonderful Year
David Stagaman, S.J.

1. Joseph Maréchal, *Le thomisme devant la philosophie critique* (Paris: Desclee de Brouwer, 1924). This is the fifth volume of his *Le point du depart de la metaphysique,* which was projected to be a six-volume work. However, volumes four and six were never completed.

2. Pierre Rousselot, *L'intellectualisme de Saint Thomas*, 2nd ed. (Paris: Gabriel Beauchesne, 1924). The first edition of this work established Rousselot as one of the genuine comers in French philosophy and theology. Unfortunately, he was killed in 1915 during the First World War.

3. This section is indebted to the "Introduction" by Geoffrey Kelly who edited *Karl Rahner: Theologian of the Graced Search for Meaning* (Minneapolis: Fortress Press, 1992).

4. Bernard Lonergan,"The Concept of *Verbum* in the Writings of St. Thomas Aquinas," *Theological Studies* 7 (1946):349–92; 8 (1947):35–79, 404–44; 10 (1949):3–40, 359–93.

5. Bernard Lonergan, *Insight: A Study of Human Understanding*, vol. 3, 5th ed. *Collected Works of Bernard Longergan,* eds. Frederick E. Crowe and Robert M. Doran (Toronto: University of Toronto Press, 2005).

6. Another important influence on Bernard Lonergan was John Henry Newman. No doubt Newman's *Grammar of Assent* played a significant role in the characterization of judgment as the virtually unconditioned.

7. Bernard Lonergan, *Method in Theology* (1973; repr., Toronto: University of Toronto Press, 1990). A new annotated edition of *Method in Theology* will be published eventually as part of the *Collected Works.*

8. For good background on how the chapter on foundations came to be, see William Matthews, "A Biographical Perspective on Conversion and the Functional Specialties in Lonergan," *Method: Journal of Lonergan Studies* 16, no. 2 (1998); 133–60.

9. Lonergan, "Religion," in *Method*, especially p. 105.

10. A recent appreciation of Lonergan's contribution can be found in Cardinal Carlo Martini, "Bernard Lonergan at the Service of the Church," *Theological Studies* 66 (2005): 517–26

11. These works by Lonergan include *Constitutione Christi ontologica et psychologica* (1964); *De Verbo Incarnato* (1961); and *Divinarium personarum conceptio analogica* (1959).

12. John Courtney Murray, *The Problem of God, Yesterday and Today* (New Haven: Yale University Press, 1964).

13. John Courtney Murray, *We Hold These Truths* (New York: Sheed and Ward, 1960).

14. John Courtney Murray, "The Declaration of Religious Freedom," in *War, Poverty, Freedom: The Christian Response* (New York: Paulist Press, 1966), 3–10; also published as "La Déclaration sur la Liberté Religieuse," 15 *Concilium* (1966): 7–18.

15. John Noonan, "Development in Moral Doctrine," in *Change in Official Catholic Moral Teachings,* ed. Charles Curran (New York: Paulist Press, 2003), 287–305, especially 291–93. The article originally appeared in *Theological Studies* 54 (1993): 662–77.

16. Murray pursued the rights of members in the Church in the following articles: "Freedom, Authority, Community," *America* 115 (1966): 734–41; "Freedom in an Age of Renewal," *American Benedictine Review* 18 (1967): 319–24; "We Held These Truths," *National Catholic Reporter*, November 1967; and "The Will to Community," in *Theological Freedom & Social Responsibility,* ed. Stephen Bayne (New York: Seabury, 1967), 112–116; see also my own discussion in *Authority in the Church* (Collegeville: Liturgical Press, 1999), 135–39.

17. The exact quote comes from Rush Rhees: "he [Wittgenstein] found him extremely good in his formulation of questions but less satisfactory in his discussion of them." See Garth Hallett, *A Companion to Wittgenstein's "Philosophical Investigations"* (Ithaca: Cornell University Press, 1977), 761.

18. Karl Rahner, "Some Implications of the Scholastic Concept of Uncreated Grace," in *Theological Investigations*, vol. 1, trans. Cornelius Ernst (Baltimore: Helicon Press, 1961), 319–346.

19. Erich Przywara taught this interpretation of analogy in Aquinas to Rahner at Pullach. See *Analogia Entis: Metaphysik* (Munich: Josef Kosel & Friedrich Pustet, 1932). Another student at Pullach, Hans Urs von Balthasar, drew his understanding of analogy from Przywara who referred to the early transcendental Thomists as "The Catholic Heideggerians."

20. George Vass, *Understanding Karl Rahner,* 5 vols. (London: Sheed & Ward,1998).

21. Throughout this section Nicholas Lash has served as my guide. See his *Easter in Ordinary* (Charlottesville: University of Virginia Press, 1988), especially chap. 15.

22. Rahner, "Concerning the Relationship Between Nature & Grace," *Theological Investigations*, 1:297–318.

23. Karl Rahner, *The Shape of the Church to Come*, trans. Edward Quinn (New York: Seabury, 1974).

24. Karl Rahner, "Reflections on Methodology in Theology," in *Theological Investigations*, vol. 11, trans. David Bourke (New York: Seabury, 1974), 68–114.

25. One day I was reading in my room in Paris when I heard a horrible-sounding shriek. The sound kept repeating itself and coming closer until a conversation ensued across the street. About a half hour later, the calm was shattered by a similar shriek—this time further up the street, rue de Grenelle. At the midday meal I learned that I had my first experience of a *bricoleur. Bricoleurs* are "handy men" who stroll through the city; their cries alert anyone who needs a repair job that help is on the way. The traditional *bricoleur* carries no tools, but uses whatever is at hand. If you give him a hammer and saw and ask him to fix your toaster, he'll do his best. Nowadays, they often carry a small sack containing a few rudimentary tools.

26. Yves Congar, *Neuf cents ans après: notes sur le "Schisme oriental"* (Chevetogne: Editions de Chevetogne, 1954); Congar, *Ecclesiologie du haut moyen age: de Saint Gregoire le Grand à la desunion entre Bezance et Rome* (Paris: Editions du Cerf, 1968).

27. Congar's renowned essay on church authority was delivered at an Anglican-Roman Catholic dialogue. See Congar,"The Historical Development of Authority in the Church: Points for Reflection," in *Problems of Authority*, ed. John Todd (London: Helicon Press, 1962), 119–50.

28. Congar, *Dialogue Between Christians: Catholic Contributions to Ecumenism,* trans. Philip Loretz (Westminster, MD: Newman Press, 1966); Congar, *Diversity & Communion,* trans. John Bowden (London: SCM Press, 1984); Congar, *Ecumenism & the Future of the Church* (Chicago: Priory Press, 1967).

29. Congar, ed., *Vocabulaire oecumenique,* (Paris: Cerf, 1970).

30. Congar, *Martin Luther, sa foi, sa reforme: etudes de theologie historique* (Paris: Cerf, 1983); Congar, *Thomas d'Aquin: sa vision de theologie et de l'église* (London: Variorum Reprints, 1983).

31. Congar, *A History of Theology,* trans. and ed. Hunter Guthrie (Garden City, NJ: Doubleday, 1968).

32. Congar, *La tradition et les traditions* (Paris: A. Fayard, 1960–63); Translated by A. N. Woodrow as *The Meaning of Tradition* (New York: Hawthorne Books, 1964).

33. Congar, *Report from Rome: on the 1st Session of the Vatican Council,* trans. A. Manson and L. C. Sheppard (London: G. Chapman, 1963); Congar, *Report from Rome II: the 2nd Session of the Vatican Council,* trans. L. C. Sheppard (London: G. Chapman, 1964).

34. Congar, *L'Eglise du Vatican II: église, people de Dieu et corps du Christ* (Paris: Cerf, 1966–67); *La charge pastorale des évêques; decret "Christus Dominum, Eglise dans le monde de ce temps, constitution pastorale "Gaudium et Spes"* Paris: Cerf, 1967); *Liberté religieuse*: *Declaration "Dignitatis humanae persona"* eds. J. Hamer et Y. Congar (Paris: Cerf, 1967); *L'apostolat des laics*: *decret "Apostolicam Actuositatem ,"* sous la direction de Yves Congar (Paris: Cerf, 1970); Congar, *La charge pastorale des évêques; decret "Christus Dominum,"* avec la collaboration de P. Veuillot (Paris: Cerf, 1969).

35. Congar, *Vraie et fausse reforme dans l'Eglise*, 2nd ed. (Paris: Cerf, 1968).

36. Congar, Esquisses du mystere de l'Eglise (Paris: Cerf, 1953); *Episcopat et l'église universelle,* eds. Congar et B. D. Dupuy (Paris: Cerf, 1962); Congar, *Priest & Layman,* trans. P. J. Hepburne-Scott (London: Darton, Longman, & Todd, 1967); *Diacre dans l'Église et le monde aujourdhui,* eds. P. Wenneger et Y. Congar (Paris: Cerf, 1966); *Lay People in the Church: a Study for a Theology of the Laity,* trans. Donald Attwater, 2nd rev. ed. (Westminster, MD: Newman Press, 1965).

37. Congar, *Eglise catholique devant la question raciale* (Paris: UNESCO, 1953).

38. Congar, *L'Eglise* (Paris: Cerf, 1970).

39. Congar, *I Believe in the Holy Spirit,* trans. David Smith, 3 vols. (New York: Seabury, 1983).

40. Congar, "Structures essentielles pour l'Eglise de demain," in *Concilium: L'Avenir de l'Eglise* (Congres de Bruxelles, 12–17 September, 1970), 147–55.

Index